W9-BVE-879

Something to Chew On

Something to Chew On

Challenging Controversies in Food and Health

MIKE GIBNEY

UNIVERSITY COLLEGE DUBLIN PRESS
Preas Choláiste Ollscoile Bhaile Átha Cliath

First published 2012
by University College Dublin Press
Newman House
86 St Stephen's Green
Dublin 2
Ireland
www.ucdpress.ie

ISBN 978-1-906359-67-6 pb

Cataloguing in Publication data
available from the British Library

The right of Mike Gibney to be identified
as the authors of this work has been asserted by him

Typeset in Scotland in Adobe Garamond,
Janson and Trade Gothic by Ryan Shiels
Text design by Lyn Davies
Printed in England on acid-free paper by
CPI Antony Rowe

For Jo

Contents

Preface

I frequently give lectures to lay audiences on some topic or other within the spectrum of food and health and I have found that there should be as long for questions as there is for the formal presentations. Quite simply, there is a hunger with lay audiences to discuss the science and indeed the controversies of food and health. Always within such a group will be one or two people with strong ideas on some issue, be it the best way to slim, the vital role of farmers' markets for our future health, or fast food as the cause of obesity. Debates with such individuals are fun and valuable and hopefully all can learn from the process. There is, however, a majority of people who simply want to learn, who are happy, most times, to be surprised by some of the things they hear, who are happy to be reassured with regard to concerns they hold and who want to go home more confident in their knowledge of food and health. They rarely get a chance to directly access someone who has spent a lifetime successfully competing at the highest international level of research in this area. Mostly, they are bombarded by media darlings who, having analysed a major problem in food and health, have the solution (the food optimists), and equally by those who have also analysed some aspect of food and health and predict dire personal or social consequence (the food pessimists). It is for that majority of the population who want to learn about food and health for which this book has been written. I don't expect absolute acceptance of everything I write about. As a scientist I thrive on doubt and uncertainty. But if as a result of reading this book a new dimension on some controversy is identified, whether accepted or otherwise, then I will have succeeded.

I set out to write this book to help non-experts gain an understanding of the complexities and challenges of some areas of great public interest in the field of food and health. Unlike the vast majority of popular books in this field, I do not promise beauty, longevity and health from this or that diet, nor do I set to provide an overarching analysis and opinions on our food supply and a path forward out of some perceived dire future. I have selected a number of areas which dominate the public's interest in this field, and I have endeavoured to provide an honest scientific analysis of each. As I mention several times throughout this book, there are many with a pre-existing opinion on some topic of food and health, which will remain so no matter what series of contrary scientific arguments are put forward. They are not really my intended audience. This is book for non-experts who want to gain a deeper understanding of the science of food and health and I don't expect such individuals to finish reading this book and agree with everything I have written. But I do hope to open minds, to surprise and even to shock some readers. After all, 'Challenging controversies in food and health' is the subtitle of the book.

Acknowledgements

I would like to sincerely thank the following colleagues who read a mid-point draft of this book, charged solely with identifying major errors: in the US, Professor Jose Ordovas from Tufts University in Boston and Professor Lenore Arab at the University of California in Los Angeles; in the UK, Professor John Mathers at Newcastle University, Professor Tim Wheeler at Reading University, Professor Tom Sanders at King's College London and Professor Jonathan Napier at the Rothamstead Research Institute. From continental Europe, Professor Wim Saris at Maastricht University and Professor John O'Brien at the Nestle Research Center in Lausanne; in Ireland, Professor Davis Coakley at Trinity College Dublin, Professor Pat Wall at University College Dublin and Professor Fergus Shanahan at University College Cork. My family and friends also read parts of the early drafts and had some excellent comments, and I would single out Deirdre Wolf from Iowa who had some extremely good advice on structures. Jonathan Williams, one of Ireland's foremost literary agents, gave me invaluable advice on communicating science to the general public and was very supportive of the project. Sincere thanks are due to my wife Jo, to whom this book is dedicated, for her endless support, her typing of many drafts and, at the end, the patient management of references. And finally to Barbara Mennell, Noelle Moran at UCD Press, thank you for your support

Declaration of Interest

In keeping with the norms of scientific writing and reporting to ensure openness and transparency, I wish to declare the following interests over the last five years. I am a member of the Nestlé Nutrition Council which advises the company on all aspects of science relating to food and health. The following companies have been involved in European Funded Research Projects which I have co-ordinated: Unilever, Philips, DSM, BASF Plant Science, Hitachi, Vitas, BioSense and consortia of companies representing the food packaging industry, the food flavour industry and the general food manufacturing industry. The following companies have been involved in nationally funded research research projects of which I am the principal investigator: Kerry, Glanbia, Carberry, Dairygold, Danone and Kellogg's.

MIKE GIBNEY

Dublin, February 2012

Abbreviations

ADI	Acceptable Daily Intake
AGRA	Alliance for a Green Revolution for Africa
ARMD	Age-Related Macular Degeneration
BMI	Body Mass Index
BSE	Bovine Spongiform Encephalopathy
CFCs	Chlorofluorocarbons
CJD	Creutzfeld-Jakob Disease
CTC	Community Therapeutic Care
DASH	Diet Approaches to Stop Hypertension
DDT	Dichlorodiphenyltrichloroethane
DEXA	Dual Emission X-ray Absorptiometry
DHA	Docosahexaenoic acid
DNA	Deoxyribonucleic acid
ECG	Electrocardiogram
ECOWAS	Economic Community of West African States
EMS	Ethyl Methanesulphonate
EPFL	École Polytechnique Fédérale de Lausanne
FACE	Free Air Carbon Enrichment
FAO	The Food and Agricultural Organisation
FFQ	Food Frequency Questionnaire
FIAF	Fasting-Induced Adipocyte Factor
GDP	Gross Domestic Product
GM	Genetic Modification
GMO	Genetically Modified Organism
GWAS	Genome Wide Association Studies
GWP	Global Warming Potential
HIV	Human Immunodeficiency Virus
IEAE	International Atomic Energy Agency
IMF	International Monetary Fund
IPCC	Inter-Governmental Panel on Climate Change
MDG	Millennium Development Goals

MRI	Magnetic Resonance Imaging
NEPAD	New Partnership for African Development
NGO	Non-governmental Organisation
NIOSH	National Institute of Occupational Safety and Health
NOEL	No Observed Effect Level
PCBs	Polychlorinated biphenyls
PKU	Phenylketonuria
PrepCom	Preparatory Committee (UN)
SARS	Severe Acute Respiratory Syndrome
SNP	Single Nucleotide Polymorphism
UCD	University College Dublin
UNICEF	United Nations International Children Emergency Fund
USDA	United States Department of Agriculture
UV	Ultraviolet
UVA	Ultraviolet A
WFP	World Food Programme
WHI	Women's Health Initiative
WHO	World Health Organisation

CHAPTER ONE

With Regard to Food

According to the great press baron Lord Northcliffe, there are four things which dominate the media: crime, love, money and food.[1] We would all like to live without crime and, whereas love and money are what makes the world go around, we can survive long periods without them. Not so for food. Food is central to our daily life. It is not just a question of fuel for life, although it is that as well. It is a deeply important part of our culture and also a very personal issue. Our relationship with our food supply is directly related to wealth. Those who struggle to find enough food to eat care little about any attribute other than its ability to sustain survival. At the opposite end of the spectrum where wealth abounds, we can get fussy about food. We can foster our own individual taste and preferences. We can opt to be adventurous in our taste or to be conservative. Most people have a general interest in food which is heightened at social events involving a shared meal and of course periodically heightened by news of great promise of some wonder diet or great gloom at some dire consequence in the event of eating this or that for whatever reasons. Some become passionate about all aspects of food or just one single aspect of food and that passion leads to widespread media coverage. It may be about chemicals in our food, about genetically modified foods, about genetics and nutrition or obesity or the use of minerals and vitamins to stave off illness. It may be about food miles and the effect of food production on the environment and global warming or about organic food or world hunger. All of these hot topics and more will be encountered in the course of this book. In order to put these issues and controversies into perspective, it is worth reflecting on our relationship with the human food chain. We need not go back too far: to our grannies' time will be sufficient. Recently, a bestselling book on food and health, *In Defense of Food* by Michael Pollan, has recommended that we should never eat anything our granny didn't eat.[2] Twenty-five years ago, I wrote a book on nutrition and health for the layperson and in it I quoted the English novelist George Orwell from his novel, *The Road to Wigan Pier*, published more than 70 years ago:

> In the highly mechanised countries, thanks to canned food, cold storage, synthetic flavours, etc., the palate is a dead organ . . . Look at the factory, foil wrapped cheese and 'blended' butter in any grocers . . . Wherever you look, you will see some slick machine-made article triumph over the old-fashioned article that still tastes of something other than sawdust.[3]

I would estimate that Michael Pollan's grandmother would have been around at the time George Orwell wrote the above and who would also have hankered after his granny's diet. As we go back in time across generations, we move away from today's highly regulated food supply to bygone eras of food shortage, more erratic food security, widespread food adulteration, utterly unregulated food control and a diet that was based on a narrow range of foods so that nutritional deficiencies were very common, contributing to poor post-natal survival and poor growth. If Pollan's and Orwell's grannies had great diets, then they were very privileged and not in any way representative of the great unwashed. We will see that the great unwashed of the British working class were so undernourished that two thirds of the recruits to the British army to fight the Boer War in South Africa were rejected.[4] The advent of the First World War, the inter-war great depression and the food shortages and rationing of the Second World War meant that food was precious. It was plain, restricted and highly valued. After the Second World War, all of that began to change.

Two major developments then occurred which would shape the area of food and health right up to the present day. The first was a huge investment in agricultural research, which would transform the mechanisation of agriculture, transform the breeding of crops and animals and transform their husbandry to achieve efficiencies beyond all expectations. Agriculture consolidated into ever more efficient units. New and sophisticated concepts of food science, food engineering and processing methods were introduced and the mass marketing of branded foods took off. Food was plentiful and food was cheap and, boy, were we going to enjoy every bit of it. Paul Roberts, in his book *The End of Food*, highlights the scale of improved husbandry efficiency.[5] New breeds of poultry were developed which, compared to the original, reached maturity in 40 days as opposed to 70 days. These chickens needed only 1.9 lb of feed compared to the 2.5 lb originally needed. US agriculture output grew 1.7 fold from 1948 to 2004 while the cost of inputs remained constant. This was due to rising efficiencies in all inputs, but especially in labour saving mechanisation. New developments in processing technology meant that new products were now a feature of the food chain. Similar efficiencies were seen right across the food chain, heralding an era of cheap and abundant food. The increase in the number of women in the workforce provided a new market for labour-saving devices in the kitchen and, with that, food products to match them. This was the era of the 'TV dinner'.

The second major development was the beginning of the science of human nutrition as we know it today. Of course this branch of science was alive and well then, but it was still rooted in the identification of essential nutrients from amino acids to vitamins and to establishing the human requirement for nutrients. The hunger of the first part of the twentieth century was still deep in the psyche of the field of human nutrition. But in the 1950s, a very famous study was conducted called the 'Seven countries study'.[6] It studied the diets of different provinces in the US, Japan, Yugoslavia, the Netherlands, Greece, Italy and Finland, with a special emphasis on the level and type of fats in the diet. The researchers also measured blood cholesterol levels. They noted that as the level of saturated fats in the diet increased, the level of blood cholesterol also increased. They then compared blood cholesterol levels against national rates of coronary heart disease and noted that if average cholesterol levels in blood were high, so too were rates of heart disease. Thus was nutritional epidemiology born. Soon after, a number of nutrition intervention experiments were carried out in humans to study the effects of different levels and types of fats (saturates, monoun-saturates and polyunsaturates) on blood cholesterol and the results showed that it was possible to accurately predict the influence of different mixes of dietary fat on blood cholesterol in humans.[7] This was followed by large multi-centre intervention studies showing that the alteration of diet could actually reduce the rate of heart disease and the era of 'healthy eating' began.[8] The dairy, beef and egg industries adopted a strongly defensive stance. Healthy eating hit the political agenda in 1977 with the publication of the first ever set of population dietary guidelines designed to move us to a healthier diet and thus to reduce the burden of chronic diseases such as heart disease and cancer.[9] We then entered an era of caring about what we ate. Foods were now marketed for their nutritional content. We saw the arrival of nutritional labelling of foods, the era of functional foods with endless claims and, most notably in Europe, we began to like 'good bacteria' in our foods. And all the time the elephant in the room, obesity, was getting bigger and bigger. It was spreading to every corner of the globe to sit side by side with malnutrition in the old-fashioned sense, the malnutrition from a lack of adequate food. And obesity was now driving food policy and the finger was turned at the corporate food sector that were surely to blame for putting their profits before our well being, spending fortunes on advertising to persuade our children to dine on empty calories and junk food.

Parallel to this development of abundant cheap food came a rising mistrust of the scientific dimension to food. We had the war in Vietnam, the growth of protest, the hippy movement and the small is beautiful concept. The Green movement arrived and the mistrust of agri-food science grew and we now had a widespread fear of the modern food supply – additives, pesticides, and packaging. Organic farming blossomed. The regulatory system reassured the consumers time and time again about the robust measures in place to keep the food supply completely safe, and then Bovine Spongiform Encephalopathy (BSE) or 'Mad Cow Disease' hit the fan and all confidence in these assurances went out of the window. The biotechnology industry waded in with genetically modified food and the environmental lobby took up the cudgels in our defence. There was a proliferation of non-governmental organisations devoted to the defence of food and their concerns were excellent media copy. Suddenly we had farmers' markets, ethical trading in food commodities, worries about food miles and increasing legislation to limit the downward spiral of the nutritional quality of our diets, especially our children's diets.

These are all the genuine concerns of today's consumers. This book sets out to put a scientific dimension to those concerns. It looks at the areas which concern the consumer as well as areas that should concern the consumer but which don't. It doesn't look at science in isolation but also links the science to the politics of the controversy.

CHAPTER TWO

Sugar and Spice and All Things Nasty

The supermarket, the farmers' market, the ethical or ethnic food shops represent the final court in the human food chain. It is here that the ultimate commercial decision is made with all the attendant media and related hype on food and health, finally culminating in real choices. Some come with lists seeking ingredients for a special social event. Most follow a weekly routine. For some, bargains matter; for others what's on the label matters; for others, convenience matters. All have a mission and it is the sum of their missions that shapes the modern human food chain. In this chapter we explore some of the things about the foods on supermarket shelves which interest or worry consumers. We will look at their concerns and interests from three angles. First we will explore the widespread concern about synthetic chemicals in food. Next we will deal with the ultimate expression of concern on such chemicals with a look at the move to organic food. Finally, we will probe the remarkable changes in the modern food supply in the last decade or so which has seen the emergence of new functional ingredients in foods bearing all manner of claims, all clamouring for that elusive euro.

We begin with a look at those aspects of the present food supply that frequently capture the headlines – headlines that tell a story of a food chain that is rife with dangerous synthetic chemicals which cause all manner of illness. This is not a view that holds up to scientific scrutiny, and in the course of this chapter I will attempt to explain why. I will argue that synthetic chemicals are subject to an extremely high level of safety testing, which ensures that whatever is added to our food is by definition safe. The same headlines, which pour scorn on synthetic chemicals, also claim that natural ingredients are universally safe and wholesome. I will now argue that this cannot always be assumed.

Plants cannot run from predators for protection or waggle their feathers like birds to accommodate the reproductive process. Rather, they have evolved some natural chemicals to repel predator insects in some cases or to attract the birds and bees in order to stimulate pollination in other cases. Plants drop seeds on to the earth to get buried under autumnal detritus only to emerge again in spring. Such seeds need sensors to recognise that springtime temperatures have arrived, to be satisfied that there is adequate water in the soil to sustain the imminent germination process and they must know which way is up and out-wards to the liberating photosynthesis of the sun. And finally, plants cannot use a toilet, which means that when a metabolic process is done and dusted, plants cannot simply get rid of the metabolic end products in urine as we do. They have to accumulate them and these also add to the plants' repertoires of natural chemicals. All of these chemicals exist for the benefit of the plant and are what give plants their beauty, colour, fragrance, taste, texture and all the other attributes that make plant foods so palatable and so interesting gastronomically.

Because these plant chemicals (or phytochemicals) are natural, they fall well outside the sphere of consumer concern. They are generally not the stuff of headlines. The experiment, so to speak, is over. We've eaten them since the dawn of humanity; we have survived and thrived so they must be safe. Think now of some of these plant chemicals: cocaine, cannabis, nicotine and hemlock. These are hardly the type of chemicals we'd like to see on our kitchen shelves. They kill. They cause permanent brain damage, addiction, depression and endless organ failure. So it cannot automatically be assumed that if Mother Nature makes something it's automatically safe. Let's take a look at some plant chemicals. One example is a plant chemical called lectin, a protein found in beans and other pulses, which bind sugars in plants. In humans, lectins can cause severe gastrointestinal symptoms and, for that reason, raw pulses such as beans need to be soaked for a period of time to de-activate the harmful lectin. One particular form of lectin, ricin, is found in the castor bean and was used as a lethal poison in the assassination of the Bulgarian dissident George Markov on a bridge over London's River Thames. His assassin 'accidentally' collided with him, jabbing a ricin-loaded pellet into his thigh from the tip of an umbrella. Ricin is also the most favoured toxin of the Al Qaida organisation. Not exactly the outcome likely to endear regulatory authorities to your cause if you were seeking permission to add ricin to the food chain. Ricin is, of course, deactivated and loses its toxicity when the castor beans are soaked in water prior to cooking. Many other examples can be given, such as chemical compounds which induce the iodine deficiency disease, goitre, compounds in potatoes which can cause nerve disorders, compounds in celery which can damage the skin, making it sensitive to sunlight, or compounds in certain types (fava) of beans which cause a lethal form of anaemia in genetically sensitive people. Indeed, so fearful of this fava bean poisoning was the father of modern geometry, the Greek mathematician Pythagoras, that when some of his adherents were fleeing from his enemy, they chose not the direct route of escape across a field of fava beans but the longer route around the field. The hypotenuse would have been the wiser option. They met their end. All in all, nature abounds with chemicals which, while beautifully natural, are nevertheless risk-laden. But just how do natural plant compounds stack up to synthetic chemicals in the standard methods used to test the safety of synthetic compounds?

Professor Bruce Ames from the University of California, who is a world-renowned toxicologist, has spent many years quantifying the extent of the nastiness of natural compounds. He points out that, in contrast to synthetic chemicals, very few natural plant chemicals, which are designed to protect the plant from pest attack, have undergone toxicological studies in rodent (rats and mice) models. Ames, working with his colleague Lois Gold, Director of the University of California's Carcinogenic Potency Project, noted that, of the 63 natural chemicals which act as plant pesticides, 35 (56%) were found to induce cancers in rats. Taking all of the 590 compounds (139 natural and 451 synthetic) that were tested for cancer-inducing properties in rats and mice, 57% of the naturally occurring chemicals and 60% of the synthetic chemicals were positive in developing cancer in rats and mice.[1] So, about two thirds of *all* chemicals tested under extreme conditions are capable of inducing a cancer in these animal models and it really doesn't matter whether the chemical is natural or synthetic. All of these natural plant compounds are on sale in your local supermarket even among the organic produce. Should that worry us? Well, we've survived an awfully long time enjoying them and so we should not be worried. We are not rodents and we could never eat the very large doses of the highly purified natural compounds used in such studies. By the same token, neither could we eat the very large amount of synthetic chemicals used in rat and mouse studies. The bottom line is that all chemicals which are synthetic are subject to intensive testing. Natural plant chemicals are not. If they were, many would not pass the rigorous standards set for their synthetic counterparts.

Let's turn now to the man-made chemicals, which are intentionally added into the food chain, beginning with pesticides. Pesticides are often thought of as 'contaminants', but according to the definition of contaminants they do not fall into that category. The European Food Safety Authority defines contaminants as 'substances that have not been intentionally added to foods'. Pesticides are intentionally used in the human food chain and as such are heavily regulated to maintain strictest safety standards. Pesticides (plant protection products) is a term used not simply to cover chemicals intended to kill pests (slugs, weevils, locusts), but also, at least in the popular meaning of the word, to cover herbicides, chemicals intended to kill weeds. Both enhance crop growth and both enhance crop yield. To most people, pesticides are to be used on the farm and should never enter the food supply. That is not at all the case. Under what is termed 'Good Agricultural Practice', residues of pesticides may be found in foods and that is taken into account when a pesticide goes through the regulatory process. In other words, if the pesticide is used as intended on the farm, in most cases the pesticide activity will be lost shortly after application and will not be chemically detectable when sold to the consumer. However, the system anticipates that this cannot always work perfectly and that pesticides will sometimes be found on foods for sale to humans. The levels recorded in the surveillance systems of most countries are almost universally below a legally established upper level and the vast majority of tests fail to detect the presence of any trace of pesticide. Some occasional occurrence is foreseen within the regulatory process and that is built in to the safety assessment. Moreover, as we have seen, the non-regulated natural plant pesticides are every bit as hazardous as synthetic pesticides. Or, to turn it around, synthetic pesticides are every bit as safe as their natural compounds.

A second example of the introduction of man-made chemicals to the food chain is that of additives. These are manufactured specifically with the intention of putting them into foods to achieve some desired effect. Food additives are also subject to major toxicological analysis and expert opinions can be and are reviewed when new data comes along. In the EU, because of the multilingual nature of that region, food additives were assigned E-numbers for any customer who wanted to avoid a particular food additive and was not multilingual: E100–E199 (Colours); E200–E299 (Preservatives); E300–E399 (Antioxidants, acidity regulators); E400–E499 (Thickeners, stabilisers, emulsifiers); E500–E599 (Anti-caking agents); E600–E699 (Flavour enhancers); E900–E999 (Miscellaneous)

It made sense to organise them in this numbering system so that E100–E199 are all colours. Again it made sense within colours to organise them into yellow colours (E100–E109) and so on. E numbers have become very feared and largely misunderstood by the media and the consumer, and many large retailers have led the battle to have them removed from foods or to have synthetic E numbers replaced with 'natural' ones. Food additives are as old as cooking. When baking powder containing tartaric acid (E472d) and bicarbonate of soda (E500) are mixed with sour milk containing lactic acid (E472b), carbon dioxide is released and dough rises to form bread. When we mix sugar, butter, flour and water to make cakes, we add egg yolks containing lecithin (E322) to make the oil–water emulsion stable. In effect, many of the basic ingredients used in traditional food preparation were included because of the functionality of just one of their constituents. The remainder played no special role or function. The chemical industry naturally saw a niche and began to market these functional chemicals in their pure form such as pure lactic acid or pure lecithin. Thus some chemicals, which represented traditional culinary practices, were replaced by newer synthetic chemicals that did the same job, better and cheaper. This was the genesis of the food additive industry.

The area that has attracted most attention in relation to food additives is that of psychological and behavioural effects in children. A group of researchers at Southampton University reported in the *Lancet* that the consumption of either of two cocktail food additives (six per cocktail), daily for seven consecutive days, caused an increase in hyperactivity in young children.[2] The study had profound policy consequences. The EU introduced a legal requirement that if a food could contain any one of the six food colours used in either cocktail, the label should warn the purchaser of possible effects on behaviour and attention in children. In itself this is bizarre. The study showed that a cocktail of six additives simultaneously consumed daily for six weeks caused the adverse effect. There is simply no evidence that any one colour could do the damage. But, as we shall see, the EU institutions do not always base policy on science. The study itself can be criticised since our group at University College Dublin has published a peer-reviewed paper showing that the doses used in the Southampton study were simply sky high and 100% beyond what might be achieved by any child allowing for all possible worst-case scenarios.[3] The EU Parliament is reassuring consumers that they are protecting them from food-borne hazards based on sound scientific evidence. They are not. Quite simply the hazards don't exist any more than the bogeyman does. In effect they are misleading the consumer and doing so in the pursuit of their *a priori* anti-science view of the food chain.

In concluding this first section of this chapter on the food chain, it is fair to say that, irrespective of what scientists such as myself might say about the safety of man-made compounds in the food supply, many consumers remain deeply suspicious of them. Hopefully, some who read this chapter will rethink their views. Some will not be for turning and will seek their redress in the court of final choice – the supermarket – and shun certain additives. Others will seek a radical alternative – the organic food movement.

In the last decade or more, sales of organic food have grown by 20% per annum in the US.[4] It is the same all over the developed world, although with the global economic downturn the premium prices of organic produce will probably lead to a slowdown of that growth. There are three major drivers of this market: a belief by consumers that they will avoid exposure to pesticides and artificial fertilisers, a belief that the food will taste better and a belief that organic food is nutritionally superior to conventional foods. Let us take these in turn, and I will draw on a Scientific Status Summary commissioned by the Institute of Food Technologists.[5] Four studies were available which compared the levels of pesticides in conventional and organic food. Averaging the four, pesticides could be detected in 58% of conventionally farmed foods, while the figure was 17% for organically farmed foods. In almost all cases, the level detected was well below the maximum permitted level and indeed well below what would be detected in those few conventional crops showing a positive presence of a given pesticide. It may surprise people that out of every six organic carrots you buy, one (17%) will have pesticide residues. The largest of the four surveys (USDA pesticide data program) estimated that half the pesticides in organic foods were due to the long-banned persistent pesticides such as DDT and others of that chemical family (organochlorines) and that the other half were due to 'drift' from a conventional farm to an organic farm. Scientists in the regulatory arena must apparently never even think that an organic farmer might break the rules. We make an assumption that all other farmers are capable of shifting to the wrong side of the regulatory divide from time to time. But it is apparently an anathema even to think that an organic farmer would do so. Hence the conclusion that, in 100% of cases, pesticides found on organic produce are never the fault of the farmer. However, leaving that issue aside, the consumer is absolutely right: there is less exposure to pesticides through the use of organic foods. Organic farmers do use pesticides, but they are natural components of plants or bacteria and, in general, organic farmers rely on preventative crop husbandry to reduce the need for pesticides.

Turning now to taste and flavour, I will draw on one well-controlled study from the University of Kansas.[6] Prior to this study, four studies failed to find a difference and one study did find a difference in the taste of organic and conventional foods. There were many weaknesses in these studies, one being the size of the consumer taste panels. Another was the difficulty in controlling for soil types, microclimate, cultivars, the harvest methods and how the crops were handled post-harvest. To overcome this, the Kansas researchers took the same varieties of tomatoes, onions, cucumbers, lettuce, spinach, rocket and mustard greens. They constructed several tunnels with plastic walls and grew the same plants using two methods, conventional chemical fertiliser and organic compost, both supplying comparable levels of the essential plant nutrient nitrogen. The micro and macroclimates were identical, as were the harvesting and post-harvesting processes, and the sample sizes were adequate to truly test the difference between the two methods of cultivation. The crops were prepared identically and the participants were asked to rate the foods for 'Overall liking', 'Flavour intensity', 'Bitterness' and 'Other attributes'. The scoring system was standardised. Absolutely no statistically significant differences were noted between the two cultivation systems. Irrespective of the passionate opinion of the organic food lobby, carrots taste like carrots, whether they originate from the organic or conventional systems of agriculture.

This leads me to nutrition, my own specialty in food and health. It is commonly believed that organic foods have a higher nutritional value than conventional foods, a belief again fostered by the organic food industry. Researchers at the University of Copenhagen conducted one very important study into the effects of organic farming on the mineral content of foods.[7] They compared three cultivation systems for their effect on a wide range of minerals from the major ones such as calcium, iron and zinc to the minor ones such as molybdenum, cadmium and cobalt. The study was carried out in two successive years. The first system of cultivation was organic fertiliser (manure) and permitted organic pesticides. The second was again organic manure but with conventional pesticides. The third was artificial fertilisers and conventional pesticides. There was no difference between any of the cultivations systems whatsoever in the levels of major or minor minerals. However, the year of growth significantly altered mineral composition, which highlights the powerful effect of microclimate on the nutritional composition of plants, a microclimate which is as variable for conventional as for organic farming. What makes this paper from Denmark highly significant is that the International Centre for Research in Organic Food Systems funded it. More recently, the UK Food Standards Agency commissioned a systematic review of all the literature relating to the nutritional quality of organic food. The review concluded: 'On the basis of a systematic review of studies of satisfactory quality, there is no evidence of a difference in nutrient quality between organic and conventionally produced foodstuffs.'[8] And finally, returning to the Copenhagen group, they examined the impact of eating organically or conventionally grown carrots on the blood levels of the pro-vitamin carotene in healthy human volunteers.[9] There was no difference in the levels of carotene in the carrots produced by either farming system. In both cases feeding the carrots increased blood levels of carotene but to the same level. The authors concluded thus: 'The expected higher content of presumed health-promoting carotenoids in organic food products was not documented in this study'. Yet again, the widely held belief that organic food is more nutritious than conventional food does not stand up to scrutiny. Neither does the belief that organic food is inherently good for the environment.

The organic farming lobby argues very strongly that their farming system is more environmentally friendly than conventional agriculture. According to a very detailed report of the UK Department for Environment, Food and Rural Affairs, this is not so.[10] For example, organic milk requires 80% more land to produce per unit volume than conventional farming. Some six times more land is needed to produce a tonne of organic vine tomatoes than for conventional tomatoes. An organic chicken requires 25% more energy to rear and grow than a conventionally farmed chicken and, moreover, the former generates 46% more of the key greenhouse gas, carbon dioxide, than the latter. My personal take on all these data is not that one farming system is 'better by far' than another for environmental impact. There are winners and losers on both sides. The key take-home message is this: the oft-stated superiority of organic versus conventional farming in terms of environmental impact quickly crumbles when carefully examined. Quite simply, it is propaganda.

The third area of the human food chain we turn to is that of nutrition. The concept of healthy eating is now everywhere and just about every food is presented or marketed in a way to help promote overall healthy eating. Health claims for foods abound across the supermarket. So let's take a look at the evolution of the healthy food industry. In the 1970s, two food categories dominated the use of health claims to sell their products. The margarine industry, dominated by Unilever, changed their product formulation to embrace the concept that saturated fats were bad for your cholesterol and that, in contrast, polyunsaturated fats helped lower blood cholesterol. These new branded margarines, rich in polyunsaturates, may have had a good story to tell but they had two negative forces working against them. The first was the politically powerful dairy industry that challenged them scientifically at every turn. The second was the widespread view that butter was the 'real thing' and that margarine was a 'poor man's version' of it. In the end the new branded margarines won out and began to occupy significant shelf space in supermarkets. The other food sector to play a major role in claiming health attributes for foods was the breakfast cereal industry dominated by the Kellogg Company. Breakfast cereals first emerged in the nineteenth century with a strong religious provenance. The design of breakfast cereals had enhanced nutritional well-being in mind but also enhanced moral well-being. To ensure optimal nutritional capacity, breakfast cereals were first fortified with iron so that the need to eat meat, seen by the breakfast cereal advocates as a route to lower moral achievement, was effectively eliminated. As the vitamins began to be discovered in the first half of the last century and their recommended daily amounts established, the breakfast cereal industry, in keeping with their respect for the nutritional value of their products, began fortifying cereals with vitamins. In the background, mandatory fortification of foods had started to appear. Margarine had to be fortified with vitamin A and vitamin D to the level found in its rival, butter, so as not to disadvantage margarine eaters. White flour was fortified with iron, sometimes calcium and certain vitamins to give it an equal nutritional footing to whole-meal flour. But mandatory fortification was below the radar so to speak and rarely mentioned. However, increasingly, foods began to be marketed for their nutritional properties, beginning with the margarine and cereal industry but slowly moving into other spheres. This advent of marketing of foods based on their nutritional properties had two sides to it. Firstly, industry had to invest in technology to develop nutritionally enhanced foods and, secondly, the consumer had to want them. As the years rolled by, more and more consumers did want them. With rising wealth and purchasing power came a more discerning consumer whose appetite for information on nutrition and health grew, fuelled by a mass media happy to report the latest finding in food and health. The concept of 'functional foods' emerged. These are foods that go beyond adequate nutritional effects and which impart some benefit to the consumer. It might be a margarine with a natural plant compound that lowers blood cholesterol or it might be a yoghurt with some highly beneficial bacteria.

The concept of functional foods took the food industry by storm. Conferences, symposia and workshops dedicated to the discussion of functional foods began to abound and soon food product after food product was introduced into the market with varying claims about their health enhancing properties. Science was often moved sideways to make room for the marketing gurus who pushed the process to its limit. If one company added an ingredient to their brand with a claim, competitors followed. It was a nutritional Klondike. And then the dam burst. The EU was the first to move into the regulatory environment, introducing legislation to examine the scientific evidence of food-based health claims. Three levels of claims are envisaged. One is a content claim: 'Rich in natural antioxidants'. A second is a functional claim: 'Rich in natural antioxidants which help prevent blood clots'. The third is a risk factor reduction claim: 'Helps reduce blood cholesterol (which will help reduce the risk of heart disease)'. The progression of claims could follow any nutrient: 'Rich in calcium', 'Helps maintain healthy bones' and 'reduces the risk of osteoporosis'. And understandably, as we progress from claims of content, function and disease prevention, the whole picture gets murkier and murkier and the cost of establishing the evidence to support the claim gets bigger and bigger. But unless significant and robust evidence is provided, the European Food Safety Authority will reject the claim. This will fundamentally change the way food is promoted in the EU on nutrition and health grounds. On the one hand it will obliterate the many nonsense claims which were in existence. On the other hand, it will push up the cost of bringing a health claim for a food product to the authorities which may alter the innovation landscape, shifting it definitely towards the very large food corporations that can afford such very expensive studies.

The facts remain that we have access today to as wide a variety of food as is imaginable which is regulated to levels never seen before and with those regulations policed at an unprecedented level. Shoppers have a fantastic choice: you can go vegan, vegetarian, follow this diet or that diet or adopt the latest advice from whatever book or magazine article takes your fancy. Moreover, we live in an era when food is studied to a remarkable level, to work out the optimal choice of foods and the optimal balance of nutrients to promote optimal health. However, as we will see towards the end of this book, this cosy food chain we enjoy today is simply not sustainable. The globe is facing major challenges of exploding population numbers, rising oil, biofuel and food prices, global warming, major weather changes and an imperilled water supply that all threaten the food chain. And again as we will see when looking at the bigger picture, the battle against hunger in this utterly altered planet will need many tools in the toolbox. One of those will be genetically modified food, which we will turn to in the next chapter. Nothing has the power to shape the human food chain other than this technology.

CHAPTER THREE

Modified Foods: Genetic or Atomic?

No area of innovation in the food supply has ever provoked such a negative reaction from politicians, the media, consumers and non-governmental environmental groups than that elicited from the question of genetically modified (GM) foods. So great is the level of confusion that a staggering one in three European citizens agrees with the statement that 'Ordinary tomatoes don't have genes but genetically modified ones do'.[1] All foods, whether of plant or animal origin, are living entities and must thus contain genes. Even with a very high degree of refinement of foods, such as the conversion of sugar beet to pure sugar or the conversion of olives into highly purified olive oil, the original plant genes are present. This chapter sets out methodically to tackle the real and the alleged effects of GM foods on our own health, on that of plants and on the environment. As with the previous chapter, where man-made chemicals were compared to naturally occurring chemicals, the present chapter will compare the effects of GM crops with those produced by conventional or 'natural' plant breeding. A fundamental point to be made is that since the dawn of civilisation humans have dominated and modified the genetic material of all domesticated animals and farmed crops. GM technology is, in my view, no more than a continuum of this process, albeit, as we will see, one that is grossly misunderstood. In outlining my case, I wish to draw a difference between two types of readers. In one case, if I do my job correctly, the response may still be negative to aspects of GM technology, but there will now be a greater understanding of the science and a greater acceptance of some of my arguments as to why we should cautiously embrace this new technology. There will, however, be another type of reader who, no matter what evidence I put forward from whatever independent sources and however unanimous these sources may be, will still reject the concept. This is basically a fundamentalist view. Many opposed to GM foods have a fundamentalist view so that, should they lose the scientific argument, they will still remain fundamentally opposed to GM technology for moral and philosophical reasons. For me, their case is lost and probably those who hold such views will not be readers of this book. But if I can respectfully put the scientific case as I see it, to those who are not so dogmatic in their views but who still hold the common consumer and media view that such foods are 'Franken-foods' (meaning of Frankenstein-like origin), I might cause some shift in their opinion. So, let us turn to the dominance of humans over the plant and animal genome of livestock and crops.

Our ancestral crop farmer gathered crops from here and there and fed his family. He then took plants and or seeds from points distant from the community settlement and began planting them near where he and his family lived. By simply moving the crop from its natural habitat to a purpose-built site, our early tillage farmer had started the long domination by humans of plant genomes. When plants from one environment are moved to another, which has a different soil and a different microclimate, some will now fare better than others. This is because they will, by chance, have a genetic make-up more favourable to the new environment, and this competition is referred to as selection pressure or genetic pressure. As the tillage farmer began to sow and reap and to cultivate crops, rather than relying on picking those growing in the wild, a new evolutionary pressure emerged. Harvesting favoured those seeds that clung tightly to the stem and which were not lost to birds or insects in harvesting. Today's wheat is strongly held to the stem by a short, strong connection. In the wild type it is a long, loose connection. The former has evolved to rely on humans to spread seeds, while the latter relies on the wind. Soon the farmer began to do what all farmers do and that is to inspect his garden. He would notice a fast-growing individual plant that yielded a lot of corn and he would have decided that this should be preferentially saved for seeds. As Darwin put it in *The Variation of Animals and Plants under Domestication*: 'a wild and unusually good variety of a native plant might attract the attention of some wise old savage and he would have planted it or sow its seed'.[2]

Humans had gained a firm grip on the evolving genomic structure of plants and it remains there to this day. There are ancient carvings going back 10,000 years in Asia of humans cross-pollinating plants, and the earliest record of humans grafting plants goes back just as far. For the ensuing centuries, the basic crossing of plants through the most traditional methods continued. As trade took off, the advent of new crops and exotic fruits and spices added to the plant gene pool. With the advent of the twentieth century and increasing trade and affluence, plant breeding and plant genetics began to take on a new trajectory. A Dutch botanist, Hugo de Vries, and a German geneticist, Carl Correns, are credited with bringing the forgotten work of the father of genetics, Gregor Mendel, to the fore. Among those who dominated the ensuing years were the flamboyant Californian plant breeder Luther Burbank and the Russian plant geneticist Nikolai Vavilov. Burbank was not a scientist and has often been described as an artist. He bred and crossbred traditional and exotic varieties and produced a plethora of extraordinary new plants. Vavilov, who visited Burbank and later wrote his obituary, described Burbank's garden-orchard thus:

> Burbank had collected a huge worldwide assortment of the genus Prunus. Crosses of a series of wild varieties among themselves and with cultured types displayed, as a result of hybridization, gigantic fruits. The largest plum in the world was created. There were plums that died on the trees, producing tree-borne prunes. Burbank found a small French plum with sour, astringent fruits, but lacking a stone. By crossing this plant with a cultured plum and repeated crossings with various plums, hybrids that combined the absence of a stone with the desirable qualities of cultured plums were developed.[3]

In contrast to Burbank, Nikolai Vavilov was one of the pioneers of genetic science in the early twentieth century. He collaborated closely with the British biologist William Bateson who is credited with the first use of the word 'genetics'. Vavilov studied plants' immune systems and amassed one of the largest seed collections in the world, gathered from every corner of the globe, in his study of the genetic basis of the evolution of agriculture. Indeed, it is said that during the great siege of Leningrad in the Second World War, one of his researchers died of starvation surrounded by seeds! These two men represent the two paths that plant breeding would take: the scientific and the commercial. This was particularly true in the US which was spared the ravages of the so-called Great War and which would transform modern agriculture. It was Hugo de Vries who foresaw the need for humans to have a bigger say in the evolution of plants. In 1905 he wrote: 'We may search for mutable plants in nature, or we may hope for a species to become mutable by artificial methods . . . indeed, if it once should become possible to bring plants to mutate at our will and perhaps even in arbitrarily chosen directions, there is no limit to the power we may finally hope to gain over nature.'[4] How right he was. In 1927 Hermann Muller of Columbia University published details on the use of radiation to create mutations. It would be one of the greatest discoveries made of relevance to modern agriculture.

The standard textbook on the use of radiation in plant breeding has been written by A. M. van Harten from Wageningen University in the Netherlands and in it he describes a very famous centre in Japan, the Institute of Radiation Botany in Ohmiya: 'The facility is circular, like a Roman amphitheatre. It sits into the ground beneath an 8-metre high dyke. In the centre lies the source of the radiation, usually buried in an underground vault shielded by either a 5-centimetre lead wall or a metre of concrete. When required, the radioactive source is raised up from its underground vault and is activated to begin its radiation emission.'[5] The plant material is exposed to a very high dose of radiation, many times higher than the doses typically used in the treatment of cancer, doses which would make people sick and sometimes lose their hair. The biological impact of this radiation on living cells is enormous but nowhere is it better described than in the speech which presented Hermann Muller to the King and Queen of Sweden on the occasion of his award of the Nobel Prize in 1946:

> This discovery aroused a great sensation already when it was first published in 1927 and rapidly led to a great deal of work of different kinds and in the most varied directions. The mechanism of the effect of rays was studied by many research workers, with Muller at their head. Greatly simplified, X-ray irradiation, as also ionizing irradiation, could be likened in general to a shower of infinitely small (even compared with the individual cell) but highly explosive grenades, which explode at different spots within the irradiated organism. The explosion itself (or the fragments it throws up) tears the structure of the cell to pieces or disturbs its arrangement. If such an explosion happens to take place in or close to a gene, its structure, and therewith also its effect on the organism, may be changed.[6]

You will not find such explicit truths in the literature of the anti-GM lobby.

As a result of this high level of exposure to atomic radiation, the vast majority of mutated plants are useless. They die, do not grow and fail to produce seeds or produce seeds which do not function properly. But some will show a trait, which could be useful in one way or another, be it size, yield, hardiness, taste, texture or colour. These delicate mutants can now be back-crossed with the original parent plant variety, the objective being to instil the desired characteristic from the mutant plant into the more genetically robust parent plant. Besides the use of radiation (gamma rays, X-rays, thermal neutrons) to induce mutations, chemicals are also used. These include, for example, the chemical EMS (ethyl methanesulphonate), which because it causes genetic mayhem in plants is a deadly carcinogen for humans. But it does a fine job of causing botanical mutants.

The global authority on the use of atomic radiation to induce plant mutations and thus to help plant breeders is the International Atomic Energy Agency (IEAE), a UN agency based in Vienna. More than 2,200 mutant species have been released in the past 70 years, most since the mid 1980s.[7] The atomically and chemically mutated varieties include rice (Basmati), barley (Golden Promise), cotton, groundnut, pulses, sunflower, rapeseed and grapefruit (Ruby Red) and many others. All of the newly mutated varieties have evolved superior traits in growth rates, drought and salt resistance, yield, cold-resistance and so forth. All have had their genomes blown to bits in their atomically or chemically fast-tracked mutation. These results unequivocally prove that mutation techniques are useful and unique as a tool in plant breeding. The process was nicely described in the *New York Times* in an interview with scientists from the International Atomic Energy Agency:

The process worked because the radiation had randomly mixed up the genetic material of the plants. The scientists could control the intensity of the radiation and thus the extent of the disturbance, but not the outcome. To know the repercussions, they had to plant the radiated material, let it grow and examine the results. Often, the gene scrambling killed the seeds and plants, or left them with odd mutations. But in a few instances, the process made beneficial traits.[8]

Are these atomically modified crops ever toxic to humans? Can they spread their mutated genes to other plants? These are questions we shall come to shortly, but they are best answered simultaneously for both the radiation mutated plants and genetically modified plants. And it is to genetically modified plants we now turn.

Stanley Cohen and Herbert Boyer were the first scientists to genetically engineer a living organism, in this case a bacterium. Cohen and Boyer met at a conference in the Hawaiian island of Waikiki, and over a late night snack at a deli they apparently agreed to co-operate, since each had an expertise that, if put together, would be larger than the sum of the parts.[9] Cohen, based in Stanford, was interested in how genetic information could make bacteria resistant to an antibiotic. Boyer, from the University of California at San Francisco, was an expert in cutting up bits of genes and putting them back together. They wondered if genetic material from bacteria that were resistant to a particular antibiotic could be cut out and inserted into the genetic material of a bacterium that was sensitive to that antibiotic. And crucially they wondered whether the capacity to resist the test antibiotic would also be transferred. And indeed it was transferred and, moreover, the newly acquired ability to resist the test antibiotic was transferred through subsequent generations. Genetic engineering was born. Humans could now target one gene in one organism and, with the cut and paste enzymes of Boyer, insert that genetic material into any other organism. The techniques have moved on a bit since then, but the basic principle still operates.

One of the first genetically modified foods to appear in the human food chain was chymosin, a little known protein used in the manufacture of cheese. When chymosin is added to milk, it forms the curd, which separates from the whey; the formation of this curd is the first stage in the making of cheese. Traditionally, chymosin was isolated from the fore-stomach of young calves and there were concerns in the cheese industry that, as more calves went on to adulthood with the rapidly rising demand for meat, chymosin would become scarce. In 1988, the first GM chymosin was produced from genetically modified bacteria and since then it has been the source of choice for chymosin in the manufacture of most hard cheeses. Nobody died. No one grew horns or started compulsive mooing. Cheese consumption continues to rise and environmental NGOs were not bothered. Another entrant into the field was a GM tomato, which had an enhanced tomato flavour and which was used to make tomato purées. The tins were clearly labelled as genetically modified and most consumers were not concerned. The giant chemical company Monsanto would change that. One of Monsanto's greatest products was the weed-killer Roundup. It interferes with the plant's protein synthesis system, but since humans and animals have a completely different protein synthesis mechanism, Roundup is of no consequence to humans or animals. But it kills plants instantly. Obviously, the use of herbicides to kill weeds requires the farmer to spray the weeds but not the cultivated plants, in this case soy, and that requires special equipment and skills; even so, some cultivated plants will suffer. What Monsanto did was to find bacteria that had a variety of the enzyme that was not inhibited by their herbicide Roundup. They found one and inserted the gene for the resistant enzyme into soybean. Now the soy plant had an advantage over the weeds. Monsanto released the product, which was a huge success among US farmers. However, they did not handle their public relations very well because the backlash from the public championed by environmental groups led to a mistrust of the technology. In the EU, in particular, the precautionary principle was invoked. 'Frankenfoods' had arrived.

Having encountered the two methods of shuffling the plant genome, let us now take a look at some of the products and consider their contribution to modern agriculture. For fairness, I shall examine two examples from each technology, beginning with conventional breeding using mutation techniques. The first example I will select is very much along the lines of the Roundup-resistant soybean crop. It is a wheat variety that goes by the name of Clearfield and it was first produced by BASF Plant Science, which is part of the German chemical giant BASF. This was a mutated crop using chemical mutagenesis to shuffle the genome. BASF produce a herbicide, with the awkward name imidazolinone, which ranks with Roundup as one of the most widely used in modern agriculture. This herbicide, like Roundup, blocks the enzyme that is responsible for the manufacture of amino acids for protein synthesis in the plant. And again, since humans and animals do not have these biochemical pathways, this herbicide has no effect on them. As Nina Federoff describes in *Mendel in the Kitchen*, the treatment with the mutagenic chemical 'beats up the DNA' and gives rise to all sorts of weird mutants.[10] The very few that look normal are retained and sprayed with the herbicide imidazolinone. Those that survive this spraying process are bred until a stable variety is found that behaves normally but withstands imidazolinone. Engineering of the crop's genome has produced both of these two plants, resistant to their specialist herbicide. The Monsanto crop was genetically engineered and is banned from the EU. The BASF crop was produced by chemically modifying the genome and that can be used in the EU. What sense does that make?

The next example I want to take is Golden Promise which is a mutated barley produced through the use of radiation. Golden Promise became a really important part of the Scottish whisky industry. It was a shorter variety than the prevailing one which gave a higher yield and which matured earlier. These two examples of non-GM plant breeding technology illustrate how the geneticists managed to make changes in the characteristics of crops that were valuable to agriculture and which led to the widespread uptake of the mutated variety.

Let us now turn to GM technology. The two GM examples I have chosen each set out to solve a major problem in the human food chain. The first involves a large multi-disciplinary project funded by the European Union Research Programme, of which I was the co-ordinator.[11] This project sought to examine how plant and animal production can alter the composition of dietary fat and then to examine how our genes interact with dietary fat, to increase the risk of developing the metabolic syndrome. Within the consortium was a work-package on plant biotechnology led by BASF Plant Science based in Germany along with the University of York and Rothamsted Research, a UK government-sponsored institute. The problem this group tackled was the availability to the human food chain of long chain polyunsaturated fats found in fish, often referred to as omega-3 oils.[12] These fats have a longer carbon chain and are more polyunsaturated than those found in vegetable oils. Because of this, they remain liquid at the very low temperatures found in the marine environment, allowing fish and other marine life to have normal cell function at quite low temperatures. Such fats play a vital role in the human diet. They influence the efficiency of the clotting system in the blood, the electrical functioning of the heart, the immune system and the development of the brain. For humans, the only dietary source of these omega-3 fats is fatty fish. Plants cannot make them nor can humans. Certain seed oils, such as linseed oil, contain potential precursors of them, but the ability of humans to make the conversion is very low and thus the only meaningful source of omega-3 fats, to all intents and purposes, is oily fish. There are a number of problems with this. Firstly, if every citizen on the planet were to achieve the recommended daily intake of omega-3 oils, then all the fish in the earth's oceans would rapidly vanish. Secondly, we use fish to feed farmed fish, so the efficiency of fish farming as a route to generating omega-3 oils is simply not a sustainable solution. Finally, the marine food chain has a high chance of contamination with mercury, PCBs and dioxin. The levels of these contaminants are low and on balance the health benefits from omega-3 oils outweigh the low level of risk associated with these chemical contaminants. Nonetheless, experts do recommend a lower intake of one to two servings per week.[13] Alternative sources of omega-3 fats must be found. One way would be to industrially grow the marine algae that are at the bottom of the marine food chain. They make the long chain omega-3 fats on which fish feed to accumulate these fats. However, the energy costs associated with the processing of these algae are high and lower cost options are being sought.

Enter genetic modification. In algae, the omega-3 fatty acids are synthesised using a series of sequential steps, each of which is regulated by a specific gene. Now, what the smart Lipgene scientists have done is to take these genes responsible for the manufacture of long-chain omega-3 fats from algae and genetically engineer them with precision into the oilseed crop, rapeseed. The result is natural rapeseed oil rich in long chain omega-3 oils. No more limits to their supply and no risk of contamination.

The second GM example takes us to Hawaii, where a major export crop is the papaya. The papaya ringspot virus is spread by aphids and can wipe out a crop. In 1978, a young plant virologist, Dennis Gonsalves, returning to his native Hawaii, witnessed the slow demise of the Hawaiian papaya and set about combating the virus. He found that a papaya containing the gene for the protein with which the ringspot virus is coated could withstand a viral attack. He and his colleagues isolated the gene encoding for the protein coat and inserted it into the embryos of young papaya. One plant, dubbed 55–1, showed resistance to the virus and this was crossbred with commercial varieties. The GM varieties known as SunUp and Rainbow, which are totally resistant to the virus, are now universally used in the United States. These examples show how both technologies, chemical or radiation-induced mutagenesis on the one hand and genetic engineering on the other, can deliver fantastic solutions to the challenges of the human-food chain and it is only by considering them jointly that we can start to reduce the suspicion the public has in GM technology.

The facts are that atomically or chemically mutated crops show far more genetic rearrangement than GM crops. In the case of the Lipgene study, some 30 genes were functionally altered in the genetically modified rapeseed relative to the conventional variety. But comparing two conventional varieties, which were conventionally bred using atomic mutation techniques, over one thousand genes were differentially expressed. These examples show that the use of atomic radiation to generate mutations causes widespread and totally unpredictable changes in the genetic code itself and in the relative level of expression of genes compared to genetically engineered approaches. The latter is intensively scrutinised and any remotely adverse effect is enough to see the project binned. This is not the case in the atomically modified foods. They enter the market freely with no scrutiny whatsoever.

In 2004, the National Academy of Sciences in the United States issued a report entitled: *Safety of Genetically Modified Foods: Approaches to Assessing Unintended Health Effects.*[14] This report highlights some unintended effects of conventional plant breeding. Lenape was the name given to a potato that was launched in the late 1960s, which was resistant to insect and blight attacks. It was a cross between common variety Delta Gold and a wild Peruvian variety. Following reports that the potato could cause acute illness, it was found to have an extraordinarily high level of a natural component of potatoes called solanine. Solanine can be very toxic to the nervous system.[15] The Lenape variety of potato was promptly withdrawn. Solanine is one of those natural plant chemicals that can have quite nasty adverse effects in humans. Fortunately, the levels of solanine in potatoes are generally very low, so we all enjoy the potato's excellent nutrition. But, occasionally, there are problems. In 1974, an outbreak of solanine poisoning affected 78 schoolboys after a lunch which included potatoes. Of these, 17 were admitted to hospital.[16] Here again we see unknowns occurring through conventional breeding. Another example is a group of toxic compounds known as psolarens, found in celery. Again, psolarens are designed by the celery plant to protect it from insect attacks. However, farm labourers working in the celery fields can suffer a skin disorder brought about by the interaction of sunlight and psolarens on the skin. Many cases have been documented by the US Center for Disease Control and the National Institute of Occupational Safety.[17] Nonetheless, breeders deliberately seek to enhance the levels of psolarens in celery varieties to minimise insect attack and thereby to maximise yield. In summary, all manipulation with the genome of a plant will cause altered metabolism, possibly with unintended side effects. In the case of GM foods, the degree of genetic interference is small and is subject to very detailed scrutiny. For example, when scientists tried to improve the nutritional properties of soybean proteins, they chose the gene that carries the genetic information for a high quality protein from Brazil nuts. Phase 1 was to insert the gene into the soybean crop. When that was successfully completed, phase 2 was to determine if the known allergenic properties of Brazil nuts were also transferred to the GM variety. And these allergenic properties were in fact transferred to the soybean.[18] The project was immediately abandoned. In the case of mutated crops using chemical or radiation methods, no such pre-release studies are needed despite the fact that, as we have seen, these technologies of mutations induce far more genetic changes than GM foods.

What about the environmental effects of GM crops? Can genes be readily transferred from a GM crop to a non-GM crop? The answer is yes. In *Mendel in the Kitchen*, Nina Federoff deals with this issue in a chapter entitled: 'Pollen has always flown'. In summertime we are used to the weather forecast telling us of the day's pollen count. Pollen is the male part of plant sexual reproduction and is released in very large quantities. A maize corn plant may release 25,000 pollen units, each the size of a grain of salt. Pollen flies and most pollen is wasted. To be successful, it has to hit the female part of sexual reproduction known as the style. Pollen from a particular plant has eyes only for the style of a similar plant, which explains why my garden looks the same every year. The lily has not become an iris and the iris has not become a rose and indeed the red rose stays red each year, notwithstanding the proximity of the yellow rose, which also manages to retain its yellow colour every year. The pollen and the style from the same plant can make the next generation. The flow of pollen in the wind has allowed a natural experiment over the millennia where varieties a great distance apart from one another can cross-pollinate. The anti-GM lobby has transformed this standard cross-pollination phenomenon into a myth of 'gene-flow'. But farmers who produce crops for seed production have always known that if they are to produce pure seeds, they need to be sure that the neighbours are not growing competitor varieties that could mar the pure seed production. Nina Federoff cites the example of canola, a form of rapeseed oil that has come to dominate the vegetable oil component of our diet. Before canola, rapeseed had high levels of a fatty acid known as erucic acid, which in moderate doses caused cardiac problems in animals. This is yet another example of a perfectly natural but toxic plant chemical. So, plant scientists methodically bred successive lines of rapeseed with lower and lower levels until they got today's canola oil, which is effectively free of erucic acid. But when they were breeding their precious plant, they had to make sure that neighbours weren't growing the traditional rapeseed whose oil was fit only for industrial purposes. The distance required for cross pollination was carefully studied and it was found that if the normal rapeseed was planted within 1,000 feet of a canola crop, 3% of the canola would be contaminated by the normal variety. However, if the reverse is considered, only 2% of the normal variety took up canola genes even as close as 140 feet. Other studies give similar results. In the case of the transgenic papaya trees, if non-GM varieties were grown next to the GM variety, a 1% transfer occurred but, if 400 metres separated the two, no cross-pollination was found. In a major study of gene-transfer in Australia, a herbicide-resistant canola, not genetically engineered, was examined under realistic field conditions. The level of transfer of the herbicide resistant plant was three seeds per 10,000. Thus, while pollen can fly, it does not fly far and it has to hit a compatible plant. It is therefore possible to allow the growing of GM crops under conditions which confine them in such a way that pollen flow is eliminated. And we should always bear in mind that pollen will also fly from atomically mutated crops carrying known and unknown genes. But, somehow, that doesn't seem to matter.

Now let us focus on the argument that the use of GM crops will significantly alter the wildlife in agricultural land. The humble monarch butterfly, the so-called 'bambi of insects', was to hit the headlines in the late 1990s with a report that corn, which was genetically engineered to kill the European bore weevil, also killed off the monarch butterfly. This piece of genetic engineering was achieved by inserting into the corn a gene that would cause the plant to produce a protein called Bt, which is a natural compound produced by soil bacteria and which is lethal to the weevil. The monarch butterfly is a wily creature. It feeds on the leaves of milkweed plants and one might ask why a little butterfly is so insistent on feeding on such a single source of nutrients. The explanation is a beautiful story of nature. The monarch butterfly migrates annually from Canada to Mexico, making the long journey successfully. Birds and other predators leave them alone. The simple reason they do so is that in eating the leaves of the milkweed plant, the monarch butterfly accumulates a plant toxin from the leaf to which it is immune but which is toxic to any bird foolish enough to dine on a monarch butterfly. Birds have long learned not to eat these butterflies. Scientists took pollen from corn genetically engineered to contain the protein Bt and they sprinkled this corn pollen on milkweed leaves and, lo and behold, this killed nearly half the population of monarch butterflies, eliciting the usual scaremongering headlines about the dire consequences from GM foods. Now it is important to remember that monarch butterflies do not eat corn but do eat milkweed leaves. So the question was asked: In corn fields, might pollen fall on milkweed leaves so that if the corn was the GM variety to contain Bt, the pollen falling on the milkweed leaf would be poisonous? To resolve that question, the US Department of Agriculture in 2000 set up a steering committee comprising scientists, civil servants and consumer groups to allocate research funds to address the risk assessment question in relation to Bt modified corn and the monarch butterfly. In 2001, five scientific papers were published in the Proceedings of the National Academy of Sciences.

The net outcome of the risk assessment was that the risk to the monarch butterfly from Bt corn was negligible. In most commercial hybrids, there is insufficient Bt protein in the pollen to cause the butterfly any harm. The overlap of the time when pollination occurs in the corn and when larval development occurred in the butterfly was just 60%. Finally, only a small proportion of butterflies use milkweed in cornfields. One variety of corn that did have enough protein expressed to damage the butterfly was phased out of use immediately. However, buried in the detail of the paper is the really important comparison between crops treated with the standard chemical insecticide and the Bt engineered GM variety. Survival of larvae that had been fed the insecticide treated leaves (conventional farming) showed a survival rate of 0–10%. In the case of the larvae fed the GM variety, survival was 80–93%.

Bt corn is intended to kill the European bore weevil and not the monarch butterfly. But, in the course of time, is it possible that the weevil will become immune to the Bt toxin, thus returning us to the starting point and maybe wasting decades of hope and concern over GM crops? The answer is yes, but again, the technology has thought of this. Farmers who buy GM seeds expressing the gene for an insecticide from a company must sign a contract that they will create small insect refuges at strategic locations around the GM crop. The refuge contains a non-GM variety of the crop. Let us imagine a thousand weevils descending on Farmer Brown's field. Because the refuge is relatively small in size we shall assign 100 weevils to settle on the refuge. The other 900 settle on the GM corn that is expressing the insecticide. If 1% of these survive, which is an unlikely high value, then we'll have 9 resistant weevils. Of the 100 weevils that landed on the refuge, let's imagine 9 died naturally and 91 are left. We now have 100 weevils that are going to mate. The probability of a resistant weevil mating with another resistant weevil is 8% and the probability of such a weevil mating with a non-resistant type is 92%. Of this 92%, all will have just one copy of the resistant gene and, under the laws of genetics, this single gene will not do the job and the progeny will not survive after dining on the GM corn. In this way, the selection advantage is against the resistant strain.

In chapter eleven, we shall look at consumers and how they see risk and so we will come back to GM foods. We will also come back to them in the final chapters when we begin to consider global hunger and the interaction of the food chain and the environment. But for now let's leave GM with some conclusions. Humans have been playing with the genomes of plants from the earliest times and what we all could agree as natural plant-breeding methods were in use up until the 1930s when mutation technologies took over. These technologies shatter the plant DNA and the vast majority of mutants are discarded, but some are kept for breeding back with the non-mutated variety. The plants acquire an entirely new genetic code, which carries the gene for the desired new trait but also carries a whole host of unknown changes in the genetic code. We know that these mutated crops can give rise to unintended effects when released and that these new genes are as likely to travel on pollen as much as on GM pollen. Some of these unintended effects are of importance to agriculturalists and some are in the realm of human health. But nobody cares. No agency regulates these new varieties. In contrast, GM crops are rigorously tested and rightly so. The National Academy of Sciences Committee issued a report on the relative safety of GM and conventional crops (*Environmental Effects of Transgenic Plants: The Scope and Adequacy of Regulation*). Two of their conclusions are worth considering here:

> In comparing conventional and transgenic approaches to crop improvement, the committee is in agreement with a previous NRC report (2000) which found that both transgenic and conventional approaches (for example, hybridisation, mutagenesis) for adding genetic variation to crops can cause changes in the plant genome that result in unintended effects on crop traits.

Based on a detailed evaluation of the intended and unintended traits produced by the two approaches to crop improvement, the committee finds that the transgenic process presents no new categories of risk compared to conventional methods of crop improvement but that specific traits introduced by both approaches can pose unique risks.[19]

So mutated crops with their genomes blitzed to pieces escape the regulatory net. It simply doesn't make sense. However, as we shall see in chapter eleven, sense is not emotion, and emotion is what drives the anti-GM lobby.

CHAPTER FOUR

The Metrics of Food and Health

The science of epidemiology studies the clustering of diseases and illnesses whether they are the infectious diseases such as SARS which erupt, spread and then rapidly disappear, or the chronic, non-infectious diseases such as cancer, heart disease or arthritis and the like. Many of these chronic diseases are now known to have a dietary element, which greatly influences the frequency with which the condition appears. This is the science of nutritional epidemiology and the present chapter is intended to give the reader an insight into how it all works. It is a branch of human nutrition that has contributed enormously to our understanding of diet and health and this branch more than any other has helped shape national and international food and nutrition policies. It was nutritional epidemiology that discovered the links between salt and blood pressure, between different types of fats and blood cholesterol, between the B vitamin folic acid and the common birth defect, spina bifida, and the link between fish intake and cognitive function to mention just a few. Once the nutritional epidemiologists have noted an association between some dietary practice and some adverse health effect, the experimental nutritionists enter to test this association both in animal models and ultimately in human studies of dietary intervention. However, as with many scientific disciplines, nutritional epidemiology also has its limitations and thus the present chapter will seek to examine all facets of the subject of nutritional epidemiology.

Nutritional epidemiology measures both nutrient intake and disease and then relates the two to reach its conclusions on healthy eating. The first side of the equation is measuring food intake and then converting that food intake into nutrient intake. Many tools are available to nutritionists to measure nutrient intake and the merits or otherwise of each one are endlessly attacked, defended and debated at scientific conferences. The bottom line, however, is that they are all flawed and the best a researcher can do is to minimise these flaws in carrying out the research and to bear these flaws in mind when analysing the data. I would argue that all of the tools are equally flawed, but different adherents to different tools would argue otherwise and usually that argument ends in the conclusion that theirs is the least flawed method. We'll come to the heart of this flaw shortly but first let's turn to the tools of the trade, the choice of which is dictated primarily by the question being posed. In some instances, as we will see later, very large numbers of people (hundreds of thousands) must be included in the study and under such conditions the tool needs to be 'cheap and cheerful'. The most commonly used such tool is the Food Frequency Questionnaire (FFQ). A set number of foods are described (126 food items in the widely used Harvard method, but others can be several hundred food items) and the respondent can tick a box to describe the frequency of consumption of the food and some indicator of portion size. In large studies it can be posted to participants who complete it themselves, accessing help, if needed, by telephone or by the Internet. The end product for the researcher is that for each participant there is a figure for the intake of all foods on the list (frequency of intake * portion size). For example: 6 eating occasions of breakfast cereal per week at an average serving weight of 30g = 6 * 30 = 180g/week or 26g/day; 4 slices of bread a day on 6 days a week and an average weight of 30g per slice = 6 * 4 * 30 = 720g/week or 103g/d.

In other instances, sample sizes are smaller simply because it is intended to be much more invasive or demanding of the subject. A typical tool for such a survey would be a food diary, which each respondent completes. In our own national surveys, respondents fill in diaries two to three days at a time with each subject visited four times in the study week. The information provided is very detailed. 'Breakfast' is not enough. Neither is 'cereals, tea and toast'. The respondents have to state clearly which cereal (we record data at brand level), what type of milk, toast, spread, juice etc. is used. For quantification of the amount consumed there is a hierarchy of approaches, such as actually weighing frequently consumed foods (slice of bread, cereal, etc.) or using food photographic atlases where respondents choose a photograph of a particular serving size from a range of serving sizes of known weight. This is all very labour-intensive and thus costly and hence the smaller numbers (thousands). The end product is the same: for each respondent there is a detailed description of each food eaten on every eating occasion and a value for the weight of the food eaten. There are, of course, other methods which achieve the same end result, but these two represent the issues that we need to understand. Now, the weary researcher can start the dreary task of entering these data into a software programme of a food composition database.

The researcher has data on exact food intake, a weight for each eating occasion and the appropriate code to the appropriate food in the database. This is enough now to complete nutrient intake. The code might be, for example, 'New potatoes roasted in vegetable oil'. We know the exact weight of roast potato consumed. The nutrition composition database tells you the exact levels of nutrients in 'New potatoes roasted in vegetable oil'. Thus we can exactly compute the nutrients ingested arising from that weight of 'New potatoes roasted in vegetable oil'. Note that the description of the food is fairly exact. Not potatoes but 'New potatoes'. Not 'roasted' but 'roasted in vegetable oil'. The nutrients in such a weight of such a food include all the known nutrients: energy, protein, fat, types of fat, carbohydrate, types of carbohydrates, fibre, all the vitamins, all the minerals, all the amino acids, all the fatty acids and so on. The detail of the output is as long as your database allows.

The real excitement begins. To researchers, new data is what it is all about. The planning, the execution and the meticulous attention to detail are over and the thrill of virgin data follows. But before your trusty nutrition researcher presses the return key on the computer to unleash the wonders of the data, remember the fact that the collection of food intake data is fundamentally flawed. There will be coal all right in the data – good coal even, but no diamonds.

But we must turn to the major flaw of dietary intake: people lie about their food intake. Now 'lie' is probably too strong a word, but a very large number of respondents do not report truthfully. Why so? The vast majority of people in those parts of the world where food is plentiful struggle with their weight. Those who don't are a rarity. Thus, on Monday mornings, the week begins with great intentions and very serious efforts not to over-indulge and to get off one's butt. Come the latter part of the week, it only needs a wee nudge, good news or bad news, good day or bad day, to collapse into a wayward life of eating and drinking and, frankly, having fun. Then, Monday comes around again and so the cycle goes on. Most people have bimodal eating patterns. Whether it's within a week, a month or a year, there are contrasting periods of restraint and indulgence.

So when a volunteer is recruited into a study, probably having been screened to exclude those too young, too old or for whatever other reason, the serious-ness of the research is explained. 'You must follow a normal diet.' 'You must follow a normal diet.' 'You must follow a normal diet.' It is drilled into them. And because people are inherently good – well, most people – they follow their normal diet. But what is normal? Is it the periods of restraint or the periods of indulgence? My guess is that people regard the Monday diet as normal and the Friday diet as a lapse. So they report on Monday-style eating patterns and during the study week they don't relapse into the weekend of abject failure or they don't report doing so. Because Monday's diet is restrictive, the overall reported caloric intake could be below credible levels.

How do we know that many people under-report food intake? A person lying in a coma is expending the lowest amount of energy compatible with life to sustain vital organ function, such as a beating heart, a breathing lung, a filtering kidney, a memorising brain and so on. The amount of such coma-level energy expended is called basal metabolic rate, but since we mostly measure people lying awake, resting rather than in a coma, this can be called resting metabolic rate. Men have more muscle and organ per unit weight than women so they have a higher resting metabolic rate because muscle is more demanding of energy than fat. And bigger men have bigger metabolic rates than smaller men and so on. Thus if we know age, gender, weight and height we can predict resting metabolic rate. Most surveys will collect such parameters and they can thus estimate resting metabolic rate for each subject. We can then match the energy or calorie intake reported and the expected resting energy expenditure. A mismatch means a likely misreporting and it is almost always under-reporting. I have seen reported average energy intakes that simply cannot be true. Either the entire sample is comatosed or is failing to correctly report their dietary habits. Since they are not the former, they are distorting the truth.

The under-reporting of energy can be studied using a technique which we needn't bother ourselves with, but which relies on 'heavy water' based on non-radioactive isotopes. They help us to precisely measure energy expenditure of free-living people. You just drink a glass of heavy water labelled with the stable isotopes of oxygen and hydrogen and then later give a sample of urine. Assuming that body composition does not change during the study, one gets accurate measurements of energy intake (equals expenditure where body composition stays constant) and a very accurate and individual picture of under-reporting. And what is the best predictor of under-reporting? The percentage of under-reporters rises proportionately with body weight. The fatter you are, the more likely you are to under-report. It all makes perfect sense. The fatter you are the more likely you are to struggle with your diet and to have more frequent cyclic periods of indulgence and restraint.

Public health nutrition generally hides this problem. Some study it to try and understand it more, but most studies linking diet to health and disease simply ignore it. The biggest problem of all arises when we want to study how patterns of food intake are related to disease, which is what we now turn to.

People have three routes to choose from when they under-report food intake. They can deny ever eating the food, they can report some but not all eating occasions, and they can under-represent the amount they eat when they say they do eat a given food. Our own research suggests two things, neither particularly helpful. First, under-reporting involves fibbing at every level: denial of ever eating, lying about frequency of eating or about portion size when eaten. Second, there is no universal targeting of particular foods such as snacks or foods commonly perceived to be 'unhealthy'. All foods are involved in under reporting. But when you read a study linking meat with colon cancer, or almond with heart disease or whatever, bear in mind that upwards of 40 per cent of people are not truthfully reporting energy intake, that energy comes from foods and thus we cannot, simply cannot, be certain that one study group (with cancer) under-reported meat or almonds or whatever more than another part of the study (without cancer). If samples are large enough, the flaw or error may be randomly distributed equally, both in the diseased group and the healthy group. We hope so, but we have no objective way of showing how true our hopes are.

The second part of the metrics of food and health is to measure health or rather its absence in the form of disease. Counting the ill and the dead is not a very pleasant job but one that epidemiologists have to do. Moreover, they have to do this for specific illnesses at specific sites in the body and they have to do so accurately. The process of studying nutritional epidemiology can be divided into two: the study of diet and risk factors for disease or the disease itself. In the case of heart disease, both high blood cholesterol and high blood pressure are risk factors for heart disease. If you have high values for either you have an increased risk of heart disease but no guarantee of it. There are people who smoke heavily, are overweight, have high blood cholesterol and high blood pressure and live to a ripe old age. And there are others, who are non-smokers, are lean and fit and have normal blood cholesterol and blood pressure and who die young. Epidemiology is not about individuals, however. It is about populations. Thus we can be certain that a population with a high concentration of smokers, with a high prevalence of obesity, high blood cholesterol and high blood pressure will have a high rate of heart disease. We cannot, however, tell who in the population will get heart disease and when. To many, that day may not be far off, as we will discuss in the next chapter.

For the purposes of this section, it will be easier to focus on two diseases – heart disease and cancer – because they represent the two extremes in challenges to the epidemiology of diet and chronic disease. The most extreme would be to opt for those who have died and who have undergone a post-mortem examination where the subsequent pathologist's report verifies heart disease. Fine for the epidemiologists but not for the nutritionists, because ascertaining dietary habits in the deceased is a dead cause. The next best would be to turn to living patients and to verify the existence of the disease in such patients through some hospital-based diagnostic imaging such as angiography and after that an ECG or stress test might do. For certain, you cannot take the word of the subject or the subject's doctor. End points, as these measures are called, must be verifiable. In the case of cancer, we can also look at a verifiable MRI scan and a verifiable biopsy. Thus for both diseases there are definite diagnostic end points which epidemiologists can use. But heart disease differs from cancer in that we can also study risk factors for the disease such as blood cholesterol or blood pressure. We know that if we measure such factors, we find either or both high in some group, and we know with near certainty that more people in this group will go on to get the disease. Moreover, we can do experiments using these risk factors and I will return to this shortly. But for cancer there are no known or easily measurable risk factors. Almost always, the end-point counted is the clinical manifestation for cancer – the lump or pain that brought you to the doctor in the first instance. The problem with this is that the visible lump or the pain from the invisible lump is the end of a long story called cancer and in this highly complex story we can only guess which aspect of diet might be linked to which chapter in the story book of cancer.

All cells in the human body divide, grow and die in the cycle of life. When a new cell is formed, it has a good chance of having some faulty DNA and an equally good chance of having any repairs to this faulty DNA quickly mended. But if a cell has faulty DNA and the DNA is not repaired, it has two choices: it can die and there the story ends or the unrepaired DNA can divide and give rise to a rogue cell line, the very first chapter in the book. Because a rogue cell has faulty DNA, which does not exactly follow the DNA sequence of its host, it will produce some rogue proteins on its surface and these will be recognised by the host's immune system. So the rogue can be eliminated at this stage by the body's immune system. Again, if that is the case, the story ends there. Equally, the small pile of rogue cells can be held in check (equilibrium) by the immune system so that they remain viable but quiescent and this equilibrium phase can continue into old age without ever escaping the hold of the host's immune system. Or, as the next phase is so named, the rogue pile can 'escape' this hold and now motor on to become a full tumour, growing and sequestering its own blood supply until finally it is a palpable lump or a pain. Thus, when an epidemiologist sets out to count cancer, he or she can only count those 'cases' that have reached the final chapter. Those subjects described as a 'control' might be free of the disease (the lump, the pain), but they could also be at an earlier chapter in the book of cancer, not yet visible or, indeed, never to become visible. These two diseases represent the extremes of the task facing the epidemiologist. For diseases like cancer, which have no obvious and easily measurable early stage biomarker, the discovery of reliable biomarkers is the Holy Grail.

So here we are and ready to start counting the dead and ill. As ever, there are many tools to choose from and the two I will use to illustrate the nature of the problem are case-control studies and prospective cohort studies. In case-control studies, people suffering from the disease are identified and then age and sex-matched controls 'free' of the disease are picked. The dietary habits of the two groups are compared. Fairly straightforward one might imagine. Dream on. It's fraught with problems. First you must find your cases. Let us imagine you wanted to study heart disease in relation to diet and for whatever reason you wanted to use a case control study. You could randomly select persons from the population and give them a questionnaire asking them if they ever had heart disease diagnosed or whether they were taking medication for heart disease and then verify the presence of the disease from hospital records of ECG or angiography studies. Then from those who don't have heart disease you get age and sex matched controls. Heart disease is fairly common (prevalence of about 10% in adult males), so you wouldn't have to have such a big initial sample to find a reasonable number of cases. But suppose you wanted to examine ovarian cancer, which is likely to affect only 1.5% of women. Sampling from the general population will make it difficult to find cases, so you may have to work up some way of recruiting from clinics. And the headache here is that when you have obtained a comprehensive list of patients with ovarian cancer from the clinic and you randomly select from that, you take the good with the bad, meaning that you will always have very advanced cases and you cannot ignore that fact just because you find it uncomfortable to interview a terminally ill patient. And then comes an even bigger headache. In assessing their diet, you don't want to know what they ate last week or even the week of their diagnosis. You need to probe their dietary habits of yesteryear to determine their dietary pattern when the disease started, which means trying to piece together a view of their diet several years ago. This recall is further bedevilled by the bias that comes from having a disease. Do people with a disease deny or not past lifestyles implicated in the disease? Nobody said it was easy.

The other tool that is commonly used is the prospective cohort study. In this instance, upwards of hundreds of thousands of persons are recruited into the cohort. If they are in any way sick or ill with a verifiable chronic disease they are excluded. Once they meet the entry criteria they are examined to study their diet, to get a blood sample and to get a clinical examination. This is referred to as baseline data. Usually, they are followed every two or so years for many years. Those who develop a chronic disease early in the life of the cohort are excluded. Then onwards in time, at a certain point into the life of the cohort, the dead and the ill are counted for a particular chronic disease. These are matched for age and sex within the living cohort and again the epidemiologist compares the 'cases' and the 'controls', but this time there is no recall problem and no bias from the presence of the disease. So why on earth do case-control studies? Well, the prospective-cohort studies require huge numbers and a massive investment to get them going and a massive commitment to keep them going. Thus the financial investment to set up such cohorts and to keep these complex entities fully functioning is very high. There is also the problem of the yield of cancers. In the Women's Health Initiative study, for example, some 49,000 women were studied over eight years.[1] The number of cases of breast cancer was 1,727, an overall yield of 3.5%. Breast cancer is very common. If one wanted to study ovarian cancer, which is much less common, too few cases would be recruited in the follow-up. For these types of cancer, the case control study is the best option despite all the faults.

Now we have reached the stage where all the data are in, both the detailed count of the dead and ill and the detailed analysis of food and nutrient intake and, in the case of the prospective cohort studies, probably blood data and clinical data. The number crunching begins and the statistical massaging kicks in. At the end of the day, the epidemiologist may declare that indeed there is an association between the intake of a particular nutrient or food category and some chronic disease and that that relationship is not confounded by any other lifestyle factors. This is what you read in your newspapers: 'Scientists at the University of Numbers have found that people who have high intakes of high teas have low levels of low back pain.' So frequent are such press releases from publicity mad universities that this type of information is often downgraded to the page filler level. The problem for the science of nutritional epidemiology is that the above effect is an association. Is it the case that people who have low back pain like high tea or is it that people who have high tea also have something else as well as low back pain? You can go on all day about what might be the case. The only hard facts are the observed association: *that people who have high intakes of high teas have low levels of low back pain.* In order for us to unravel cause from effect, we have to complete a dietary intervention trial. These dietary intervention trials to test some hypothesis derived from nutritional epidemio-logical studies, the outcomes of which have huge societal implications, are not for the fainthearted. They are large, expensive, high-risk, lengthy as in many years and with an audience of vested interests in attendance, half of whom want you to fail and half of whom want you to succeed, almost at all costs. Carrying out a study to test the hypothesis that the type of carbohydrate sugars used in carbonated soft drinks causes obesity will be watched by that industry, by government, by scientists of different leanings as outlined in chapter ten and by non-governmental organisations which exist to clobber this industry or foster that industry. The studies have to be large enough to be 95% certain of finding a statistically significant effect. A study which does not have sufficient power would be rejected by the relevant ethics review committee because it would discomfort a large number of people with no hope of success. So these studies tend to be large as in hundreds or very large as in thousands. Moreover, the effect may become evident quickly as in months or slowly as in years. I have chosen two dietary intervention trials to serve as case studies.

The first involves the DASH (Diet Approaches to Stop Hypertension) study.[2] About one in four adults in developed countries suffer from high blood pressure (hypertension). A number of dietary factors are associated with this condition, including high salt intakes, high alcohol intakes and being overweight. Many other factors have been implicated including dietary fat levels, potassium intake, and the intakes of fibre, magnesium, calcium and protein. All of these were implicated within nutritional epidemiology studies and had not been part of any cause–effect type analyses. The literature was full of studies, which looked at villain number 1 sodium (salt is sodium chloride), but there was precious little on the other nutritional factors. The DASH study set to address that question. Three intervention diets were used. All subjects began with a control diet typical of the US standard diet and they were on this diet for three weeks. They were then put on one of two diets. The 'fruit and vegetable diet' had increased levels of fruit and vegetables at the expense of snacks and sweets and was intended to provide high intakes of potassium and magnesium and moderately higher fibre intakes. The 'combination diet' was also high in fruits and vegetables but in addition it had reduced total and saturated fat intakes and had higher magne-sium, potassium and calcium intakes.

The dietary intakes of the subjects were monitored throughout the study and, by and large, the intervention was a success and all of the target intakes were met. When all was done, the results showed that both interventions worked and both reduced blood pressure, but the best effect was seen with the combination diet, high in fruits, vegetables and low fat, low saturated fat dairy products. Everybody was happy. The epidemiological findings were upheld.

The second example I have chosen is the Women's Health Initiative (WHI) study.[2] When the association between diet and heart disease first emerged in the 1950s, it was a 'man thing' and the executive man thing at that. In the course of time the profile of the afflicted changed somewhat but it was still a man thing. And then, in the 1980s, the issue of women arose and it became politically correct to include 50% of your research sample as women or risk having your funding application rejected. Postmenopausal women were now seen as no more different to men in terms of risk factors for chronic disease. In time, the idea of a women-only study emerged and hence the women's health initiative was born. The primary disease end points for the women's health initiative were breast cancer and colon cancer, which together account for the major burden of cancers in women. A secondary end point was heart disease. The hypothesis, based on many observational epidemiological studies, was that a reduction in the intakes of total and saturated fats with an increase in fruits, vegetables and wholegrains would significantly reduce the incidence of these diseases. Two dietary treatments were used. The 'Usual diet' was a typical US diet for women of that age at that time. The second was an intervention diet, which was a low fat–low saturated fat diet, high in fruits, vegetables and fibre. The dietary intervention was generally successful. Although there was a big reduction in dietary fat intake by year 1, showing an 11% reduction in the treatment group compared to the control group, this waned a little over time so that by year 9 the difference while still real had dropped somewhat. The intakes of both saturated fats and of fruits and vegetables in the intervention group remained elevated, as planned, throughout the study while the intakes of wholegrains tended, like total fat, to wane somewhat over time. The results were not as expected. There were no significant differences of any form between those women put on the experimental diet or those left on the usual diet in the level of any of the targeted diseases during the course of the study. Then the questions flowed. Was the study long enough? Did the intervention group really achieve the original dietary targets set? Were there changes in the control group over the nine years? And on and on. Some of my nutritional epidemiology colleagues consider the study to have been flawed. Some say the intervention was not successful and cite a sub-study, which used stable isotopes to measure under-reporting.[3] But the reality is that under-reporting was found with both those given the low-fat test diet and those who maintained their normal diet. The former under-reported more than the latter. However, that is not an explanation of why the anticipated outcome wasn't found. There are those who will use the results of the women's health initiative study to bolster their views that all this dietary advice is a load of codswallop. There are others for whom this negative outcome will not check any of their highly committed views. But some of us will be worried by these findings in the sense that the very attractive hypothesis that was tested, based on extensive epidemiology, was refuted.

Measuring the link between diet and disease is not easy. The tools used are crude and it takes a huge effect to be verified in intervention studies. These tools will get better and in the next chapter we will explore the sharpening of these tools in the post-genomic era.

CHAPTER FIVE

Personalised Nutrition: Fitting into your Genes

In the previous chapter we saw that if epidemiologists are given data on key aspects of lifestyle, they can predict, on a population basis, the probability of occurrence of a given chronic disease. They can predict at the average population level but not at the individual level. Equally, we saw that when a population has its dietary patterns changed epidemiologists can predict the average response in terms of risk factors such as blood cholesterol or blood pressure. Again, they can predict at the average population level but not at the individual level. However, it has long been recognised that this variation between individuals in their response to some dietary intervention has a high genetic component. Since the sequencing of the human genome, our ability to better understand this effect of genetic influence on dietary factors has greatly increased and it fast led, as we will see, to the belief that we are now at a point where we can tailor our nutritional advice to one which is optimal for a given person. That is likely to happen, but I will argue in this chapter that there are many serious hurdles yet to be overcome before we reach that point.

One way for the non-expert to understand the human genetic code is to compare it to an encyclopaedia. The encyclopaedia has 23 volumes (chromosomes) and within each volume there are individual chapters (genes). So far, these technical terms are commonly used but two less commonly used terms are about to be encountered. Within each chapter (gene), there are words (codons) and within each word (codon) there are letters (nucleotides). Where it now begins to differ is, firstly, the alphabet. In the standard encyclopaedias that we are all familiar with, each word is made up of a selection of one or more of the 26 letters of the English alphabet. In the genetic code, each word (codon) is constructed from a genetic alphabet of just four letters (nucleotides): A, C, G, T (adenine, cytosine, guanine and thymine). The second difference between the encyclopaedia and the genetic code is that, in the encyclopaedia, the words can range from just one letter long to very, very long words. In the genetic code, the words (codons) can only have three letters of the four genetic code letters (nucleotides A, C, G, T). Each codon is the unique codon for one of the 22 amino acids which make up the proteins in the body; these proteins play a central role in regulating metabolism. The sequence below lists the 176 codons which carry the genetic code for the synthesis of a protein involved in the regulation of our appetite – leptin.

atg cat tgg gga acc ctg tgc gga ttc ttg tgg ctt tgg ccc tat ctt ttc tat gtc caa gct gtg
ccc atc caa aaa gtc caa gat gac acc aaa acc ctc atc aag aca att gtc acc agg atc aat gac
att tca cac acg cag tca gtc tcc tcc aaa cag aaa gtc acc ggt ttg gac ttc att cct ggg ctc
cac ccc atc ctg acc tta tcc aag atg gac cag aca ctg gca gtc tac caa cag atc ctc acc agt
atg cct tcc aga aac gtg atc caa ata tcc aac gac ctg gag aac ctc cgg gat ctt ctt cac gtg
ctg gcc ttc tct aag agc tgc cac ttg ccc tgg gcc agt ggc ctg gag acc ttg gac agc ctg ggg
ggt gtc ctg gaa gct tca ggc tac tcc aca gag gtg gtg gcc ctg agc agg ctg cag ggg tct
ctg cag gac atg ctg tgg cag ctg gac ctc agc cct ggg tgc tga

In reality, there are no spaces between codons, and the genetic code above follows the rules of the genome using CGAT as the 'letters' and having all 'words' using only three 'letters'.

For any gene, the sequence of these four letters, organised in bundles of three, varies quite significantly within the population. If genetic material were written in stone, never to be altered, then we would be rather simple single-cell creatures if we existed at all. Basically speaking, common variation in the genetic code may at certain times be neither a disadvantage nor an advantage. But if the environment changes then some common form of genetic variation might have an advantage over all other variations. This 'selection pressure' now leads to the genetic pool being enriched in the advantaged form. Imagine two families of some animal species in evolutionary times. One is excellent at making vitamin C and one is hopeless at this process. In times when there is little vitamin C in the diet of this species, the efficient vitamin C manufacturers win out. But when these nomads wander into the orchard, as it were, the non-synthesisers win out because they don't have to waste precious energy making vitamin C when they are awash in it in the orchard. The genetic change which comes to dominate is the *one most suited to survival at a given time point*. Unlike our ancestors who survived as the fittest of the prevailing and somewhat challenging environment, we are now masters of our environment. We can make it hot or cold. We can grow food, kill malaria, divide labour, order society and of course continue the tradition of warfare, greed and savagery. Thus we don't have the same selection pressure as our ancient forebears. Notwithstanding the fact that we're at the end of the evolutionary line, at least for now, we have inherited all the genetic variability of the most recent survivors of evolution. We may all share the same genes. But as we will see, we don't always share exactly the same genetic code on each gene. Only now are we beginning to see the consequences that can arise from subtle changes in genetic sequence leading to altered protein function because of a single change in amino acid sequence. Until a decade ago we could read only some of the genetic code meaning that our capacity to exploit this knowledge was limited. This all changed with the sequencing of the entire genetic code which heralded the genetic revolution, a revolution which has implications for human nutrition.

In humans, genetic variation can exist at two levels. First there are variations which involve major changes. These are very rare and can cause very serious disease. In the disease PKU (phenylketonuria), a key protein is missing which is involved in amino acid metabolism. If untreated, it will lead to permanent mental retardation. It is detected by a heel prick at birth and can be very successfully treated with diet. The second type of variation involves a single codon where the nucleotide 'letters' are jumbled. Thus one might have a codon with the nucleotide sequence 'ATG' (the first codon in the leptin example we have just seen) and where this is changed to 'ACG'. The former codes for the amino acid 'methionine' and the latter codes for the amino acid 'threonine'. This changes the sequence of the amino acids in the protein and this may have no consequences or some consequences which lead to an altered activity of the protein. This second type of genetic variation is referred to as a Single Nucleotide Polymorphism (SNP) and the frequency in the population will be anywhere from 10% to 40%. To try to understand how genetic information can be used to fine tune our dietary habits, we will consider three examples.

The first example involves one SNP on a gene involved in the metabolism of the B vitamin, riboflavin. It encodes for a protein (MTHFR) and at codon 222, one of the letters of the genetic code, the nucleotide C is replaced by the nucleotide T (from GCC to GTC). This simple change which affects about 30% of the population has quite significant metabolic effects. Because you inherit both maternal and paternal genetic information, you can inherit the variation in either of two ways: GTC and GTC which is referred to as the TT type or GCC and GTC which is known as the CT type. A group of researchers at the University of Ulster and Trinity College Dublin found that if they identified people who were being treated for high blood pressure and who also had the TT gene sequence and with low levels of riboflavin in their blood, correcting those low levels with a supplement of riboflavin dramatically lowered blood pressure.[1] Nothing happens to blood pressure for those receiving the riboflavin supplement who do not inherit the TT variant. This is truly personalised nutrition.

The second moves from looking at one SNP to looking at many SNPs. Researchers in the US used advanced computational methods to select not one but a suite of five SNPs that they used to predict the exact diet most suited to someone wanting to lose weight.[2] For some, it was predicted that a low fat diet would be best. For others, a low carbohydrate diet might be best. For yet others, an overall healthy diet was predicted to be best. They put this theory to the test. They had access to data on weight loss using a variety of diets among women all of whom had lost weight over a one-year period. The women had been randomly assigned to one of four diets to lose weight and no account was taken of genetic make-up because such knowledge was not available at the time. The researchers subsequently approached the women to get a sample of their DNA from cheek swabs. They then examined the genetic code of each woman and, based on their computer predictions, they were able to say whether the woman was lucky enough to have been assigned to the 'right' or 'wrong' diet for her genetic sequence. Those who by chance were assigned to the right diet for their genetic sequence lost twice as much weight as those assigned to a diet not suited to their genetic make-up. Once again, this is personalised nutrition. If you want to lose weight, doesn't it make sense to pick the weight-loss approach most suited to your genetic make-up?

The third example moves now from a suite of five genes to the examination of SNPs in hundreds of thousands of genes. This is known as 'Genome Wide Association Studies' (GWAS).[3] In GWAS, we read the whole genetic code and record all variation from the norm. Sometimes we are mightily surprised that an unexpected gene pops out as being important. For example, a group at Tufts University in Boston used GWAS to study the factors in the genome which might lead to variation in plasma levels of vitamin B_{12} which, as we will see later in this book, can be a determinant of impaired cognitive function in the elderly. They found that the gene encoding for a protein FUT2 was markedly associated with plasma levels of vitamin B_{12}. FUT2 is a protein involved in a number of biological processes including tissue growth and development, the generation of new blood vessels and in helping the gut manage a nasty little bug we will soon meet which is strongly associated with stomach ulcers, H.Pylori. Without this unbiased scoping nature of GWAS, it is nigh impossible to see how we could have predicted a relationship with such a protein and plasma B_{12} levels. Such genome wide studies are now the bees knees in genomics studies but, to date, few have included nutritional data in them simply because they use very large numbers of subjects with or without some medical condition and rarely are these groups well characterised by diet. That will change in time. These three examples and the first two in particular throw light on the best dietary options for individuals with particular genetic make-up. That we could tailor diet and overall medical treatment to exactly match an individual's genetic make-up heralded a great deal of very high expectations for personalised health and personalised nutrition.

On 26 June 2000, in an event transmitted around the world, two hitherto competitive bids to sequence the human genome came together to announce the first 'working draft' of the human genome. President Clinton in Washington and Prime Minister Blair in the UK heaped praise on this milestone in biological research. The hype surrounding this event is worth recalling by way of some quotations from that day:

'Today we are learning the language in which God created life': *Bill Clinton*
'We have to focus on the possibilities, develop them and then face up to the hard ethical and moral questions that are inevitably posed by such an extraordinary discovery': *Tony Blair.*
'I can see this technology making the wheel obsolete': *Mike Dexter, Director of the Wellcome Trust for Medical Research*
'We now have the possibility of achieving all we ever hoped for from medicine': *Lord Sainsbury, UK Minister for Science.*[4]

Given the hype of Clinton, Blair and the global press surrounding the sequencing of the human genome, it was not surprising that the hype hit the food and health sector from academia to industry. And, of course, some entrepreneurs began to see a commercial niche whereby people would pay to find out what common genetic variations they had and accordingly to ascertain what was the optimal diet for their genetic make-up. Seduced by the prospect of Euros, Dollars or Yen, the personalised nutrition industry bloomed and promised much. Lest I be accused of colouring the scene to suit myself, here is an extract from the website of Sciona, a leading company in personalised nutrition:

Sciona is a privately held international company that provides personalised health and nutrition recommendations based on an individual's diet, lifestyle and unique genetic profile. The company began on June 8th 2000, the same day President Clinton and Prime Minister Blair announced the completion of the first draft of the human genome project. Sciona was founded on a simple premise: to use the scientific information uncovered in this landmark research project for the benefit of consumers and consumer product companies.[5]

Sciona went bankrupt in 2008. It was a good company, employing excellent people working with the world's best scientists in the field and engaged with the regulatory authorities. It was not as though the entrepreneurs behind Sciona were acting contrary to perceived wisdom at the time. The prestigious Institute of the Future at Palo Alto in the US produced a report in 2003 entitled: 'From Nutrigenomics to personalised nutrition – the market in 2010' in which they predicted that 'The Direct Market Will be Sizeable . . .Our conservative forecast indicates that at least one third of consumers will be making some changes in their nutrient intake in response to personalised nutrition by 2010'.[6] The clever people at Palo Alta got it wrong as did the entrepreneurs behind Sciona. Why were they so wrong?

To begin with the science base of personalised nutrition was at the time extremely weak and it continues to be so. The avalanche of scientific papers linking an SNP with some aspect of diet and some health attribute continues to this day. All of them with the exception of the first two studies cited above are 'associations'. For example, a study might show that people with a particular SNP who have a low intake of, say, polyunsaturated fats have a high level of blood cholesterol. For those without this SNP, there is no link between polyunsaturated fats and blood cholesterol. The inference, then, is that in personalised nutrition someone with this SNP would be advised to avoid low intakes of polyunsaturated fats. That all seems fine and straightforward. However, this is simply statistical association at this stage. The theory might be true or it might not be. The problem is that in order to establish the truth or otherwise of this association, one needs to actually test it. That would mean recruiting equal numbers of those with the SNP and without the SNP and rotating them through diets high and low in polyunsaturated fats to see if blood cholesterol does in fact respond as the theory predicts. Without that, the science base is very weak. The weakness also extends to the unknown effects of modifying an individual's diet in one direction based on genomic data when, unbeknown to all concerned, there is an as yet undiscovered genomic association which would suggest that this dietary change will in fact have an adverse effect. Intervention studies will provide assurance that this is not the case, but association data cannot protect individuals with some unknown adverse effect.

Personalised nutrition is only going to work if it is accompanied by what I call customised solutions. In other words, it is not enough to be told that you should have more of this nutrient and less of that nutrient. You need to have advice on food choice and this leads us to the issue of how the food chain might respond to the concept of personalised nutrition. The following little story illustrates how it will be impossible for the food chain to adapt to personalised nutrition in the way many, including the smart people in Palo Alto, once thought.

Jack and Jill bought into a personalised nutrition service, meaning that they paid $400 to an on-line company who sent them tubes and a little brush and they took swabs of their cheek cells with the brushes, popped them into the tubes and sent them back for genetic testing. They are now armed with their own personalised nutrition information:

Jack: Avoid low intakes of selenium, copper, vitamin E, folic acid and ribo-flavin and avoid high intakes of iron and calcium.
Jill: Avoid low intakes of selenium, iron, calcium, vitamin E and n-6 PUFA and avoid high intakes of saturates, copper, folic acid and vitamin D.

Jack and Jill toddle off to the supermarket and soon find themselves being escorted outside by the shop security. They had been fighting in the aisles over what went into the trolley. Some foods that were 'good' for Jill were 'bad' for Jack and vice-versa. So they kissed and made up and went to another supermarket and this time each took their own trolley and each filled it as best suited their genes. A week later, Jill was back with her mother, sobbing about how impossible it was to accommodate two lots of shopping in one fridge and how terrible it was never to dine together since what suited him didn't suit her and vice versa and since the cooker could only deal with one meal at a time (sob . . . sob). Jack on the other hand was in the pub, crying into his beer at the loss of his beloved Jill: 'The food companies are like dinosaurs compared to Jill and me (sob . . . sob). We have embraced the very technology that Clinton and Blair had blessed. It's not as though I am asking Kellogg's to make cornflakes for every conceivable genetic variation but some effort that would help people like myself and Jill who are trying so hard would at least be a beginning and at least provide some options.' Not long afterwards, Jack was distraught, disconsolate and hitting the beer hard. This was precipitated by his mates ordering a round of soup, assorted sandwiches and a platter of chicken wings, sausages and pork crackling.

This little tale is rather tongue in cheek, but it does illustrate the challenges to consumers and the food industry in meeting the challenges of personalised nutrition. If Jack and Jill had a cat, then there would be no problem in delivering their cat with personalised nutrition because cats eat the same food every day from the nice pet food manufacturer plus the bits and pieces they scrounge from the dinner table. So it would be possible to envisage a pet food chain capable of delivering a range of diets specially blended to optimise the diets of individual pets. However, our food supply is more complex. In any modern food composition database there are about 5,000 foods described. How these are combined is determined by individual food choice, and the number of permutations and combinations is so great that the possibility of delivering a food chain for personalised nutrition is simply out of the question. If we are to exploit the advent of the genomics era for optimised nutrition, we need to think a little more laterally. There is another way of looking at person-alised nutrition. As a concept it emerged alongside overall personalised health and from the beginning was genome based. My argument would be that this is the wrong place to start and I envisage three graded and interrelated levels of personalised nutrition.

The first level involves personalising food choice. At present, we read the food pyramid and head to the supermarket to make choices and where we are not buy-ing fresh produce we read the label to make choices based on the nutrition profile. That of course is the theory which in reality is rarely practised. But let's play along with the theory. There is nobody on the planet who at the end of the shop can integrate all the nutritional information in the supermarket trolley into a final analysis of the adequacy of their choice across a full spectrum of nutrients. Help is needed. One option would be to hire a nutritionist to walk behind you, pushing a laptop on wheels doing the sums. Not an option. However, one could see the day when the supermarket would give shoppers a personal hand-held device to scan the barcode which would contain the required nutritional information and which at the end of the shop could reveal the nutritional content of the foods purchased. I can certainly see that happening. However, it will have its limitations. There is firstly no personal nutrition planning in advance, but maybe that could be built in by way of information on the shopper's loyalty card. Secondly, in the event that, for example, your overall choice led to a very high salt intake as indicated by your handset, you might want to make a change. Rummaging around the trolley to find the offending food would lead to aisle rage.

In reality, the real service will be Internet delivered and there are several commercial companies offering their services for personalised dietary analysis. You log on to a personalised dietary analysis website and enter your personal details: age, sex, weight, height, any medical conditions, location, meal-eating patterns, personal food preference, where you do your weekly food shop, where you buy lunch, how much you like to spend and so on. You then enter your typical daily food choice data using a questionnaire on the website. This is then processed by the personalised dietary analysis service through a standard food composition database producing a wealth of data on your average daily intake of calories, proteins, different fats and carbohydrates, your minerals, vitamins and fibre. In effect you have your own personal e-dietician. Your nutrient intakes are then compared to recommended daily amounts and you receive advice as to the strengths and weaknesses of your nutrient profile. Consider, for example, the case where your salt intake is quite high. The service can tell you which of the foods you eat contribute most to salt intake. It's then up to you to decide which changes in food choice you want to make to reduce that intake and next week you can see how this has improved. This level of personalised nutrition is a commercial reality today and no doubt will be extended to more sophisticated levels, possibly offering detailed options at daily menu level to help people optimise their diet.

The next level of personalised nutrition involves an examination of your phenotype: your height, weight, blood cholesterol, glucose, fats, etc., your heart rate, blood pressure, bone density and so on. Your phenotype is your physical, biochemical and clinical characteristics. Commercial companies exist which offer biochemical screening through the postal service. You receive in the post a little kit in which you prick your thumb and allow some blood to drop on to a piece of absorbent paper. This is then put into the small tube provided and mailed back to the service provider, who extracts the blood and analyses it for those aspects of your biochemical phenotype which are important in person-alised nutrition. They can measure your blood omega-3 levels and, if these are low, can advise you on how to improve things; this can be extended to other biochemical markers of dietary patterns. You will also receive data on blood metabolites which are influenced by diet such as glucose, cholesterol and vitamin levels. Thus someone who opts for this level of personalised nutrition will know for sure what their 'nutritional phenotype' is and, if combined with the first level of personalised nutrition, they will have a very deep knowledge of their personal nutrition without ever going near their genomic data. But this level will also go beyond just blood samples and there is a big commercial interest in the development of electronic devices to help people monitor their health. The first level of personalised nutrition might tell a person that their calcium intake is low. The second level, which delivers nutritional biochemistry data, might tell them that their vitamin D level is low. When they visit their GP, a new heel-based scanning device can measure their bone density. To minimise the risk of falling, they might train their walking habits using electronic gait-tracking systems. All of these are commercially available. You can also personalise your physical activity patterns using portable devices which you wear on a belt that measure your physical activity and which can then upload that data to a web service via a USP port. The web service then gives you options for improving your physical activity. When you have chosen the one you want to follow, data is then downloaded from the website into your portable device. Philips, the Dutch electronics giant, offer such a service.[7] When you wake up in the morning your device is activated and a small red diagonal line appears on the device. As you accumulate the agreed level of exercise, the light slowly turns to green and will be fully green when you have achieved your target. We have now arrived at the point where nanotechnology is helping us to develop smart textiles so that we can wear a vest to monitor our lung and heart function which is transmitted wirelessly to your doctor's computer. This whole area of electronic devices that enable people to get feedback on their health is central to person-alised medicine and to personalised nutrition.

Increasingly, however, we are seeing the term 'personalised nutrition' being used to define the needs not just of individuals but of clusters of individuals. Indeed, many believe that the future will be in the use of clusters. We can use smart data mining techniques in which the software searches a large database and sorts people out into groups which have some common attributes. For example, when we analyse the Irish national food consumption database for food intake patterns we find that the population falls into six clusters. They can be given titles to explain why one group might differ from another. One might find a group entitled 'Traditional Irish diet', another called 'Healthy eating diet' or another called 'Fast food diet', depending on the food choices for each cluster. We are also able to do the same for blood biochemical values. In time, we will be able to use simple dietary questionnaires to classify people into specific dietary clusters and then give them advice on how to move from a cluster with a generally poorer nutritional quality to one with a superior nutritional quality. Dealing with up to ten national clusters will be far easier than dealing with an entire population at individual level, at least in the medium term.

Personalised nutrition thus has a bright future, as long as we start at level one and only work our way upwards on the basis of good quality science. Understanding the gene sequence and its variation poses a huge challenge to us. But the phenomenon of 'epigenetics' makes it an order of magnitude more complex and it is to epigenetics we next turn.

CHAPTER SIX

Plastic Babies: The Phenomenon of Epigenetics

The birth of a newborn baby is a very joyful occasion and it is impossible not to comment on how perfect their features are. But miniature adults they are not. Most organs such as the heart, the lung, the kidney, the gut and the skin will grow to adult proportions with three to five divisions without any great change to their overall design. That is not the case for other organs such as the brain or the sexual organs, which will grow both in size and in complexity as part of normal postnatal and adolescent growth. The three to five divisions that most organs will undergo after the infant is born (3.5 kg total weight at birth going to 7.0 kg, then 14.0 kg, then 28.0 kg, then 56.0 kg in just four divisions) until adulthood pale into insignificance when we think of the 50 + divisions that will have occurred in the womb where the vast majority of complexity is built and where, relatively speaking, growth has seen maximum change. This is of course not unique to humans; it is the way all mammals undergo development. However, there are some very important differences in the way human babies grow, distinctly different to even our nearest cousins, chimpanzees.[1]

Most of the main determinants of growth in size are in the third trimester of pregnancy, the period of maximum growth of fat. Human babies are unique in being born fat, although dolphins are also born fat and that is not the only thing we share with dolphins, as we will see. There are two important features of this baby fat. The first is that this fat, which the baby has accumulated, is located just below the skin as subcutaneous fat. In other animals, any little fat in the newborn is fixed to organs within the body which allows the skin to slip and slide over them without any abrasive damage. In human babies alone, this generous quantity of fat is fixed to the under-part of the skin all across the body giving us lovely fat babies with fat cheeks, necks, arms, legs, tummies, backs and so on. The second striking feature of baby fat is the rate at which it is synthesised. With just ten weeks to go to birth, the foetus will have accumulated about 80g of fat. Some five weeks later, this will have trebled to 240g, and in the last five weeks the fat mass will double again reaching about 500g at 40 weeks. This represents a gain of about 45g/d of fat in this last ten weeks. For an average adult at 70kg body weight and 20% of that body weight as fat, an accumulation of 45g/d of fat would lead to a doubling of the adult's entire fat reserves in just ten or so weeks with a net ten-week weight increase from 70 to 84kg. Thus the rate at which a normal human baby accumulates fat in the last ten weeks of pregnancy is never seen again in life. Even Sumo wrestlers don't match this. To understand why babies accumulate so much fat prior to birth, we need to go back in time, right back to the evolution of the human race.

A big brain was our main evolutionary advantage over other species. In absolute terms, elephants and hippopotami have bigger brains than humans, but as a proportion of body weight we have the biggest brain. A second and related evolutionary event was the move from a quadruped life (walking using all four limbs) swinging in the trees to a biped life (legs only) on the ground where humans could stand tall and most importantly free their hands for important aspects of dexterity which included managing fire, hunting and making tools. The decision to stand up had implications for the female of the species. Think about a more familiar four-legged animal, a cat or a dog. They let their organs hang down towards earth, held up by a strong diaphragm; for quadrupeds, a fat gut just hangs down. The pelvis does no more than connect the backbone to the leg-bones. When mum's ancestral cousins decided to stand up, the pressure from these organs and the gut weighed directly on the pelvis and thus a typically female pelvic anatomy evolved for considerable bone and muscle strength.

We now have three features to consider: a baby to be delivered who has a uniquely large brain in a large skull and is fat, and a mother, who in adapting to walking on two legs, has made the birth passage more difficult with a much strengthened pelvis. Three compromises are made, two by the baby and one by the mother. The latter compromises by rendering the bones of her pelvic region softer and which facilitates delivery. The first compromise the baby makes is not to complete development of the skull at birth. The skull of a newborn baby is not fully formed and consists of a series of bony plates, interlinked but not fully overlapping. We've all seen in newborn babies their fontanelles, a small soft patch on the top of the head below which lies a layer of fat directly above the throbbing brain. During birth, these bony plates slide over one another, reducing the volume of the skull and making passage possible through the birth canal. As Elaine Morgan points out in her book, *The Descent of the Child*: 'This is one time in life when a hole in the head is indeed an asset.'¹ The second compromise the baby makes is to enter the world with a brain that is not nearly fully formed – the intention being to complete growth and development in the next 24 months or so. The joint decision of the baby and mother to manage the bony skeleton and pelvis respectively are fairly easy to understand. But why doesn't the human baby just emerge with a fully functioning brain? Why do babies accumulate so much fat? The two questions are interlinked.

When a foal is born, it quickly stands on its feet and begins to suckle its mother. Within minutes, the foal is beginning to run with the herd. It has to do so because if it doesn't it is easy prey for predators. Soon the foal is eating grass although nobody sat down with the foal and explained what to do. Mares don't have to teach foals to graze grass. The art of eating is a major parental struggle in the early years of a human's life. In order for the foal to survive, its brain has to be hardwired to its immediate needs after birth. In contrast, a newborn baby is so poorly developed relative to the foal that it cannot even hold its head up. It can cry, it knows how to suck and, when put on the breast, the baby knows how to swallow. This extraordinary dependence of human babies on their mother is linked to our bigger brain and the need for that brain to absorb whatever the relevant society it enters deems fit. An Arabic foal and a Shire foal do exactly as is written in the genetic manual of horses. A baby born into an Arabic society will be expected to learn different things from a baby born into a Western society. They will both learn to speak but to speak different languages. They will both learn the difference between right and wrong but with different nuances as to each. They will both learn to feed themselves in different cultural contexts with different foods. Because of this need to learn postnatally, the human baby cannot be born hardwired for performance. It therefore follows that brain development must continue for a period after birth and that, throughout life, the human brain is sufficiently plastic to be amenable to all forms of new knowledge.

We have now explained why the pelvic and bone structures had to adapt to the phenomenon of birth and why the maximum development of the human brain cannot take place in the womb. We still have to explain why babies accumulate so much fat. The reason for accumulating an enormous reservoir of fat so fast is that there is a price to be paid for having such a large brain relative to other species. To begin with, the brain is an energy costly organ. In an adult, around about one quarter (23%) of calories consumed are used by the brain. If you go to a five to six year old, this rises to twice that (44%). At four to five months it is now 64% and for a newborn baby it is a staggering 74%. Pay attention: three quarters of the calories consumed by a newborn baby are headed upstairs to the brain to help to grow and grow and grow because if it doesn't do it then the window of opportunity is lost forever. The first 20–30 months or so of life make our adult brain. Some areas of the brain are more demanding in the newborn baby in terms of energy needs. Top of the list are those regions of the brain involved in hearing. Without hearing (not really necessary in the womb), there can be no speech. Speech is central to the community the baby is born into and speech and language are one of the defining attributes of humans. So with such an expensive organ in terms of energy, a serious reserve of energy after birth is a distinct evolutionary advantage. But it is also a high-octane energy source. The brain is the centre of the nervous system and the nervous system operates by the transmission of electrical signals down interconnected nerves. Like all electric cables, adequate insulation is required because otherwise we get cross firing and short circuits. In the animal world the nerves are insulated by a fat known as myelin and an integral part of myelin is both cholesterol and a particular fatty acid, which falls within the category that most people understand as 'omega' fats, which we met in chapter three when discussing the n-3 polyunsaturates of marine oils. This fatty acid is abbreviated to DHA (docosahexaenoic acid). Many will associate omega fats with brain function and this is the reason in a nutshell. Now, when a pregnant mother eats some oily fish and absorbs the omega fats therein, one would imagine that the DHA would wing its way to the mother's brain and nervous system, where it is needed. In fact the data show that the fat transferred by the mother to the foetus is preferentially rich in DHA so that foetal fat has four times the level of DHA as maternal fat. Thus the fat with which the baby is born will provide an energy reserve but also reserves of DHA, which will greatly kick-start postnatal brain growth. Hopefully, we have now covered all of the factors linked to the uniquely large human brain, the need for the delivery of a baby with an incompletely formed brain inside a flexible skull that passes through a birth canal with a level of flexibility that makes the birth of a baby possible where the baby is armed with an energy source which helps feed the demanding brain and the specialised fats needed to build the insulation needed for brain growth.

The honours student among you might have spotted an obvious question. If the anatomically simple single cell algae in the ocean can make the omega fats upon which fish feed on and which we then feed to get our brain food, why did evolutionary pressure not favour the inevitable mutation which allowed some humans to directly make such a valuable nutrient? That would be an evolutionary advantage in a species that relies on a long period after birth for brain growth and when a postnatal supply of DHA might not be guaranteed. The answer lies in the most likely choice humans made to live after abandoning the forest.

There they were, our ancestral cousins, swinging around in the forests, playing, preening, having sex, feeding, suckling, sleeping, screeching and occasionally sitting in on the big Saturday night fight of alpha males. The evolutionary pressure here was zero. That every reader of this book can see such ape-like happiness in our mind's eye from countless TV documentaries is living proof of their wonderfully sophisticated and harmonious society. So what went wrong or right? Once upon a time, our ancestral cousins experienced a major climate change for which, unlike modern times, they were not responsible. The forests that provided shelter, fresh water and abundant vegetation for food began to shrink. Nature's supermarket grew smaller and there were many fights in the aisles. Some of our ancestral cousins looked outside the forest to other options. Conventional wisdom argues that they migrated out to the Savannah where they became hunters and eventually hunter-gatherers. Now, however brave adult males are in their hunting skills, if they cannot nurture their young to a reproductive age, then the line ends and that group becomes extinct. The capacity to nurture the neonate is thus the first stage in the survival of any species as Elaine Morgan points out. And nurturing the neonate means finding a sustainable source of brain food. The Savannah is not a sustainable source of brain food. In contrast, as Stephen Cunnane points out in his book *Survival of the Fattest*, the riverbank or the delta of the river mouth is just ideal.[2] It is rich in fish and shellfish, which provide an abundant source of DHA. It is rich in birds who feed on the fish and lay eggs rich in cholesterol. And it is rich in another brain food, iodine, a deficiency of which causes reduced cognitive function, which if it occurs at severely deficient levels in pregnancy can cause cretinism, an advanced form of mental retardation. Iodine is much more abundant in the oceans that in the earth's crust and it is partly volatile. This iodine evaporates into the earth's atmosphere and returns to the ocean with rainfall. Rivers and the seafood that lives therein are thus rich in the iodine of rainwater. Therefore, in such an environment, there was no evolutionary pressure for humans to waste their energy and vital nutrition making any brain nutrient that was in abundance all around them. Nor was there any need for the large-scale storage of iodine. And that is how we evolved to depend on an external source of DHA and not to have any iodine stores. Elaine Morgan, who has written extensively on evolution, argues persuasively about the aquatic origins of humans in her book *The Aquatic Ape*.[3] I don't wish to enter this great debate on where our evolution took place, but it is rather intriguing that we share two things in common with the smartest aquatic creature of all, the dolphin: a baby with lots of fat and subcutaneous fat at that and a big brain. Wouldn't it make one wonder about mermaids?

We have evolved a system of gestation, delivery and growth that allows that us to sustain the evolutionary advantage we inherited. But what happens when it goes wrong in the food and health sense? What happens if within this evolved norm the expectations of nutritional well-being are not met? We will answer that question by first looking at pregnancy.

Poor nutrition during pregnancy can significantly hinder foetal development, but mainly in the latter phases of pregnancy when, having built the complexity of human life, the final stages are primarily growth to normal birthweight. The outcome of such deprivations will be a smaller baby – smaller than its true genetic potential. Small doesn't mean a proportionate shrinking of all features. Limbs will shorten, as will the trunk and all that is in it. However, the brain will show very little shrinkage. Nature recognises the singular importance of the brain over all other organs and protects it. Small adults and large adults share similar brain size. When the baby is born, a period of undernutrition will lead to a period of reduced growth rate so that gradually the child will fall behind the expected height for a given age. If this period of undernutrition is short and adequate food is eventually made available to the baby, then the baby will undergo a period of accelerated growth and will catch up with its peers returning to the correct height for age. However, if the young infant or toddler suffers prolonged energy shortage where adequate food levels never materialise, then the reduced height will become permanent. This is called 'stunting' and we will return to this in chapter twelve. Once again, we need to treat brain growth and development separately. If in the first few years of life an otherwise well-nourished child is denied access to an adequate supply of those nutrients critical to the development of the brain, then the result will be a permanent reduction in cognitive function. In the two or so years after birth when the brain reaches its optimum size, it is very vulnerable to an inadequate supply of brain food. The loss of cognitive function is irreversible and again, in chapter twelve, we will take another look at this from the point of view of nutrition in the developing world. These concepts were at the heart of my lectures on nutrition in growth and development for decades and during that time it never dawned on me to ask the key question which, with today's knowledge, is so obvious. Who or what overruled the genetic code? Let's just think about it. Imagine two identical twins, which means we are considering two babies who share 100% the same genetic material and who shared the same journey from conception to delivery in their mother's womb. At a certain point in postnatal development, let us imagine a period when energy insufficiency occurs and both twins show a slowing down of growth so that they are beginning to fall below the norm of height for age. After a period of time one twin is given access to food and shows an accelerated growth response, returning to a normal height for age. The other twin continues to suffer energy shortage to a point where, when adequate food is eventually restored, catching up with the other twin is no longer an option. These identical twins will grow up with two different heights. They were both born with identical genetic instructions and, in the case of one twin, this was overruled. Who or what did this? Similarly, a child born of short stature because of energy insufficiency in the last trimester of pregnancy will remain of short stature throughout life. Who or what overruled the inherited genetic potential for growth?

We now know that whereas we inherit our genome from our parents and nothing at all can ever change that genetic code in terms of the sequence of genetic information, the expression of particular genes can be 'tweaked' upwards or downwards during pregnancy and early postnatal life. Let's try to get behind the concept of gene tweaking, which carries the technical term 'epigenetics'. In every cell in your body you carry the full genetic code you inherited from your parents. That is why in forensic medicine any piece of biological tissue with DNA can uniquely identify you. We saw in chapter five that genes can be active (expressed or up-regulated) or dormant (not expressed or down regulated). So think of each person's DNA being akin to them having their own unique piano in every organ, each with a full set of keys. In my brain, the piano plays John Lennon's 'Imagine'. In my heart muscles, it plays Rod Stewart's 'You're in my heart'. In each case, only some keys are played: some in the brain but not the heart and vice versa. And some are not played in either organ. Some are played *fortissimo* and others *adagio*. That is the way with our genes. In every organ they are all present but some are switched on and others off and some only slightly turned on while others are, so to speak, fully on.

The critically important point to note is that, when the cell's DNA is tweaked during the epigenetic process, that's it for life or for a very large part of it. That cell will divide and keep on dividing right through life and at every division the tweaking that was first done in the womb or in the very early years of life is carried on. Epigenetics is forever in many but not all cases. When one reflects on the process, it makes eminent sense as nature always does. The human body and its functions are so complex that there has to be a certain rule of law. Because every step in biology has massive knock-on effects elsewhere through the body, constant changing of key operational procedures would lead to mayhem. Thus there is a very strong adaptive mechanism, but this elasticity is only allowed within certain bounds set in the critical periods of growth. This tweaking of genes was seen as an adaptive mechanism for the foetus and the newborn to optimise its gene expression to suit the environment. It was a baby thing and long forgotten into adulthood. That thinking was to change in the late 1970s and early 1980s with the advent of the concept of foetal programming of adult onset disease. The story is truly fascinating.

David Barker, an epidemiologist with the UK Medical Research Council based at Southampton University, was puzzled by the geographic pattern of coronary heart disease in the UK. It seemed to mirror the voting pattern of the Labour Party in that the pattern was strongly influenced by the proportion of the population then referred to as 'the working class'. If you were to look at the map of childhood mortality 50 or so years earlier, you would see that they exactly matched the heart disease map that David Barker was looking at and so the question was asked as to whether the pattern of heart disease, prevailing at the time in the 1980s, was related to events more than 50 years ago. Thus began the amazing story of what is now known of the Barker Hypothesis of the foetal programming of adult disease. The following account of the story is taken from an article in the *British Medical Journal* by David Barker entitled: 'The Midwife, the coincidence and the hypothesis'.[4] To explore the hypothesis, the team had to identify (*a*) individuals with proven cardiovascular events alive and well in the 1980s and (*b*) detailed birth records of the same individuals. As it happened, the only realistic option was the other way round: find archived birth records from 50–60 years ago and trace the surviving individuals to the present day to ascertain their prevailing health status.

By all accounts, the British working class was in poor health at the dawn of the twentieth century. In 1902 it was reported that almost two thirds of potential recruits for volunteers in the Boer War in South Africa were rejected because of poor physique. This prompted the British government to establish a committee to look into child health. The conclusion was that the health of British children was nothing short of atrocious. Among those to respond to this appalling state of affairs was the medical officer for the County of Hertfordshire in declaring: 'It is of national importance that the life of every infant be vigorously conserved.' He was soon to appoint the country's first Chief Health Visitor and Inspector of Midwives, Ethel Burnside. By 1911, Burnside had a cadre of nurses trained to attend women in childbirth and in the care of infants in the very early years of life. This included weighing all infants born in the country at birth and at one year of age. A separate ledger was retained for each village.

David Barker and his group at Southampton became aware of these ledgers soon after his search of national archives. His first request to study the archives was refused by the county's senior archivist who wished them to remain closed for a further 50 years to protect the midwives whose not uncommon harsh remarks about individual mothers were deemed to be sensitive. By a bizarre coincidence, David Barker had lived in a Hertfordshire village with the quaintly English name of Much Hadham with his mother during the war to escape the bombing blitz of London. His sister was born there in 1943 and, on the basis that Barker had a mother and sibling listed in the archives, he was given access on condition that they be kept under secure conditions back at Southampton University. A quick call to the head of the university revealed that such conditions could readily be met since the university also housed the private papers of the Duke of Wellington within secure archives. Thus Miss Burnside's archives were deposited alongside the private papers of the Duke of Wellington and, in keeping with the promise to the county archivist, they remained there, with David Barker and his team given access at agreed times to transcribe the detail. And then the search began to locate those persons whose birth records for the period up to 1930 were available. Some 15,000 men and women were traced and their health in the 1980s was linked back to their birthweight in the 1920s. Thus began the Barker hypothesis of the foetal origins of adult disease. Many other records were uncovered not only in the UK but elsewhere, all adding to the body of evidence to support this hypothesis.

I can clearly recall an occasion, shortly after the first of these papers was published, when a prominent cardiologist recoiled in horror at the mention of this research. It was ridiculed because it was uncontrolled, confounded by a world war, a cold war, an economic depression, a post-war boom and anything else you think of to belittle this upstartish hypothesis. For anyone to suggest that your mother's diet during your gestation was a bigger determinant of your present-day likelihood of getting heart disease than your present dietary patterns was beggaring belief. Such is the tenacity with which scientists adhere to theories. We will return to the subject of the tenacity of scientists to stick to pet theories in chapter ten. Fortunately for David Barker, his colleague in the Institute of Human Nutrition at Southampton University (my alma mater) Professor Alan Jackson developed an animal model to test the hypothesis.[5] Rats were fed normal diets, then mated and following successful mating (easy to tell in a rat) the protein level in the diets of pregnant rats was reduced. The reduction in protein was enough to sustain a perfectly normal pregnancy but was also enough to upset the ability of the embryo to have optimum protein synthesising ability. The moment the litter was born, the mothers received the correct level of protein, ensuring that protein was a limiting nutrient only in pregnancy and not in lactation, weaning or early growth. The young pups grew into adult rats and by all accounts looked perfectly normal. However, they all developed elevated blood pressure. These rats didn't suffer economic swings or world wars or cold wars and so an animal model would not only provide supporting evidence but in time would at least in part unravel how all this was happening.

There are endless studies which can be cited to show evidence that birth-weight has a profound effect on health in later life. I will take three examples to illustrate the evidence, each introducing a new nuance to the story. The first is the association of adult chronic disease, in this case type 2 diabetes (determined by an oral glucose tolerance test) in 370 men aged 59 to 70 years for which birth data were available.[6] Those with a birthweight in the range 3.0 kg to 3.4 kg had five times the risk of developing diabetes as those with a birthweight of 4.3 or greater. This rose to sevenfold if birthweight was less than 2.5 kg. This is a staggering effect. The lightest babies go on to have a 6–7 times greater risk of diabetes than those with the highest birthweight.

The next study introduces the placenta into the equation.[7] The placenta is an interesting organ. The embryo and the placenta share the same genome and as such can be seen as twins. The placenta is also connected to maternal blood supply and has to balance the signals it receives from the foetus and the mother, signals which may sometimes be conflicting. In this study, the researchers looked at blood pressure in men and women aged 50 years and ranked them according to both their birthweight and the weight of their placenta. At any placental weight, adult blood pressure was highest among those with the lowest birth-weight. Equally, at any given birthweight, as placental weight rose from less than 454g to greater than 681g, blood pressure also rose. Thus the worst scenario was to be a light baby with a heavy placenta and the best scenario was to be a heavier baby with a light placenta. These blood pressure differences were not minor. They were very significant.

The final study I have selected introduced a measure of growth after birth. A cohort of 13,517 men and women born in Helsinki between 1912 and 1944 was studied.[8] Body size was available at birth but also at years three and eleven. Once again, the data showed that the incidence (%) of type 2 diabetes and high blood pressure increased with decreasing birthweight but the scale of the difference was also influenced by subsequent growth. At the highest birth-weight, it did not really matter what the weight of the children at 11 years was. However, at lower birthweights it did and, for adults who had birthweights less than 3.0 kg, the level of diabetes in those who gained most weight in the first 11 years of life was doubled above those who gained the least.

Those are three samples of studies from a huge array of literature which leaves us with no doubt but that the health of men and women in adulthood can be traced back to their growth *in utero*. This is not to say that, as with genes, we blame our mothers, throw our hands up in the air and dive into the French fries. In adulthood, through diet, exercise, proper medical care and a healthy lifestyle, we can seriously reduce our risk of disease, irrespective of what level of contribution came from our short life in the womb. Experiments on pregnant women to examine birth outcomes are 100% unethical and thus much of what we know about this area comes from famines of which the Dutch famine at the end of Second World War is the most informative.

In the latter stages of the Second World War, the allies launched Operation Market Garden to secure a number of key bridges across the Rhine. The oper-ation was partly successful, but the bridge in Arnhem could not be captured and became immortalised in the title of Cornelius Ryan's novel and subsequent film *A Bridge Too Far*. The exiled Dutch Government organised a railway strike to help the allies. The occupying German army retaliated by putting an embargo on food transport into the region. As the winter of 1944–5 set in, a major shortage of food ensued and the Dutch Hongerwinter (Hunger Winter) ensued. Caloric intake fell to 1,000 calories a day at first and then to 580 calories in February 1945. Some, 10,000 Dutch citizens died in the Hongerwinter, which started in September 1944 and ended in May 1945 – a full nine months.[9] Now the fun-loving Dutch continued to procreate so that some pregnant mothers entered the famine in September 1944, thus affecting the latter stages of preg-nancy. Some were pregnant entering the famine. Some were pregnant for the duration of the famine and some became pregnant late in the famine which thus affected the early stages of pregnancy. A study of 300,000 male military recruits aged 19 years of age in 1964, exactly 19 years after the Hongerwinter, showed that those whose foetal life was nutritionally disturbed in the latter period of pregnancy showed least effect. Those whose foetal life coincided with maternal caloric restriction at the earlier stages of pregnancy were more likely to be obese at 19 years of age. The early stages of pregnancy are about building complexity more than size while the latter stages are about building size rather than complexity. When caloric restriction of mothers occurs early in pregnancy, the design genius of foetal development takes the message very seriously and re-jigs the design of the baby. This is adaptation and adaptation is the engine of survival and evolution. Those who can adapt to environmental changes survive; those who cannot are lost to the species. Our gene pool is rich in survival options.

The phenomenon of epigenetics and foetal programming of adult disease is one of the most interesting areas of research in diet and health. We will return to it briefly in chapter eight when we come to consider one of the most important public health problems of our time, obesity. But first we need to tackle another unlikely aspect of human biology which may also come in to its fore in obesity, the human gut.

CHAPTER SEVEN

Your Inside Is Out: Food, the Gut and Health

When we were children, my younger brother swallowed a small coin, a three-penny piece. We shared the initial anxiety that such a non-food item had entered his body but then waited with excitement for it to re-emerge from his body and it did. Was the coin inside him? In the layman's term, yes it was in him. In strict biological terms it wasn't in him. It entered his gut which is a long tube, a very long complex convoluted tube that goes through the human body like a hallway in a block of apartments, goods in, goods out. But you can enter this hallway one end and exit it another without getting inside an apartment. To be truly 'inside' you, one has to cross over the barrier that keeps the inside in and the outside out. In the apartment block the barrier is the front door, secure, alarmed and fully protected. In the gut, the barrier to the external world is one that the gut shares with many parts of the body. It covers the barrier parts we can see, such as the eye and the skin, and the barriers we cannot see such as the lining of the lung or ear or urino-genital tract or lactating nipple. Bar the gut, which has one entrance in and usually another entrance out, the others are cul-de-sacs. So the gut is outside you and this chapter explores this amazing organ as it pertains to food and health. The gut is, as we will see, the no-man's-land between the outside of us and the inside of us and it is an organ of unique intelligence. In terms of food and health, get the gut wrong and the rest will sadly follow suit.

The gut is about five to eight metres long, which compares to the Olympic long jump record of just less than nine metres. It is divided into very broad sections: stomach, small intestine and large intestine and one can take any one of those and find whole textbooks on anatomy. This chapter will focus on the remarkable relationship humans have with these gut bacteria, the huge role played by the gut in our overall immune system and the dialogue the gut has with the brain in the regulation of food intake and in many other quite surprising areas. Let's start with the latter.

Early in the formation of a human embryo, a small clump of cells, the neural crest, becomes evident which soon splits into two parts. One migrates upwards so to speak to form the human brain. The other migrates to form what is known as the 'enteric nervous system'. In time the embryo will come to connect these two nervous systems via the vagus nerve. The enteric nervous system comprises a highly complex set of nerve wiring which runs in strands along the length of the gut wall from mouth to anus.[1] It contains a network of 100 million nerve cells (neurons) with all the same features of nerve transmission as the brain. It has a greater nerve transmitting capacity than the whole of the spinal column which feeds from the brain. Again as in the brain, there are several central command areas, each called a plexus. These talk to the brain via the vagus nerve, a massive superhighway of nerves that emanates from the gut, which goes upwards on your right-hand side to enter the spinal cord at junction 19 (19th vertebra of the vertebral column). The command centres of the gut rule the roost. The vagus nerve can act to turn up the level of activity, but the nerve impulses that flow to and from command centres in the plexus of the gut are effectively independent of the brain. Think about such common terms: 'butterflies in my tummy', 'gut feeling', 'gut instinct', 'threw up at the sight of it' or 'haven't the guts for it'. Without being students of neurobiology, the reality of the gut as an adjunct brain has entered the common vernacular. Why 'two brains'?

Millions of years ago, our ancestors emerged from the primordial pool, plonked themselves on watery rocks, eels-out-of-water, snake-like, lying there, doing nothing but waiting for some prey to walk close to a swishing tongue to be gulped into the mouth – not very demanding in the brain department. Then as species evolved and grew legs and learned to walk, to run, to hunt and kill, a bigger, more complex and more sophisticated brain was needed, and so our cranial brain evolved. What about the gut brain? What was the evolutionary advantage? That is always, always, always the key question to ask in biology. Let us first imagine an evolutionary process where the gut-brain was abandoned as not necessary for this sophisticated hunter, orders of magnitude more intelligent than his eel-out-of-water forebears. To do so we need to consider the gut. It is a most hostile and inhospitable environment. It is dark, wet, swirling and lacking oxygen. It has parts awash with hydrochloric acid and other parts awash with enzymes that mindlessly break down proteins, carbohydrates and fats with the charm of muggers. Incredibly strong detergents are secreted into the gut. It's not a straight tube but twists and turns, this side up, that side down and worse than the worst roller coaster. And in certain parts there are great explosions of gas, inflammable gases like hydrogen and methane or odious gases such as hydrogen sulphide that would stink you into embarrassment. It is populated by gazillions of bacteria who have their own agenda. All this before you eat. And you might eat a new plant which is highly toxic or get a bug from filthy water which could grow, invade the gut wall and release into your blood the botulinum toxin, the most poisonous toxin on the planet. Those who evolved without a gut-brain just didn't survive, because by the time the brain realised that something was wrong in the nether regions of this utterly horrible environment, it was too late. The damage was done. But those who evolved with a gut-brain that did its own thing did survive. If something nasty is sensed, its 'vomit or diarrhoea time' and 'sorry, brain-brain', action is need now. The brain-brain sees a predator and the gut brain picks up the signal. Together they act – 'flee and no bathroom stops allowed'. You are to visit a dentist. You're apprehensive. 'Don't eat' says the gut brain: 'That way you will avoid the massive rush of blood to the gut as happens when we eat. Better keep it for the brain-brain which can see and co-ordinate things from the flight deck.' The brain-brain may be the master of most controls, particularly those of a higher order associated with the advanced human neo-cortex. But the gut-brain is master of the gut and that is no small organ and it is the master of many aspects of our survival and emotions. That the gut-brain can act independently of the brain-brain is evident from the once fashionable approach to the treatment of ulcers which involved cutting the vagus nerve. A gastric ulcer was seen as an event of stress. This stress is recorded by the brain-brain which, according to this theory, stimulates the vagus nerve leading to excess acid release in the gut thereby causing ulcers. Cutting the vagus was supposed to help.[2] As we will see later in this chapter, ulcers are now known to be caused by an infectious agent working in the gut and we will come to these in due course. For the many treated for ulcers in this way, the severance of the brain-brain and gut-brain links didn't diminish the latter in any way, such is the independence of the gut-brain.

The gut is the border keeping inside in and outside out. It is an amazingly complex border and for the purposes of this chapter we will look at only some of the sophisticated armoury at the gut's disposal to patrol this border.[3] To understand how it all works, we need to consider some simple anatomy. The cells lining the outer part of the gut, the one which meets the food you eat, have an unusual structure. They have hundreds of long protruding pieces which reach out into the gut, waving away like fans at a rock concert, thousands of long arms aloft waving in motion to the music of the night. This serves two functions. It swooshes bits and pieces of undigested food to the centre of the gut, away from the gut wall until they are fully digested and capable of being absorbed. It also offers a very large surface area for the absorption of nutrients. And it stops bacteria from gaining access to any point of entry to the gut. These cells secrete a thick mucus-like substance to help reduce damage to themselves from the debris and mayhem of the swirling gut and the bristles are very pliable, swishing this way and that with the vagaries of the tides of flowing gut contents. Along the length of these gut cells lies a wide range of really smart defensive mechanisms to keep the outside out. But what exactly is the gut so afraid of? Who are the enemy?

To understand that, it is time to turn to the inside. Once you traverse the gut, you enter the serenely beautiful and peaceful interior where there is strict law and order. Everything in there, except for the matter absorbed from the gut, is made to measure and the supply chain runs all the way back to your genes. The police in this orderly interior are the proteins and they are made to the strict blueprint of our genes. Everything in this orderly environment is 'self' and the enemy is 'non-self' that might illegally traverse the border from the gut's no-man's-land. As we have seen, within the serenely peaceful interior, every protein can be traced back to a part of the genetic code inherited from the mother and father. The proteins we eat in our diet were designed by some other organism's genes whether that be a milk protein designed by cow genes, a wheat protein designed by wheat genes or a protein on the outer surface of a bacteria, made to the bacteria's genetic rule-book. Should such proteins illegally cross the border, there is a sophisticated immigration control system to deal with these non-self intruders of which more later. As we will soon see, the gut is awash with bacteria, but the gut and the bacteria have signed a treaty and the two live peacefully together. The enemy is any protein or bacterium that crosses the gut.

Let's take a look at the defence arsenal of the gut. The most basic of weapons is no more than the mucus secretion we just mentioned. This is similar to your nose which traps the airborne non-self bits and pieces you inhale from your atmospheric environment and for which you occasionally need your hand-kerchief. In the gut, mucus secretion is pretty well ongoing, but if too many bacteria get too close, the output is considerably increased. The bacteria get trapped in the mucus which is shed and released into the tidal and downward flow of gut contents. The next level of defence is the release of very small proteins which are like smart military rockets, homed in on microbial cell walls. Once there, they simply punch a hole in the bacterial cell wall which is instantly fatal for the marauding bug. If things hot up, so to speak, a form of cells like our white blood cells (neutrophils) can be released into the gut to patrol the gut wall itself, devouring any bacteria in sight or indeed any protein or particulate matter that for some reason has become too close for comfort. Without sending out cells, the gut has protrusions of another set of white cells called dendritic cells. They are octopus-like cells and in the case of the gut they can manage to stick one of their tentacles from the 'inside' zone out into the gut, periscope-like, more than happy to engulf unsuspecting rogue bacteria that have no respect for the bacteria-gut treaty.

And of course, the gut defence arsenal contains a stealth weapon, known as Peyer's Patch. Throughout the external side of the gut are aggregated areas where the gut offers a soft spot to intrusive bugs or proteins. It's a soft spot, deliberately vulnerable because it lacks the swooshing long arm-like protrusions and the attendant goo-like mucus covering and because it is two-faced: one side just outside and one side just inside. But lurking beneath the flimsy and deliberately vulnerable cells, just inside our true inside, lies an array of very well trained elite white blood cells known as M cells who devour bacteria and proteins. They do one other really smart thing. They don't quite fully digest proteins from bacteria. They temporarily retain some of these proteins intact and hand them over to a type of white blood cell known as a B-lymphocyte, an elite police force within the sophisticated immigration control system. Remember, this microbial protein left over from the M-cell vultures is derived from a gut bacterium and thus it is 'non-self', that is, not made from our genetic code. One B-lymphocyte will be recruited from the garrison to produce an antibody to this protein. And this conscript lymphocyte will clone itself to perpetuate this information until death, not their death – your death. This is part of our immune 'memory'. Once seduced into the Peyer's Patch, once sampled, never, ever forgotten. The B-cell conscript, armed with the exact details for the manufacture of the antibody to eliminate an exact foreign protein, sampled through this system, emerges from the gut and eventually enters the bloodstream. And where does it go? It goes to the borders where inside meets outside. We have focused on one border, the gut. But there are others: the lung, the urino-genital tract, the lactating breast, our tear ducts, ears etc. The conscript B cell sends clones to all of these borders. And in return, the B-cell conscripts recruited through a similar mechanism at all the non-gut borders also flock to all other borders. This is a seriously joined-up defence system. The B cells home in to the gut right along its length and secrete these antibodies to protrude into the swirling violence of the digesta. When the targeted protein is encountered on a live bug cell wall, it is handcuffed and left to the devouring neutrophil to demolish the culprit.

Of all the non-gut borders that engage in this process, there is one that merits very special attention – the breast. It may not normally be thought of in the same breath as the gut, but the connection is enormous and, given any reflection at all, the connection is obvious: the breast makes a food which will encounter a very special gut, that of the suckling infant. Oliver Wendell Holmes, a highly revered American Supreme Court Judge renowned for his eloquence, once wrote: 'A pair of substantial mammary glands has the advantage over the two hemispheres of the most learned Professor's brain in the art of compounding a nutritive fluid for infants.' The judge was spot on, in all but one aspect. Successful lactation does not require mammary glands to be substantial!

The mother's gut, lungs, urino-genital tract sample the bacteria and other non-self proteins in the immediate environment of the newborn and synthesise thousands of A-type antibody clones targeted at very specific non-self targets. Not only does she deal with the immediate environment but she has a library of these relating to past encounters of non-self. These A-type antibodies accumulate at high levels in breast milk, especially in the first few days when the milk is referred to as colostrum. These line the baby's gut like an antiseptic paint: total protection. Now, note please that this maternally derived antiseptic paint is not a permanent gift. It makes evolutionary sense for the baby to learn how to do this itself since mammy will not always be around. But while she is, the young baby gets a very sophisticated helping immune hand. Another protein unique to breast milk (not found in cows' milk) is called lactoferrin and it reduces bacterial growth by sequestering free iron in the gut. For bacteria to proliferate in the gut, they need nutrients. Breast milk is very low in iron compared to that of cows' milk and most of the iron is sequestered on the lactoferrin. Moreover, lactoferrin when secreted in milk isn't fully saturated with iron and so lactoferrin can take up free iron from the gut. Bacterial growth is limited by the low levels of available iron, most of which is sequestered on to lactoferrin. And of course, lactoferrin readily gives up its iron load to the gut of the nursing baby for its growth and development. Thus A-type antibody and lactoferrin contribute to the maintenance of gut integrity and immunity. So too do the many complex carbohydrates in breast milk which function as caviar for certain types of bacteria in the gut and, having alluded to these bugs several times this far and to the gut-bug treaty, it's time now to delve into detail about our gut microbes.

We've all seen documentaries on major hospital surgery and how it is possible to create an asceptic environment in which surgeons can open up our innards, exposing inside to out, fix us, stitch us up and send us back to the ward to recuperate and go home. The efforts that the team has to make to create a sterile environment are humungous. Bacteria like warmth and moisture and spare food and they are not bothered by the absence of oxygen. Thus our gut is perfect for them and, bar living in a sterile bubble, eating sterile food and breathing sterile air, there's precious little we can do about it. Early in evolution, the two sides came to understand one another – you, the 'host' and they, the microflora. Obviously, if we have to entertain a microbial colony in our gut, we don't want it to be dominated by nasty bugs which could proliferate to overcome our gut defence systems and infect us. This does happen with food poisoning and gut infections but, in general, there is peace. In effect it's in the interests of the gut bacteria to keep the bad ones out because if they get to dominate it's curtains to all – us and them. As one reviewer put it, we live mostly with 'armed peace' and, occasionally, we break out into 'open warfare' with our bacterial squatters.[4] So, from an evolutionary point of view, we got a peace treaty and we will come to that, but that alone is only part of the deal. The other part is that the microflora can digest things we cannot digest and those that could eke out every last scintilla of nutrition from a begrudging diet were evolutionary favourites. First the stats, and they are remarkable. There are more than 100 trillion bacterial cells in the human body, the vast majority in the gut. This is ten times the number of cells that make up the human body as such. About 1.5kg of our body weight is microbial matter. In all, the gut microflora has a staggering 100 times more genes than we ourselves have. We are a minority in our own bodies in some respects. These stats are impressive but the biology is awesome.[5] These bacteria generally feed on (*a*) fibrous material we eat but cannot digest, (*b*) gut cells that have passed their use-by date and which are sloughed off into the swirling tidal flow of digesta, (*c*) material secreted from the gut which has finished the scheduled job including enzymes, mucins etc. and (*d*) one another, since bacteria will live for 20 minutes, die, decompose and be eaten to enter the life-cycle all over again. To begin to explain this from our point of view we will first address (*a*) above, material available to bacteria of dietary origin, effectively known as dietary fibre.

When a wheat seedling shoots out its first green leaves to the photosynthesising sunlight, it is full of soft and pliable cells. The cells have walls like we have skin and, inside, the little baby wheat cells do whatever little baby wheat cells do. And one thing they do is reproduce and grow – 2, 4, 8, 16, 32 and so on. Soon, the little shoot starts to get heavy and the bit nearest the ground gets thicker, less green since it is more interested in acting as a scaffold to the growing green bit at the top than growing itself. Soon, the structure is so heavy that the stem is now pure straw. Taking the mature wheat, there is only one fraction we can digest: the starchy content of the grain along with a tiny fraction, the wheat germ. The rest, which we call bran, is a mixture of quite complex carbohydrates that we cannot digest and which pass through our gut to reach our squatting bacteria. They now secrete enzymes which release the sugars from these fibrous components which the bugs now live on. Now, because we live in an oxygenated environment, we can fully burn sugars. Because bacteria do not have access to oxygen in the gut they take the energy extraction process from glucose only part of the way, extracting just a fraction of the energy that we do. The bits they leave behind cross the wall of the colon and thus they are available to us to burn further for energy. With the help of these bacteria, we have extracted the last scintilla of energy from plant foods. In return, we let them keep enough to feed themselves and to hand their leftovers to us.

This is an important part of the deal with our bacteria, especially as we have relied from time to time on very coarse vegetable food. Until recently, that was how the gut bacteria were regarded: a simple bioreactor. But that is a gross simplification. We will return to the bioprocessing part of the gut-bug treaty later but, first, let's consider the relationship between the host and the microbes. As we have seen, our microbial allies live in a dark, swirling, smelly biomass, peppered by bursts of gaseous energy. It's a violent, dog-eat-dog life with no graveyards for has-beens. But it is a life that is at harmony with the gut because, if both parties respect the treaty, it is a win–win scenario. At the risk of annoying my colleagues in gut microbiology, we can divide all the bacteria in the gut into a rather small number of clans so to speak. Within each clan are different families and in any clan there may be very many bacterial families. Normally, in such a stormy biomass, diversity would appear to be a good thing: lots of different types of bacteria, which rise and fall like warring clans or in microbial terms like 'blooms' in polluted lakes. But that is not the case in the gut micro-flora. The number of major clans is quite small, surprisingly small.[6] How, therefore, does such a small range survive the vagaries of this violent biomass? Do some clans get clobbered with one stress and flourish with another? No, there is much greater stability and that is achieved not by a huge array of families with different genetic repertoires, but a small number of clans with very large genetic repertoires. Thus a typical clan will open up that part of their genome, which encodes for complex carbohydrate digesting proteins when such complex carbohydrates abound. But when they don't abound, that part of their large genome is shut down and another one opens up.

The dialogue between the gut bacteria and its host – you – is quite amazing. One such dialogue goes something like this: 'There's no grub here and under the terms of the treaty you have to provide me with some.' And so certain bacterial clans (a big one with an unpronounceable name which we'll call

BTIM) secrete a signal that the gut wall cells recognise and which switches on a gene in the gut cell to make a special type of sugar called fucose glycans which it then secretes to the dining table of the gut microbes for their lunch, thus fulfilling its part of the treaty.[7] Just in case it escaped your attention, this is an adaptive microbial genome ordering your genome about. Another example of this can be seen when our gut microbial allies sense a rising population of bacteria that have not signed the peace treaty and which if allowed to proliferate would be like the rebels taking over the fort. In these circumstances, the bacteria send a message to special cells in the gut wall to release compounds which don't damage the signatories of the treaty but which are lethal for the rebels. Who is master and who is servant?

To fully understand this mutual relationship, it is best to study germ-free animals, usually mice. These animals are derived from generations of mice born and bred in specialised sterile germ-free conditions. When these germ-free mice are inoculated in their large bowels with bacteria from conventionally reared animals and thus cease to be germ free, there are dramatic changes to the colonic anatomy itself: it gets thicker, develops a bigger mucosa, enterocytes divide more rapidly, it secretes more mucus and it becomes richer in blood supply.[8] How does the advent of these bugs cause the gut function to change so much? That remains a mystery but it does seem that the microbial genome can talk to the human genome. And, to complicate matters, the same is true in reverse: the human genome talks to the microbial genome. Studies have shown that different individuals in different environments have different arrays of microbial clans and that, over periods as long as six months, those differences persist. Moreover, studies with identical twins from different families showed a high level of similarity in twin–twin microbial flora compared to twins from different families.[9] Of course it could be argued that since twins share the same environment, that is the basis of them having the same colonic microflora pattern. However, in the same study, when a twin was compared to their married partner, also sharing the same environment, there was a poor correlation in their gut flora. This suggests that our genome is dictating the composition of our gut flora. Hence that is why twins have similar gut flora, because they have identical genes. But a counter argument can be made if your colonic microflora is determined by your mother at birth. That might explain why twins are similar. Some animal studies support this. Three female rats were involved.[10] Mother 1 and mother 3 were sisters, born in the same litter. Each produced one litter. Mother 2 was unrelated and produced two litters. The microbial patterns of mother 1 and mother 3 were similar and their offspring, cousins, also showed comparable microbial patterns. Mother 2 was unrelated and she had a different microbial pattern. That same microbial pattern was passed on to both her litters. The extent to which our genotype (our genetic potential) or our phenotype (what we look like) might shape our gut microbial population is a moot point and the exact role our mothers play in this is not clear. But it is an area of explosive interest because, whether we like it or not, obesity is now related to our gut microbial pattern.

Jeffrey Gordon at the Washington University School of Medicine in St Louis has pioneered this work. The experiment was as follows.[11] One group of mice was raised in sterile germ free conditions and fed a standard diet, which was sterilised. These were germ free and lacked any gut microbial colony. A second group of mice of a genetically identical strain were fed the same diet under conventional conditions. They were not germ free and had a standard mouse gut microbial colony. The comparison thus far might seem fair – same genetic strain, same diet; one germ free and one not. But living in germ-free conditions might in itself have an effect: no tender warm hands from a smiling animal technician. Rather it is a case of hoods, remote handling, gloves, masks and all the paraphernalia that make germ-free conditions possible. So a third group was created. Some germ-free animals at seven weeks of age, in an isolated facility, had their coats smeared with faeces from non-germ-free mice. Thus in time these mice developed a colonic microflora but lived life as though they were germ free. They were non-germ free but living life in germ-free conditions – false germ free we can call them. The researchers looked at body fat and food intake. There were no differences between the non-germ free or the false germ free. But the true germ free had a lower percentage body fat with a higher food intake. Because the germ-free animals lacked any gut microflora, they could extract only a fraction of the calories in the mouse diet and thus they had to eat more just to get enough to grow on. But they couldn't extract enough energy to deposit fat. In contrast, the non-germ-free mice, awash with treaty-abiding bacteria in their colons, were so clever at extracting every last ounce of calories from their feed they could eat less and still get fat.

Gordon and his colleagues went one step further and looked at a protein called Fasting-Induced Adipocyte Factor (FIAF). The cells of our gut wall can produce this protein but our normal gut bacteria suppress its manufacture: yet another example of their genome telling our genome what to do! FIAF blocks the uptake of fats from blood into our adipose tissue stores. By slowing down FIAF release from the gut, the bacteria are now allowing fat to move from blood into adipose tissue. In germ-free animals, there is no such suppression and FIAF blocks the uptake of fat into adipose tissue. Gordon and his team genetically engineered these mice to block FIAF synthesis. The germ-free mice now got fat. Thus, in addition to making a good bioreactor for the extraction of maximum calories from food, the gut microbes keep a check on FIAF allowing fat to move from blood into adipose tissue. That our gut bacteria talk to our adipose tissue via FIAF might wake us up to pay more attention to their welfare.

As a conclusion to this remarkable piece of work, we switch away from mice that are conventional or germ free to mice that can inherit a gene for obesity. Some mice inherit two copies of the gene and become massively obese. Their littermates with one or no obesity gene are normal weight. The obese mice were found to have a different pattern of microbes to their lean littermates.[12] They then turned to humans and did the obvious experiment.[13] They took 12 obese subjects and put them on a calorie-restricted diet for 12 months. The fall in body rate ranged from 5 to 25% of original weight. Just as was seen with the obese mouse, there were differences in the pattern of gut bacteria flora between lean and morbidly obese subjects. But as they lost weight things changed and they now began to have gut microbial flora very similar to those who had always been lean. The interpretation of this fascinating but complex data on the role of the gut microflora in obesity is challenging, although some scientists have gone so far as to speculate that the rise in obesity parallels the rise in the use of antibiotics, which of course can distort normal gut flora. The stark truth is that this vein of research is wildly exciting and needs to grow before we make rash judgements.

To conclude this chapter on the gut microflora, we move upwards to the stomach, a region of the gut so hostile to living matter that it was long thought to be sterile. The stomach is the holding region for the most recently eaten food before it passes down the extremely long corridor of digestion into the extremely long small intestine prior to meeting the bacteria we have just described in the large bowel. The process of digestion begins in the stomach. Many protein-digesting enzymes are secreted in the stomach and they need acid conditions to function properly and to that end the stomach releases daily about two litres of hydrochloric acid which doesn't bode well for living organisms. An Australian clinical pathologist Robert Warren noted the presence of some form of corkscrew-shaped bacteria (Helicobacter Pylori or *H Pylori*) in the stomachs of those suffering from gastric or duodenal ulcer and, moreover, that these bacteria were almost always present when there was a gastric ulcer. At the time, the prevailing wisdom was that the ulcers were caused by stress and a poor diet, leading to excess acid production which caused the damage to the gut that was an ulcer. A colleague, Barry Marshall, decided to try and grow these bacteria and failed miserably to do so. Then, during the Easter holidays in 1982, a dish containing the bacteria was accidentally left in the incubator over the holidays. They grew to the level that Marshall was able to prove that the cultured bacteria were identical to the bacteria that Robert Warren had noted to be ever present when gastric ulcers were found. These two scientists were to win the Nobel Prize in medicine in 2005 and in the presentation address the audience was informed that:

> In order to prove that the bacterium that had been isolated caused a disease, Marshall tried to fulfil Koch's Fourth Postulate. This implies that an infectious agent that has been isolated must cause the same disease in an experimental animal as in humans. In the absence of a suitable animal model, Marshall decided to drink a bacterial culture containing Helicobacter and he suffered a severe inflammation of the stomach.[14]

The reason why this bug can survive in the hostile environment of the acidic stomach is that the stomach has a very thick gooey mucus layer to protect the cells from the acid conditions. At the tip of the cells where H Pylori lies, the pH is neutral. Within the thick mucus layer the pH falls to 4, which indicates a quite acid environment and then outside the thick mucus layer, where the proteins are being digested, the pH is 2, which is very severely acidic. Besides hiding behind the thick mucus layer, the H Pylori also secretes an enzyme which breaks down a compound found widely throughout the body, urea, which gives rise to a locally produced antacid effect.

The impact of the work of these researchers is enormous. Globally, on the African, Asian and South American continents, some 80–90% are H Pylori infected. In the EU and US the values are lower ranging from about 30 to 70%. Those infected with H Pylori will get ulcers at the rate of 1% per annum so that, over a 40-year period, 40% of those infected will suffer this debilitating disease. Nearly everyone with a duodenal ulcer is H Pylori positive, but in the case of gastric ulcers we need to add in aspirin and related drugs as a cause. One in five persons in developed countries below 40 years are infected and 50% of those above 60 years are also affected.

In conclusion, the heart is loved for its romance and courage, the brain for its creativity and mental prowess, the lung for its love of clean pure air and our muscles for strength and beauty. The gut is unloved, not least because of its toiletry functions. But the biology of the gut will dominate the food and health agenda for the next 20 years and will yield many surprises. So learn to love your gut. Feed it on fruit, vegetable, fibres and yoghurts.

CHAPTER EIGHT

A Tsunami of Lard: The Global Epidemic of Obesity

The global epidemic of obesity which, fairly or unfairly, I refer to as the tsunami of lard now reaches into the nether regions of the globe, to the poorest of poor countries and to ever younger and older victims. And in its wake the tsunami of lard leaves behind it the depressing statistics of those diseases most associated with obesity: raised blood pressure, diabetes, cancer, gall bladder disease and the less attractive correlates of poor self-esteem, depression and the stigma that goes with obesity. The World Health Organisation classifies it as an epidemic. However, for those of us not expert in this field, we see epidemics as things that suddenly appear, spread and then wane. Think of polio, TB, HIV, CJD or SARS. Obesity, as we shall see, is here to stay.

It is often said that the problem of obesity is simple: if the energy consumed from our food exceeds the energy we expend through our various activities including physical activity, you get fat. Conversely, if the energy consumed from our food falls below the energy we expend through our various activities including physical activity we lose weight. Simple! You could say the same of cancer – a simple case of the wrong cells multiplying inappropriately. And just as this simple analysis of cancer is childlike, so too is the simple-minded view of obesity as an excess of calorie intake over physical activity expenditure. Why do some people eat more than they should? Is it the sight of food, the thought of food or the smell of food? Is it a lazy lifestyle, or is it mood or genes or the biology of the gut, the brain, the fat stores or muscle, or was it what happened in the womb? The questions are endless. In my view, if we give obesity a biological complexity score of 100, then cancer scores ten and heart disease one. And by the time this chapter is finished, I hope you will agree at least in principle

In the past, the ability of a child to survive long enough to pass on its genetic material to the next generation was determined by many attributes, one of which was (*a*) the capacity to feast and fatten when food was abundant, and the other (*b*) the capacity to use this fat to survive the long lean periods in between the periodic abundances. In later centuries, where poverty abounded, the rich lived in luxury and with ever-decreasing periods of food scarcity many of them became obese. As affluence exploded in logarithmic growth after the end of the Second World War, food became plentiful, accessible and, for the vast majority, affordable. Within decades, obesity began to spread. As long as we are affluent and live in an environment of food abundance and general physical inactivity, which we refer to as an 'obesogenic environment', obesity will be with us. Obesity is an excess of body fat stored mostly just beneath the skin and around certain organs such as the kidney in what is technically known as adipose tissue. To understand the problems obesity causes, we need to spend a little time exploring this adipose tissue.

Not so long ago, adipose tissue was seen as a fairly inert slab of lard that played a broad role as an energy reserve but which really did nothing else. Today we know otherwise. It is an organ that manufactures key compounds, mostly proteins, which are released into blood to communicate with the brain about food intake, to the gut about absorption of ingested nutrients, to the muscle which takes up fat released from adipose tissue, and to the female reproductive system to warn about the danger of breeding with perilously low fat reserves. It is a highly dynamic organ where fat is stored. These stores of fat are constantly undergoing synthesis and breakdown, leaving the adipose tissue and returning again in cycles related to our pattern of food intake. At night, as we fast, fat flows from adipose tissue into the blood to the various tissues, such as muscle, to provide energy. After a meal, fat leaves the gut, enters the bloodstream and is taken to the adipose tissue for storage in the fat cells of adipose. The trouble is that, as we gain weight and store more and more fat, these fat cells grow in size and, as they grow, their ability to facilitate the entry or re-entry of fat falls. The hormone insulin facilitates this process of the entry of fat into fat cells and enlarged fat cells are less sensitive to the effect of insulin than normal fat cells. Insulin also facilitates the uptake of glucose into fat cells, and as fat cells enlarge their reduced ability to take up glucose leads to increased blood glucose levels. In a strange twist, the higher blood glucose levels send a message to the pancreas to release more insulin to deal with the problem, but there is precious little this extra insulin can do with enlarged fat cells since they continue to be insensitive to insulin-mediated glucose uptake. So we have high levels of blood glucose and high levels of blood insulin. And that is a form of diabetes known as type 2 diabetes, which is at the heart of the ill-health consequences of obesity.

Let us now move to the question of why some people become obese and others don't. Obviously it is because they consistently eat more calories than they expend, so let's explore why they experience this positive energy balance. At most meetings of nutritionists, two major arguments are put forward. The first focuses on social class and the second on the food chain. For the first, it is argued that obesity has a strong social-class gradation, being more common in the lower social classes. We will not argue with that since typical data such as those from the UK would suggest that this is indeed the case. Twenty per cent of males holding a degree in the UK are obese. Among those with no qualification, the prevalence is 30%.[1] Thus there is a 50% higher rate of obesity in the lower as opposed to the higher educated men. The next phase of the explanatory process outlines the social and environmental reasons for this gradation. A lower level of education and of knowledge about diet and health are generally proposed. This is followed by examples of the obesity-fostering environment in which the socially disadvantaged live, referred to as an 'obesogenic' environment, a term we will use frequently throughout this chapter. This implies an environment which promotes a sedentary lifestyle, and where high calorie foods are abundant and where serving sizes are on the large side. It is also argued that this social group has inadequate income. Their schools and canteens serve junk food with very limited options for healthy eating. They live in 'food deserts', by which is meant that their nearest supermarkets are in fact out-of-town hypermarkets with limited access by public transport. What local shops they have access to do not stock healthy foods or, if they do so, these foods are not at affordable prices. Taken together, the only solutions to this problem are social and economic ones and, since the 'free market' is part of the problem, it cannot be part of the solution. Food policies will impose solutions. Thus is obesity politicised, and with the statistics at hand it is difficult to argue otherwise.

However, the 'statistics at hand' are only part of the true story. Now let us look at that part of the true story which in this approach is not factored into the problem and which therefore cannot feature in any solution. Using exactly the same statistics, we can say that among UK males holding a university degree 80% are *not* obese, and among UK male workers with no formal educational qualification 70% are *not* obese. The percentage decline in the prevalence of the non-obese when moving along the social gradation of higher to lower is now a mere 10%. Effectively speaking, seven to eight out of ten UK males, irrespective of educational level, are *not* obese. This is now quite a different story. Let us look again at the male workers with the lowest level of education. Some 30% are obese, while 70% are not, and let us look at the previous explanations distinguishing risk of obesity across UK social groups: education, income, school and work meals, food deserts, public transport access and local access to affordable healthy foods. Are those arguing the case for these factors as an explanation of why there is a social gradation of obesity now arguing that the non-obese male poorly educated workers somehow escape these factors and live in a quite different environment from those in the same social class who developed obesity? And how come, among the male professionals with university degrees who apparently do escape such social and economic pressures, some are obese and others are not? What part of the environment of the UK professional male is uniquely obesogenic to professional men and not to either lean professional men or male manual workers, obese or otherwise?

I am afraid I don't buy into this simplistic notion that obesity has a strong social gradation and that economic and social deprivation is the root cause of the problem. We all live in an obesogenic environment, an environment which is multi-faceted so that the facets which bedevil the world of the unskilled male Briton are different from those that haunt their professional counterparts. It is quite possible that in the lower social classes the facets of the obesogenic environment are stronger or more prevalent. But, equally, the strength and prevalence may not be an issue and the response to the environment may differ through different levels of education and different attendant worldviews. I will return to the issue of social class shortly when we come to consider genetics and obesity.

Strongly embedded within this view that the socially and economically deprived are faced with a unique obesogenic environment is the parallel view that this obesogenic environment is dominated by an excessive intake of cheap, energy dense, sweet, fatty and highly processed foods. The super-sizing documentary proves it! Well in reality it doesn't. If a particular pattern of food intake was uniquely associated with obesity, then across time and geographic locations we should expect this association to crop up again and again. In truth, it doesn't, which shouldn't surprise us. Many a middle-aged woman who is overweight never visits fast food outlets. There are many who are fond of a weekly visit to McDonalds who are slim as a model. It is not like dental caries, always associated with a high frequency of intake of sugary foods. It is not like tobacco and lung disease. The fact is that every food category plays a role in obesity. For some it is fast food. For others it is big lunches and big dinners. For some it is alcohol and for others it is confectionery or bread or chips or curries or cheese or whatever. As we shall see in chapter eleven, blaming fast food, snack food, soft drinks, food-vending machines and the like may make us feel good, but it is avoiding the truth: all foods play a role in the development of obesity, the exact menu varying on personal taste and preferences. On the issue of food choice and obesity, it would be well to remember the phenomenon of the under-reporting of food intake discussed in chapter two. As body weight rises, the rate of under-reporting of food intake increases. So beware of those carrying 'data' on food choice and its role in obesity.

Which brings me back to the original question, slightly rephrased: Why in a ubiquitous obesity-inducing environment do some people develop obesity and others do not? The answer I give is unpopular with the adherents of the social and economic theories of obesity: why, in the same environment, some people get fat and others do not lies in your genes. In an environment which is universally promoting obesity a very large number of people will gain weight, some more so than others and some more easily than others. A good number of these but not all will go on to become obese. In such an environment, the susceptibility to weight gain is very strongly genetically determined.

The evidence for the role of genes comes from work done in the 1980s, mainly by Alan Stunkard and Claude Bouchard. One study looked at a set of identical twins and focused on those reared apart.[2] Thus they had identical genes but lived in different parts of the world, experiencing dissimilar environments. Irrespective of the fact that they lived apart, if one twin was fat there was a 70% probability that his or her identical twin would be fat. In a second study, data were available on 5,000 adopted persons.[3] The weight of the adopted person correlated very well with their biological parents but not with their adoptive parents. Finally, since both these studies are associations where cause and effect cannot be readily separated, we turn to an intervention study.[4] Twelve identical twin pairs took part in a 100-day intervention study where they received an extra 1,000 calories per day. All gained weight ranging from 4 to 13 kg. The greatest predictor of any identical twin weight gain was the weight gain of the other twin. All three studies lend support to the previously mentioned statement that in an environment that is conducive to the development of obesity, some will fare worse than others and some of that variation will be genetic. In fact, Wim Saris from Maastricht University has calculated from these twin studies that, when humans are overfed, the efficiency with which the additional energy is converted into weight gain ranges from 33% to 100%.[5] This variability in the efficiency of converting food energy into body-weight gain has long been known in the animal feed industry and, over decades, breeding has gradually driven up that efficiency. That it exists in humans should come as no surprise. More recently, another study of obesity in twins was published and, since this took account of the dramatic growth in the obesogenic environment since the 1980s, it is a very important paper. Professor Jane Wardle of University College London made use of a registry of twins in the UK.[6] Parents were asked to record the twins' weight and height and they obtained data on over 10,000 children. Of these, one-third were identical twins sharing two things in common: the same genes and the same environment, the same home, the same meals, and the same school. The remaining two thirds also shared the same environment but not the same genes because they were not identical twins. The data showed that 77% of the variation in fatness was attributable to inherited factors or genes. A mere 10% was due to shared environment (home) and some 13% to non-shared environment (different sports or different pastimes).

What is striking about this paper is the ease with which Professor Wardle and her colleagues set out the challenge to those who have agendas about the home as the cause of the problem:

> Probably the most controversial finding from twin studies is the relatively low shared-environment effect, a finding that has been observed for behavioural traits. Discussions about the obesity epidemic almost invariably ascribe a key role to the family, but, in the present study as in other twin and adoption studies, siblings from the same family were only slightly more similar in adiposity than would be expected from their genetic similarity, and the shared environment effect was just over 10%. The fact that siblings' experience of being served the same food, being given the same options for television viewing and active outdoor play, seeing the same behaviours modelled by parents and going to the same schools does not make siblings more similar is a challenge for the etiologic model that highlights the home environment as a root cause of obesity. This finding will however come as no surprise to parents who are well aware that their children come in different shapes and sizes despite having a similar background. What is important is this finding that 'blaming' the parents is 'wrong'.

These authors went on to tease out the genetic role and the role of social class.[7] They followed two sets of children from age four to age eleven. One set were the children of obese parents and the other set had lean parents. Among those with lean parents, the level of obesity barely changed over the seven-year study, from 8% to just 9%. In contrast, the level of obesity in the children of obese parents at age four was 17% and it soared to 45% by age eleven. If you now separate the children in each group into those from high or low socio-economic status, absolutely nothing changes in relation to obesity levels for the children

79

of the lean parents. In the case of the children with fat parents, obesity rose in both those with a high and a low social class, but it rose much faster in those of the lower social class. So if social class is important in obesity, it is only if it is associated with a genetic predisposition to obesity

A final piece of evidence comes from two economists from the US National Bureau of Economic Research and from the Federal Reserve Bank.[8] Using publicly available data sets, they studied the link between school 'junk food' availability and obesity. They were able to show a positive association between the availability of 'junk food' in schools and the levels of obesity. However, when they factored in the weight of the children's parents, they found that this entire association was wiped out because, in truth, the apparent junk food/obesity link was entirely driven by overweight adolescents who had one or more overweight parents. Don't blame fast food or fizzy drinks or whatever prejudice takes your fancy. Whipping them may make you feel good but it is not going to solve the problem. We have an obesogenic environment and, for different individuals, different responses to different aspects of this environment are drivers of weight gain. Guessing who is susceptible to what has still to be worked out.

Clearly, the decisions to eat, to stop eating or to refrain from eating are choices we consciously make and the basis for those decisions lies in our brain. One part of the brain, the feeding centre, turns on the desire to eat. Another, the satiety centre, turns off the desire to eat. Evidence that the brain sends and receives signals via the bloodstream to eat or not eat or to stop eating came in the 1950s through the use of a technique known as parabiosis, which is where two animals have their blood circulation artificially connected.[9] If the satiety part of the brain is deliberately put out of action, rats lose their appetite regulation and they become obese. If some of these rats have their blood circulation connected to normal rats with a normally functioning satiety centre, their regulation of appetite returns and they assume normal weight. Something that was missing in the blood following the malfunctioning of the satiety centre in the brain was obtained from the blood of the normal rat. It was to be another 40 years before some candidate compounds in blood were identified as the go-between for brain and the rest of the body. Jeff Friedman at Rockefeller University discovered a protein in blood which he called 'Leptin' after the Greek work for thin, leptos.[10] He too was working with different strains of genetically obese rats. He would go on to show that one strain had a mutation on the gene which coded for leptin production by adipose tissue leading to abnormally low levels of leptin in blood. However, if these mice are injected with leptin, they quickly develop into completely normal non-obese mice. Leptin helps suppress appetite. When first discovered, it was believed that leptin would be the magic bullet for the treatment of obesity but the enthusiasm soon waned. Since leptin is produced by fat stores to tell the brain to ease off the calories, it was not surprising to find that fatter people had more leptin than leaner people. What was surprising to discover was that, despite this big 'stop-eating' signal from adipose tissue, the brain wasn't listening and this led to the theory that a defect at the brain leptin receptor might exist. Although some progress has been made using leptin injections to facilitate weight loss, the idea of daily injections, not without some side effects, is not an attractive one, especially given the high cost and the highly variable response in terms of weight loss. Where leptin has scored spectacularly has been in the very rare genetic disorder where the leptin gene is completely malfunctioning and only minute levels of leptin are found in blood.[11] In these very rare cases, children become grossly obese by the age of five and giving them leptin injections normalises their weight and so saves their lives.

Many other proteins play a role in the regulation of food intake and many are just as exciting as leptin. But at the moment it seems that leptin is the conductor of this very complex orchestra. Such is the scale of the market that drug companies are investing billions in trying to understand the music that this orchestra makes. One of the big problems in the use of animal models to study the biological control of food intake is that humans are fundamentally different from animals. We may share the same biology as the mouse and our regulatory orchestra may play the same symphonies, but we have a higher level of regulation – the neo-cortex. The neo-cortex comprises the bulk of the human brain and is the seat of learning, language, memory and everything that makes humans human and not mouse. So why is this section of the brain more important than the leptin-led orchestra? I test my students thus. Imagine you are really hungry, having gone for several days with nothing to eat. I then ask them to close their eyes and to really try to imagine absolute hunger and starvation. I then tell them that I have in my hand a fully nutritious meal containing all the nutrients they would need. Then they open their eyes. Universally they decline to eat it because it is cat food. It appears to a logician of the Mr Spock of Star Trek variety to be an absurd decision since the cat food is abundant in all the nutrients they need and is subject to food safety regulations every bit as stringent as human food. A rat would snap it up and sleep in peace. But my students listen to their cortex. Obviously, there would come a time when they would have no choice but to eat the cat food. But they are not at that point yet.

There are other examples when we behave very differently to rats. You have just had a delicious dinner with your boss and could not eat another bite. Then she brings in an apple pie she has made herself with apples grown in her own back garden. Everyone else says yes. So do you.

In the study of food intake there are two related worlds. One starts the moment a food crosses the metabolic threshold and enters the mouth. From then on everything is metabolic and regulated by all sorts of biochemical bells and whistles. For the most part, this was where, until recently, the genetic component of obesity was sought in genes regulating the production of hormones, of enzymes, of receptors and the like. But new twin studies point us to the other world: that before the mouth. This is a world of the sight, the smell, the thought or the memory of delicious food. It is the world of supermarket shelves, of plates, menus, patisseries, boulangeries, charcuteries and fast food logos. It seems that identical twins have a high probability of selecting the same foods, of seeking common nutrient profiles and of switching off their appetite after a meal at the same time. Thus we now know that the normal variation in our genes which determines the likelihood that one person will go on to gain weight and another will remain at normal weight also operates on the behavioural side of the appetite coin. Now we must learn to integrate the study genetics with that of nutrition and with social and behavioural sciences. Things have got more complex, which is always a good sign in science.

The biological complexity of obesity also extends to its treatment. The five-year cure-rate for any disease is based on the percentage of people who have been cured of the disease at a given time, and who remain cured of the disease five years later. Here is what the Council on Scientific Affairs of the American Medical Association had to say about obesity: 'The 5-year cure-rate for obesity is worse than the 5-year cure-rate for the worst cancer';[12] grim beyond belief, but regrettably true. The dieting industry is enormous and people spend hard-earned money chasing dreams sold by chancers. All the wonder pills, all the gadgets, all the fancy therapies cannot alter the first law of thermodynamics. For the system to shrink, you need to put in less energy than you take out. The majority of people, at some time in their lives, go on diets to lose weight and the vast majority are successful in the short term. In the longer term, it requires a heightened neo-cortex to consciously, day in day out, curb food intake. A few people succeed. The vast majority do not.

We do not understand how the body resists weight change and why, after weight loss, so many people regain it. The concept of a set point for weight is widely accepted without a great deal of serious biological evidence. The set point is like the thermostat in our central heating system. It is switched on when the temperature falls below a critical (set point) temperature and is switched off when that is exceeded. When I first heard this concept explained, the use of the word 'ratchet' did the trick for me in conceptualising the notion of a set point. An individual gains weight and does so with respect to its existing set point. Then things get out of control and there is further and sustained weight gain. And then the set point is ratcheted up and once it passes each ratchet there is no going back. The ratchet is the biological set point and it can be easily driven upwards, but it is very difficult to drive it downwards. I will try to explain this using the fat cell theory, which I find useful to convey the basic message to students.

For argument's sake let's assume the average fat cell contains about 0.4 micrograms of fat each. A person who might gain weight would see their average fat cell load expand to 0.6 micrograms. That is acceptable and when weight loss is attempted it is tolerated with fat cell levels falling back to 0.4 micrograms per cell. That seesaw can go on forever. But when the weight gain leads to the accumulation of 0.8 micrograms per fat cell, a tipping point is reached and the fat cell divides. Now we have two fat cells each with 0.4 micrograms. Click, click! That was the ratchet turning irreversibly. Let us imagine that we want to return to the previous weight. To do so, we need to lose half the fat we gained. The problem is that each cell now has the standard fat load of 0.4 micrograms each and to halve this to just 0.2 micrograms per cell requires us to get the cells to live a life they simply do not like. If we listen to our cortex, we can win out over the disgruntled under-fat cells with a below par quota of fat. But all the time the basic animal biology will be waiting to return to 0.4 micrograms per cell. Then along comes a wedding, the annual holiday and a 40th birthday and whoosh – you took your cortical eye of the ball but the fat cells had never rested. In the blink of an eye, we have regained most of the weight. The body is back to the new set point realised when we went beyond the last set point and hit a new ratchet. This may be a Walt Disney view of body-weight regulation, but it helps me understand the problem of easy weight gain and easy weight loss but a weight loss that is ever so difficult to sustain.

Now let's turn to the other side of the obesity coin – physical activity – and we'll look at this from three angles: physical inactivity as a causative agent of obesity, physical activity as an antidote to the woes of obesity and, finally, physical activity in weight loss. Let's start with the role of physical activity in the development of obesity. Andrew Prentice and Susan Jebb, then at the Dunn Nutrition Centre in Cambridge, published an analysis showing the relationship between the average intake of calories in the UK and obesity on the one hand, and between cars per household and obesity on the other.[13] As the prevalence of obesity rose over a 20-year period, caloric intake in the UK showed no tendency to increase. But the number of cars per household exactly matched the rise in obesity. This is an observational study and cause and effect cannot be separated. Maybe as the UK grew richer, the richer became fatter and bought more cars. Maybe they got lazier. Maybe, maybe. However, it is difficult not to link the two together – the rise in obesity has paralleled a marked decline in physical activity. The Nurses Health Study is one of the most detailed ongoing studies of any population. Led by Walter Willett from the Harvard School of Public Health, this study began in 1976 with the recruitment of over 120,000 nurses who were very carefully studied at baseline for diet, health, lifestyle, blood biochemistry and so on. And at baseline, you had to be healthy. In a sub-study over a six-year period starting in 1992, 50,000 women were studied with nearly four thousand developing obesity and nearly half of those with diabetes.[14] The women were questioned in detail about TV or video watching, about time spent sitting at home or at work and about driving. Those at the top end of TV viewing had a 94% increased risk of becoming obese and a 70% higher chance of developing diabetes and these statistics were adjusted to take account of all known confounding effects. This study now combined hours watching TV against the average level of physical activity. Those who were the least physically active and who watched the most TV had 2.9 times higher risk of getting diabetes compared to those with the most physical activity and least TV viewing. The results showed that 30% of obesity cases and 43% of type 2 diabetes can be prevented if a modest level of physical activity is pursued (<10 hours per week watching TV and 30 minutes of brisk walking per day). Clearly, the present 'epidemic' of obesity has a strong link with an ever-increasing sedentary society.

Let us now turn to the issue of physical activity as an antidote to the woes of obesity. At the Centre for Integrated Health Research at the Cooper Institute in Dallas, Stephen Blair and his team studied several thousand men aged 23–79 years who had clinically diagnosed diabetes at the outset.[15] With over one decade of follow up, nearly 3,000 deaths occurred. Higher levels of fitness minimised the risk of death from diabetes complications *irrespective* of body weight. The relative risk of mortality was four to five times higher in the least fit group, whether one looked at perfectly lean subjects or those who were overweight or even obese. The same group recently studied 6,000 women who at baseline were free of cardiovascular disease, cancer or diabetes. They had their cardio-respiratory fitness assessed on a treadmill and were ranked into low, moderate and high fitness levels. After 17 years follow-up, 143 cases of type 2 diabetes were observed. Those who were moderately fit had only 86% of the risk of death of the least fit and, at the top end of fitness, this fell to just 60%. The protective effect of fitness held true for persons who were overweight and even obese. Those who are on the fit-and-fat-is-good side argue that a slim sedentary person is a higher risk than an overweight person who is fit. Others argue that the slim fit person is still the ideal. My personal belief in this extraordinary battle against obesity and its health effects is to take all the gains you can. Fit and fat is better that unfit and fat and certainly better than lean and sedentary.

We now turn to the last area of consideration of physical activity and obesity: exercise and weight loss. The net energy cost of jogging is about one calorie per kilogram body weight per kilometre jogged. So let's say an 80kg male runs 6km three times per week – that amounts to 1,440 calories or 206 calories per day, equivalent to just one chocolate bar or about two apples. The argument is made that this is not significant and that if one wanted to drop from 2,500 calories per day to 1,500 calories per day, half from food and half from exercise, then you'd have to jog 5km every day of the week. Since that is beyond most people, exercise is downgraded in the weight-loss stakes. Many studies show, however, that exercise is a good adjunct to dieting in weight loss and this often attributed to the sense of well-being that exercise brings and to its sense of a public declaration of intent to pursue a healthier lifestyle. All in all, physical activity for weight loss generally loses out to management of dietary habits. Wrong, wrong, oh so wrong. Step in Professor James Hill who co-founded the US National Weight Control Registry and Professor of Pediatrics and Medicine at the University of Colorado Centre for Human Nutrition. He has written a book called the *Step Diet* in which he urges us to count steps, not calories.[16] Years of work within this field and with the National Weight Loss Registry have led to one absolutely vital point: unless you expend 25 per cent of your total energy expenditure each day through exercise, your chances of maintaining weight loss are really very small. Hill in his book converts all forms of calories to the equivalent energy in the form of steps. In my case, if I drive to work and drive home, my total daily steps measured on a pedometer are about 4,000. According to Hill's formula, for my age, weight, height and gender, my resting metabolic rate is equal to 27,000 of my steps. Thus the 4,000 steps I take on an average day are just 12.5% of my resting metabolic rate (27,000 steps). I need to make it 25%. And I can easily achieve this by walking to work, 40 minutes each way, which gives me 9,200 additional steps. Most people find that their overall physical activity is only 12–15% of daily energy expenditure.

Professor Hill advises a gradual increase in physical activity to achieve 25% of total caloric output. Of course he also adds some fairly simple dietary advice to go with the exercise plan: whatever is put in front of you, leave a quarter of it behind.

And so, as we reach the conclusion of this complex topic, let us explore how obesity affects the lives of those who suffer this condition. These are the words used to describe the obese person: mean, stupid, ugly, unhappy, incompetent, sloppy, lazy, socially isolated, undisciplined and lacking personal control. That's just about as offensive as you can get without citing criminal traits. This view of the obese is shared by obese persons and is shaped in childhood. Janet Latner from New Zealand and Albert Stunkard from the US carried out a simple study in 2003, which had previously been carried out in 1961.[17] It involved showing fifth and sixth grade US schoolchildren drawings of six children. The first ('healthy') was a perfectly normal child. The second ('crutches') was of a child holding a crutch with a brace on his leg. The third ('wheelchair') was of a child sitting in a wheelchair with a blanket covering both legs. The fourth ('hand') was of a child with no left hand. The fifth ('face') was of a child with a facial disfigurement on the left side of the mouth. The sixth ('obese') was of a child who was normal in appearance but was obese. Boys received drawings of boys and girls received similar drawings of girls. The task was simple. The children were asked to study the pictures carefully and then to select the one they liked the best, then the second best, third best and so on. Each selection yielded a score of one to five according to the child's ranking. A low score indicated a popular choice and vice versa for a high score. The results showed that the average score for the obese child was 4.97 (almost maximum dislike) in 2004 compared to 4.56 in 1961. Thus, consistently over time, obese children were almost universally seen as the least liked. The other scores were (for 2004): 'Healthy', 1.97; 'Face', 3.09; 'Crutches', 3.39; 'Hand', 3.70; 'Wheelchair', 2.86. These results are shocking, but if you read the literature on the stigmatisation of obesity you will not find these results shocking. They are the norm. Susan Wooley of the University of Cincinnati outlined the scale of the problem: 'Once, in an attempt to obtain pictures of obese and lean children for a study, we spent 3 days in public places such as a zoo and an amusement park, asking parents for permission to photograph their child. No parent of a lean child ever refused and no parent of an overweight child ever agreed.'[18] So we have as our norm a remarkable prejudice against overweight and obesity. Overcoming such deep-rooted social prejudice will take a major effort, involving employers, teachers and the like. But it's not going to happen. On the scale of things to worry about, it doesn't hit the radar.

staggering 70% of that increase was found and the rise in weight from 1961 to 1991 accounted for only 20% of the overall weight gain over the full 125 years. This tsunami or wave-like pattern is also evident from the studies of the Danish epidemiologist Thorkild Sorensen.[22] He used data on 19-year-old recruits into the Danish army. In 1948 only a few per cent were obese. By 1970 it had reached 10% but it remained at 10% for the next 20 years. In 1990 it began to skyrocket from 10% to reach nearly 35% in just a decade. There are no obvious answers to the question as to why obesity has not grown steadily and why it has grown in different wave-like patterns in different countries. These data illustrate how easy it is for conventional wisdom to move along some simple track, which upholds some conventional tenet such as obesity never really being around in the early part of the last century and gradually spiralling upwards thereafter.

It would be wrong to say anything other than that obesity is caused by eating too much relative to physical activity. But why do some people eat more than others or exercise less and why is it that when subjects are overfed some gain weight more than others? For certain, genes are playing a role. But they can't explain everything. The mere availability of obesogenic food isn't the explanation. Someone has to eat it to get obese. Why do some partake more than others? That is the key question. But nutrition is locked into identifying which foods are the drivers of the increased food intake and fast food and soft drinks are the popular culprits. But with the inherent errors in measuring habitual food intake confounded by under-reporting, this is a gross waste of public money. *Why do some people more than others choose to eat more than they need to maintain an acceptable body weight? That is the key question and it is not being adequately addressed.*

CHAPTER NINE

Greying Matters

Obesity, you could say, is the elephant in the room. In fact it is a very noisy herd of elephants. Obesity dominates every aspect of public health nutrition policy and is a subject journalists are in love with. Were one to mention malnutrition, then that would upset people because they would naturally assume that you are talking about the starving masses of the developing countries and that, juxtaposed to a conversation on obesity, makes for discomfort. Most people who read the European Parliament's White Paper on nutrition are taken aback when it states that malnutrition, which particularly affects older people, costs European healthcare systems similar amounts as obesity and overweight.[1] Now where is the elephant? From the perspective of challenges to human nutrition, particularly challenges with a proven cost-effective solution, the malnutrition of the older population in developing countries is elephantine in dimensions. Consider obesity, which is associated with high levels of elevated blood pressure, elevated blood cholesterol and elevated blood glucose. They are readily detected by a GP and readily treated with drugs. However, as people get older, they develop more serious aspects of disease and are far more likely to be admitted into hospital. Ample research shows that the malnourished elderly enter hospital more frequently, stay longer, have more complications and are readmitted more frequently. This is the mega-expensive side of the health services and explains why malnutrition in the elderly costs more than obesity. The former accounts for 10% of the UK health budget and the latter 5%.[2] And just as obesity is growing, an increasingly ageing population will ensure that age-related malnutrition will continue to outstrip obesity in health-care costs

The demography of the planet is constantly undergoing change and it is an increasingly older world. According to the US Institute of Aging, between 2005 and 2030 we will see an increase globally of 104% in those aged 65+, rising to an increase of 151% in those over 85.[3] Apparently, the numbers of persons over 100 years of age has doubled every decade since 1950 and thus between 2005 and 2030 there will be a staggering 400% increase in persons over 100. It has been calculated that since humans arrived on earth the probability of reaching the century in terms of age has fallen from 1 in 20 million to 1 in 50 for females in low mortality countries such as Japan and Sweden. Some countries will show a decline in overall population due to low fertility rates, such as in Russia where by 2030 the population will be reduced by 18%. The population of Japan will fall by 11% by 2030 and by then one in four Japanese will be 85 years or older. As we grow older, we grow weaker in every aspect, bar wisdom. For the younger readers of this book to whom all of this might seem a long way off, please note that this decline starts in the third decade of life and continues to decline almost linearly thereafter. So although you might be young, investment in good nutrition will pay off in spades decades from now.

Our body composition changes as we get older and so we gain proportionately more fat and lose proportionately more muscle. One direct consequence of this is that we need fewer calories since muscle has a higher energy requirement than fat. A lower energy requirement may lead to a lowered food intake which, as we will see later, can be augmented by declining taste capacity. Inadequate protein intake can then lead to even more muscle loss known as sarcopenia, a major cause of frailty, disability and loss of independence among the elderly. On the other hand, if energy requirements fall and our body doesn't heed the message, due to our dear friend the neo-cortex (see chapter seven), then obesity can set in. Being frail is one thing. Being obese is another. But being both is a horse of a different colour and represents a very growing phenomenon, no pun intended. A group of researchers at Washington University in St Louis studied three groups of 50+ older subjects per group in the mid 1970s.[4] The subjects underwent an assessment of physical frailty, which involved a series of physical performance tests together with the 'activities of daily living'. The first group was the one we all want to be, non-frail and non-obese. The next group was the classic frail elderly group but not obese. The third group was obese (BMI 30kg/m²). For all of the tests carried out on these subjects, the obese were always found to be frailer than the 'just frail'. Now you could argue that because people are obese they suffer more disorders such as hypertension and osteoarthritis. But even when these were controlled for, the elderly obese were frailer than the recognisably frail elderly non-obese subjects. For example, muscle quality (muscle strength per unit area) fell from 16 (nm/kg) in the non-obese, non-frail, to 14 in the frail and to 12 in the obese. The obese fared perfectly well on the measures of emotions, social functioning and mental health, which reinforce the point made in the previous chapter. Ronen Roubenoff from Tufts University in Boston (which houses the USDA Human Nutrition Research Centre on Aging), writing on 'Sarcopenic obesity: the confluence of two epidemics', explained the phenomenon thus. As we age, our physical activity levels fall, which remove the biggest stimulants to good functional muscles we have. Equally, as we age, we tend to get fatter and as we get fatter we get more insulin resistance which in turn reduces the uptake of amino acids by muscles.[5]

Whilst ageing may alter energy requirements, it is also associated with a growing inability to regulate energy balance, i.e. to match calories in with calories out. A classic study again from Tufts University illustrates two points.[6] Under strict metabolic ward and out-patient conditions, a group of young and a group of old volunteers were overfed for three weeks by almost a thousand calories per day. Both groups gained weight. However, when the subjects were returned to normal food intake, eating to their own appetite, the young men readjusted their weight to pre-test levels. But the older men did not make the adjustment. They remained overweight. When the mirror image experiment was conducted, where the subjects had energy intake restricted (by 750 calories per day), both groups lost weight. But when they returned to their normal food intake, the young responded and regained the weight. The older men did not. They kept the weight loss. There is only one explanation. Older people, when they are asked to either over-eat or under-eat, continue to do so after the study. They have poor regulatory control of appetite. The same group went one stage further – they underfed younger and older males for six months. Then they returned to normal appetite. The younger men regained all the weight loss but the older men only regained 20% of the lost weight. As we saw in chapters seven and eight, there is an array of signals released from adipose tissue and the gut, the 'leptin orchestra', which through a complex web of loops regulate food intake. One has to assume that it is within this orchestra that the explanation will be found, but the search is of the needle and haystack variety.

The biology of flavour declines with age and it is worthwhile to take a look at this.[7] Flavour encompasses three sensory abilities: taste, smell, chemesthesis. Taste buds are located on the tongue and soft palate and they can distinguish five basic tastes we met in chapter two: sweet, sour, salty, bitter and umami, the latter being a recent addition which detects the monosodium glutamate type of flavour. Smell (olfaction) is managed by the olfactory lobes in the nose. This smell can be due to volatile compounds, which waft up the nose, the distinctive aroma of coffee or roast lamb. However, a related olfactory lobe receives signals when a food is eaten. An apple doesn't smell but an apple tastes differently if it is eaten as per normal or with your nose tightly pinched. The eating releases a smell that this lobe detects. In fact, if you have different flavoured jellybeans, one won't be told from the other with a tightly pinched nose. Animals have over a thousand genes to detect smells but we have far fewer, nearer 30. The last element of flavour is chemesthesis, which allows nerves (trigeminal) on the tongue, lips, nose and eyes to detect chemical irritants: the fizz of champagne, the 'cooling' sensation of menthol, the burning sensation of curries. It is the trigeminal nerve endings in the eye which make you cry when you cut an onion, or comparable nerve endings in the nose which give the burning sensation of mustard. In the elderly, it is mainly the sense of smell which declines with old age. The threshold to detect a given smell goes up and the number of identifiable odours falls. Does a decline in smell really matter? After a meal, a flood of hormonal signals enters the blood in response to the arrival of food in the gut. But a smart way to trick the gut is to use a technique known as sham feeding. Here subjects put the food in their mouth as per normal, chew it as per normal, but instead of swallowing it, they spit the chewed food out. Just as with normal feeding, sham feeding induces a significant flow of the same hormones into the bloodstream, as does normal eating. Thus chewing food, releasing its volatiles, stimulates these hormones and studies have shown that both sham feeding and normal feeding have an equal effect on inhibiting the desire to eat. To my mind, these data suggest that a decline in the capacity to experience the effect of sham feeding in the elderly may be linked with dysregulation of appetite. Whatever the mechanism of appetite dysregulation in older subjects, the outcome is that we will continue to have the frail elderly and we can expect to find increasing numbers of the frail obese. If appetite regulation is partly under the anonymous control of the leptin orchestra, physical activity is within the control of the vast majority of those getting on in years and the benefits are profound. It could be argued that the frail elderly and the frail obese elderly are unlikely to go jogging or power-walking, but the evidence shows that older people do not need such vigorous exercise. The evidence clearly shows that the use of less intensive, resistance exercise training (chest and leg process, knee extension and flexion etc.) for 45 minutes on three occasions per week by older persons will result in very significant improvements in glucose and insulin function, in blood pressure control, in blood lipid management and in weight control.

Sarcopenia is a word that is not in common usage, but osteoporosis and osteoarthritis are high visibility terms. Both relate to the bony scaffolding which supports our muscles. Osteoarthritis in the US accounts for 25% of all visits to the family doctor and it is estimated that 80% of the population above 65 years of age will have had x-ray-based evidence of some osteoarthritis with 60% of 65 year olds exhibiting symptoms. Once again, the first line of remedy might be exercise, which strengthens muscles around joints, and weight loss, which reduces the gravimetric burden on joints. A number of alternative therapies are often prescribed or self-prescribed. Two, which come to mind, are glucosamine and chondroitin. Glucosamine is involved in the synthesis of connective tissue, which softens bone-to-bone contact. The theory is that the availability of glucosamine is a limiting factor for connective tissue synthesis and thus taking glucosamine pills will improve cartilage and strengthen joints. The evidence just doesn't stack up and I know that this will annoy the many people who appear to or in fact have achieved relief from osteoarthritis using glucosamine. I turn to the Cochrane Library for assistance in these situations. The Cochrane Library is a non-profit international organisation, which houses a database of reviews of the evidence for all sorts of medicinal substances. Thus the Cochrane reviews claim to represent the highest level of evidence on which to base clinical treatment decisions. The review of glucosamine (2009) for the treatment of osteoarthritis showed no evidence of a consistent effect on outcomes of pain, stiffness or function.[8] Some studies showed an effect but no effect was seen if only the top-quality studies were included. In 2009, a review of all available data (a meta-analysis) linking chondroitin to bone and joint health carried out at the University of Bern in Switzerland concluded: 'Large scale, methodologically sound trials, indicate that the symptomatic benefit of chondroitin is minimal or non-existent.'[9] All in all, there is little supporting evidence for an effective 'dietary' therapy for osteoarthritis other than physical activity and weight management.

In the case of osteoporosis, there is abundant evidence of the role of diet, lifestyle and exercise. Osteoporosis literally means porous bones. Globally, almost 2 million people present with osteoporosis-related fractures each year, and with the increase in longevity that figure will continue to rise for the foreseeable future, reaching as many as 6 million by 2050. Asians and people of African descent have higher bone density and are much less susceptible to fractures than persons of European descent and the reasons are not clear. For example, the low rate of osteoporosis in Chinese women has been attributed to several factors such as the practice of squatting to prepare food that is thought to strengthen thigh and buttocks muscles and also to the Chinese respect and care of the elderly. However, as the globe assumes a more even lifestyle, we can expect osteoporosis to rise even in Asia and Africa. There are two reasons we develop osteoporotic bones. One is inadequate bone growth up to the early twenties when peak bone mass is achieved; the other is because of excessive loss of bone from the early twenties onwards. Two nutrients are the kingmakers in bone – vitamin D and calcium.

Vitamin D is a little bit unusual as vitamins go. If sunlight is adequate, we don't need vitamin D in the diet because UV light in sunshine can help stimulate the skin to manufacture the first form of vitamin D, because as we will see vitamin D is more of a collection of related metabolites than just one as is the case for vitamin C or E. The UV light acts on an intermediary in the process of cholesterol biosynthesis. Regions of the globe 40^0 above or below the Equator have very little light of the right UV range (276–290 nm) in winter and so blood levels of vitamin D are lowest in spring after the dark winter and are highest in autumn after the summer sunshine. During winter at latitudes above or below 40^0, the angle of the sun's rays fall, the UV quality falls, daylight falls, winter woollies are donned and the warmth of indoors all contribute to this diminished vitamin D status. But in sunny climates such as Australia, there is the opposite problem: high intensity summer sunshine, the great outdoor culture and a very aggressive campaign against skin cancer. As a result of the Australian 'Slip-Slop-Slap' campaign (slip on a shirt, slop on the sun cream and slap on the hat) to reduce skin cancer, vitamin D deficiency began to appear because sun protection creams block UV light from hitting the skin.[10] Melanin is the main factor determining skin colour and is increased in individuals with darker skin colour. It reduces the effectiveness of UV light in producing vitamin D, which is fine in sun-drenched Africa where humans first evolved. As humans moved further north or south, those with less melanin (fairer skin) were evolutionarily advantaged. Those with darker skins now living in regions with reduced sunlight struggle more to obtain the same level of vitamin D as fairer skinned people. As we age, our ability to make vitamin D in the skin declines and our kidneys also become less productive at converting the vitamin D the skin makes into the most active metabolite of the vitamin D family.

The second of the kingmakers of the skeleton is calcium and, when combined with phosphate, the two create the 'concrete' of bones known as hydroxyapatite. Bones are very active living tissues and the problem in osteoporosis is with the 'concrete' pipes of bones rather than the bone marrow where most blood cells are made. Two cells keep bone in balance: one type makes bone (osteoblast) and the other type breaks bone down (osteoclasts). The bone-making cells first secrete a sticky protein, collagen, and then mineralise it. The main role of vitamin D is to maximise the absorption of calcium from the diet and, if blood supply of calcium falls, a hormone (parathyroid) ups the conversion of less active vitamin D to the most active form known as calcitriol.

In the case of the skeleton, the ageing process begins in our early to late twenties when the body's bone mass reaches a peak and then begins a gradual decline. Because men are bigger, they achieve a higher peak bone mass and do so at the same age as women. In both sexes from the late twenties or early thirties, bone loss occurs at the same rate – at about 1%–3% per annum. By about 50, both women and men have reduced their bone mass to that of a late teenager. However, in females, the menopause now accelerates bone loss so that at 70 women may have the same bone mass as a 13 year old. For women aged 50 to 70 osteoporosis is often called post-menopausal osteoporosis, and after 70 it is referred to as age-related osteoporosis. The advent of the menopause and the consequent loss of the female reproductive hormone oestrogen leads to a shift in the balance away from the bone-forming cells to those responsible for bone demolition. Osteoporosis does not come with recognisable symptoms. Bone density can be measured very easily using a scanning system known as DEXA (Dual Emission X-ray Absorptiometry), and thus women can establish whether their bone mineral density is above or below normal for their age. Addressing the issue of osteoporosis from the point of view of food and health requires us to look at the two sides of skeletal growth – the creation of the skeletal architecture and its demolition. The problem is that the period of bone growth in the second and third decade of life is not the period of maximum concern about health some four decades ahead. By the time post-menopausal women decide that they want to look after their bone health, the deed is done – maximum bone density was achieved long ago. They are now into minimising bone loss and the options for optimising bone growth and minimising bone loss are slightly different. Let's take them in chronological order.

I have said that there are two kingmakers when it comes to the skeleton – vitamin D and calcium. But the kingmakers have a staff which includes vitamin K, silicon, salt, protein and the acid–antacid balance of our diet. To optimise bone health we need firstly to optimise the kingmakers and, like the child who once wrote to Santa Claus with the request to define 'good', we can ask the question of how to define 'optimum' for calcium. Whether you live in the UK or the US, for example, will lead to a different interpretation of the level of calcium needed to optimise bone growth in the second decade of life. In the US, the expert committee decided to identify the optimum amount of calcium to (*a*) maximise peak adult bone mass, (*b*) maintain adult bone mass and (*c*) minimise bone loss in later years. The recommended dietary allowance is about

1,200 milligrams of calcium a day. In the UK, the experts disagree and feel that there is no benefit to bone health with calcium intakes above 750 milligrams of calcium a day. So as the average Briton flies from London to New York, they move from adequate to inadequate calcium intake without any change in their diet. Since the average reader of this book is not an expert, an average intake of calcium-rich dairy products, preferably lower fat where possible, should be the target for growing children. As regards vitamin D, the problem is the strict regulation of exposure to sunlight in climates where sunshine in winter is very restricted. Come the summer, it is 'Slip-Slop-Slap' time. Sooner or later, the experts who are curbing our exposure to sunlight will have to come to terms with the growing evidence, from the renowned Harvard School of Public Health, that low levels of plasma vitamin D are associated with increased risk of breast and colon cancer and also of that cluster of heart-disease-related symptoms known as the metabolic syndrome. In Australia, it is now recommended that in the summer period one should have a minimum of five minutes' and a maximum of 15 minutes' exposure to sunlight twice each day, before 10 a.m. and after 3 p.m., but between these times sunscreen must be worn. During the Australian winter, two to three hours of exposure of the skin to sunshine is needed each week and sun block is not needed in wintertime. This balancing act of promoting vitamin D status to optimise bone health and to reduce breast and colon cancers and the metabolic syndrome on the one hand, and reducing exposure to sunlight to reduce the risks of skin cancer on the other, is likely to become an increasingly hot topic in the coming years. There are other nutrients involved in bone health including vitamin K. Although a direct deficiency symptom of vitamin K is unknown, blood levels can be considerably influenced by diet and can be increased with green leafy vegetables. High intakes of animal protein and of salt can impair bone development. However, the kingmakers remain vitamin D and calcium.

Let us now switch from bone growth, which ceases in the mid twenties and turn to bone loss, which continues from the third decade onwards. How can that loss be minimised? Since postmenopausal osteoporosis is associated with the decline in oestrogen synthesis in women, hormone-replacement therapy (HRT) might seem a sensible option. HRT is associated with a number of adverse conditions and an increased risk of chronic disease; if HRT is used for any reason, it is usually short term and not for life. Although HRT improves bone strength, it doesn't have a lasting effect and it is therefore not an appropriate treatment for reducing bone loss. Calcium and vitamin D supplements have been shown in large trials to slow down bone loss and to reduce fractures. Weight-bearing physical activities are also associated with enhanced bone strength but non-weight bearing exercises (swimming, cycling) are of no benefit. Finally, there is the public health enemy number 1: smoking. Bone loss is considerably increased with continued exposure to the noxious niceties of tobacco smoking.

Brittle bones can break easily, but falls are responsible for most fractures in the ageing population. Do older people fall more frequently than younger people? Well, leaving aside the frequent falls of bouncing toddlers, yes they do. Among free-living older persons aged 65, an incidence of 0.3 to 0.6 falls per person per year has been recorded which means that for every 100 such persons per year there will be 30 to 160 cases of a fall annually with one in 20 leading to a fracture. By age 75, these numbers double and among people living in long-term care the figures rise to between 60 and 360 falls per 100 such persons annually. So, more older folks fall. Why? Well, as we age, everything begins to wear itself out. Our nervous system declines and so our reflexes are not as sharp as they once were. That instant recovery from a near fall doesn't materialise as we get on in years. Sarcopenia means our muscle mass and its quality fall. Our gait becomes stiffer. Our cardiovascular system doesn't function so well that we may get dizzy after rising suddenly. Drugs may impair many of the sensory functions involved in falls and, of course, failing sight is an age-related problem and this is one area that directly involves our diet.

In chapter twelve, we will see that the vast majority of blind people on this planet have lost their vision through an inadequate diet, specifically from insufficient intake of vitamin A. However, declining sight in the elderly is not of this nature. In the ageing population, the leading cause of impaired vision in developed countries is age-related macular degeneration (ARMD), the macula being an area of the eye's retina. About one in ten people from their mid-sixties onwards will have ARMD and, ten years on, this figure will rise to nearly one in three. Over the past two decades, there have been many studies on the potential of antioxidants to prevent ARMD. Perhaps the big attraction to study this relationship lies in the fact that the macula contains two antioxidants, which must be supplied in the diet: lutein and zeaxanthin. Initial studies by the US National Eye Institute suggested that macular degeneration could be reduced with supplements of a mix of anti-oxidants, including zeaxanthin and lutein. However, on balance, the evidence doesn't stack up and the general consensus is that a balanced diet containing a good mix of coloured fruit and vegetables will deliver all of the nutrients required for the maintenance of optimal vision.[11] However, google the terms lutein, zeaxanthin and macular degeneration and the supplements industry will tell you otherwise.

Let us pause for a moment and look at the story so far. As we get on in years we lose muscle and gain fat, our joints are stiffer, our bones are weaker and our vision fails. But when people think of things that can go wrong with ageing, none of those is anywhere near the top because the undisputed leading fear of growing old is declining cognitive function. Most people can live with frailty, with obesity, with the odd fall and even a fracture. But please don't let me lose my marbles. It is a given that as we get older we get more forgetful and indeed it can have its charm, bonding the grandparent with the bemused grandchild. But while the odd 'senior moment' is tolerable, the thought of serious cognitive impairment strikes fear in most people for it inevitably heralds total dependency. Memory is thought to exist in one of four categories.

Episodic memory: This is the area where ageing does the most damage. It is that part of memory which recalls personal experiences: what you had for dinner last night; what you did for your holidays.

Semantic memory: This is about facts and concepts. It is a fact that grass is green and we need always to recall that. As regards concepts, we know that although a fork and a comb share some physical similarities, we don't confuse them. We understand them conceptually and we recall them accurately.

Procedural memory: This allows us to store and retrieve information on behavioural and cognitive skills which enables us to do things on 'auto-pilot' – shift gears while driving a car; tie our shoelaces or ties; dialling a telephone.

Working memory: This involves attention, concentration and short-term memory. You look up the number of a restaurant, recall the number and dial it. Minutes later it is gone from memory and something else occupies the working memory.

One in eight persons in their seventies will have mild cognitive impairment and among such individuals the likelihood of progressing onwards to Alzheimer's disease is increased three to fourfold. From the point of view of diet and health there is strong evidence that nutrition will play a critical role in maintaining good cognitive function primarily through the maintenance of both episodic and working memory. Three nutrients have been most extensively studied: omega 3 fats, vitamin B_{12}, and the B vitamin folic acid. The evidence, however, is a challenge, to put it mildly. I will give examples of epidemiological studies linking one or more of these three nutrients to cognitive decline in the elderly and suffice it to say that for every one observational study I use to corroborate this effect, I could have picked at least a half a dozen others of high-quality studies from the best researchers in the world. The first I will cite is the 'Banbury B_{12} study' which was co-ordinated by Robert Clarke of Oxford with collaboration from groups in Sweden, Norway, Denmark and Ireland.[12] A sample of a thousand individuals aged 75 years or older were recruited into the study. Cognitive impairment was measured and blood samples were taken. Persons with the lowest B_{12} status had three times the risk of being found with cognitive impairment compared to those with the best B_{12} status. In the same study folic acid levels were measured in blood and the findings were pretty similar. In the case of the role of omega-3 fats and cognitive impairment, a number of longitudinal studies recruited elderly people who had normal cognitive function, measured their intakes of omega-3 fatty acids and then followed them over time, eventually comparing those who developed impaired cognitive function with those whose cognitive function remained normal. The Zutphen Elderly Study in the Netherlands and the Hordaland Health Study in Norway both show that there is a linear decline of the risk of developing mild cognitive impairment associated with the consumption of up to a maximum of about 70g of oily fish per day which is about two to three servings of salmon per week.[13]

Other examples could be selected and they would all show the same output. Now, as was discussed in chapter four, these studies are observational and do not prove cause and effect. For that we need to turn to dietary intervention studies. In the case of omega-3 dietary fat intervention studies, there is some, but limited supporting data. Most studies have been inconclusive. In the case of folate and B_{12}, that point is even stronger with little or no evidence from intervention studies. The first conclusion we could reach here is that there is no cause and effect. Something, which we don't yet understand, is causing impaired cognitive function and at the same time is causing either (*a*) blood levels of these nutrients to fall for some reason and (*b*) older people to dislike eating fish. On balance, to this writer, that argument doesn't stack up. That there would be some unifying but unknown pathology which would cause loss of body levels of two nutrient categories as different as omega-3 fats and two water-soluble vitamins is impossible to envisage. And if it were solely a loss of body levels of omega-3 fats, then we should not have seen lower real intakes of oily fish. There is another possibility: supposing a long-term low intake of omega-3 fats or B_{12} / folate leads to impaired cognitive function which is not readily or at all reversible. Then no amount of intervention could be effective. And there is another possible explanation. If a poor diet interacts with some specific genetic variation then, when we carry out our epidemiological studies, the people we find with cognitive impairment collectively have a higher prevalence of some genetic variant or mix of variants. Unless your intervention sample contains a higher proportional number of such genetically sensitive persons, your study will be inconclusive.

To link this topic to that of the previous chapter we need to think about associations between body weight in middle age and the risk of subsequent loss of cognitive function. And I'm afraid the news is not good. Consistently the evidence is that being overweight in mid life increases the risk of Alzheimer's disease later on. Let me take one US study as an example.[14] As part of a medical-care programme, men and women were studied when they were aged 40 to 45 years between 1964 and 1973. In 1994, there were 10,276 such persons still within the programme. Between 1994 and 2003 their cognitive performance was examined. Compared with those who were normal weight at mid life, those who were obese in mid life had a 74% higher chance of developing impaired cognitive function. The figure for those who were overweight but not obese in mid life was 35% higher than for those who were normal weight.

Now let us return to the fact that among the elderly population in developed countries we have a high level of malnutrition. This malnutrition will be largely due to poor eating habits brought about by many factors from loss of appetite to social isolation or economic poverty. The tip of the iceberg will be the overall caloric and protein deficiency that will be associated with thinness and sarcopenia. At the level of biochemical assessment, a plethora of nutritional deficiencies will be uncovered affecting all of the areas we have discussed: muscle, bone, taste, appetite, sight, cognitive function and so on. The greater the level of malnutrition, the more likely it is that the person will be admitted to hospital and the more likely it is that they will have a prolonged stay with complications and a higher chance of readmission after discharge. All of this costs the health service vast sums of money. There is, however, a large body of evidence to show that with the use of oral nutritional supplements in older persons, admissions to hospital fall but, most importantly, the duration of hospitalisation halves and with it the cost per patient.

One of the great social challenges in the next half-century will be the greying of the globe. It will bring with it many challenges to food and health and to nutrition in particular. It will require us to focus more and more on the health of younger people, because the greater the investment in nutritional well being in early to mid life the greater the reward. The big challenge is telling a teenager to worry about the other side of life. But we will also need to develop effective screening programmes, which can detect malnutrition in the elderly and upon which we can build effective intervention strategies to improve the quality of life of our older citizens.

CHAPTER TEN

Food and Health: The Science, Policy and Politics

In 1820, Frederick Accum, a German chemist working in London, published a book entitled *A Treatise on Adulterations of Food and Culinary Poisons*. It was an enormously controversial book at the time because it documented the common practice of adulterating food with all sorts of nasty chemicals. Ultimately, it contributed to the development of our present-day food legislation. This legislation today covers all aspects of the safety of the human food chain and also its nutritional attributes. Today, there are very few if any aspects of our daily life more regulated by government than the food we eat. This is itself understandable since consumers who vote governments in and out of office have a passionate interest in a food chain that is both safe and nutritious. Among consumers are those who take it upon themselves to champion the cause of a safe and nutritious food supply. These consumer groups are linked across the globe through social networks. From time to time, they raise issues with governments seeking changes in legislation to ensure that some existing practice, which they see as a threat to the concept of a safe and nutritious food chain is controlled. Frequently, that puts them in direct conflict with those whose livelihoods depend on the food chain, the farmers and the food industry.

The food industry is also organised globally and is also in the business of lobbying for legislation to safeguard its position or to reduce its barriers to trade. In my time as a scientist I have seen industry lobby on such issues as how dietary fibre is defined, the reference values to be used for nutritional labelling, the issue of nutritional profiling with the use of Guideline Daily Amounts, the area of dietary guidelines, nutritionally based health claims and so forth. This tension between consumers, producers and regulators is part and parcel of what is now called participatory democracy. It is a dog-eat-dog drama, dripping in adversarial politics with a dash of science. So let's meet the players.

There is a villain of the piece. It is an unloved, untrustworthy, feared and constantly suspect villain – the food industry. And by the food industry we don't mean the honest farmers who toil daily close to nature or the small player in food manufacturing, little removed from a food artisan. We mean large corporations, preferably global players and ideally household names across the planet. And the villain has collaborators tainted with the villain's largesse, from politicians to bureaucrats, from journalists to scientists. The role of the villain of the piece and the support of his collaborating hoards regularly feature in major news items in books and in documentaries, often in the 'shock and awe' mode. So much of what is seen to be wrong in the world can be better dealt with when we know the villain, police the villain and punish the frequent villainous transgressions. This almost always makes us feel good. However, in the majority of cases, the piece is far more complex than is explained by our villain. And the topic of this book is certainly no exception.

The ultimate sin that the food industry is accused of is that of behaving like the tobacco industry. The tobacco industry sells a product, which dramatically increases the risk of developing a wide array of chronic diseases. So too, you could say, does the industry responsible for the manufacture and sale of trans fats which were used in large quantities until recently in many manufactured foods and which are strongly associated with increased risk of heart disease. The tobacco industry withheld scientific data, which incriminated their product in the development of many chronic diseases. So too, one could argue have certain areas of the food or the food biotechnology industry. However long these apparent similarities are sustained, there is one dissimilarity that is so strong that the comparison instantly collapses. The tobacco industry *is* the problem. It could be taken away if the political will existed and the problem *in toto* would disappear. However, the food industry cannot be seen in that light as being the 'problem' because, quite simply, the food industry must be the solution. In the case of trans fats, industry responded when the scale of the adverse evidence emerged and when it became competitively disadvantageous to include trans fats. Those who see industry as the villain might continue by arguing that the processed industry is the true problem and that alternatives such as farmers' markets or consumer co-operatives are the way to go. To address this point, let me construct a scenario, which is never going to happen and which, it will be said by some is a grossly unfair scenario.

Consider London, as we know it today. It has a population of 7,512,400 and covers an area of 157,731 hectares. Its total protein requirement is of the order of 166,000 tons per annum.

Let us now hypothetically isolate London from the outside world to the point where processed food cannot be delivered to London. Rather, we are going to make London self-sufficient in food for nutritional purposes and we are going to take protein needs per person per day as a test of self-reliance. From the 40 by 40 kilometre area of London, let us extend it by 10 kilometres on each side giving a new and additional adjoining landmass of 90,000 hectares. We will leave all roads, services and utilities intact, but otherwise obliterate all buildings, returning the land to an arable condition. The allotted land mass in, say, dairy farming would have the capacity to yield about 59,000 tonnes of protein per day which is just one third of the protein needs of the population. Were we to extend the landmass of arable land to meet the protein needs of all Londoners, then it is goodbye Reading, Epsom, Dartford and Harlow and all towns between these and London. This is manifestly unfair and downright stupid but sometimes it is necessary to construct a manifestly stupid scenario to begin to understand that the direction being mooted is a dead end.

The human race has undergone a social evolution, which led to the concept of the city. In return for generating wealth through non-food procuring endeavours, we pay others to prepare our food. Unlike our colleagues in the animal kingdom, we trade our food and, uniquely, we engage in the division of labour. That sets the limits as to how the food chain can be reinvented for whatever reason. In small rural villages, we can easily isolate the outside world and engineer the good life of self-reliance on local food production. However, modern humans are mainly urban and hence the need for the symbiosis: 'I'll insure your tractor driver if you harvest my potatoes' and 'I'll make you a nice movie if you make me frozen French-fries'. The remainder of this chapter assumes that for the moment we must live with the existing reliance of the urban population on a rural population to produce primary agricultural produce and for an industry to purchase, ship, transform and otherwise fiddle with this primary produce to produce the modern food supply for sale to you and me in modern retail and catering outlets. In chapter thirteen we will then entertain the argument that all aspects of food production and all links in the food chain will need to be revisited, not for issues of nutrition and health but for the sustainability of our planet. For the rest of this chapter, let's stick with the here and now.

Have you ever seen the protesters at a G8 conference burning effigies of the Central Café in Blackrock, Dublin? No, I didn't think so. Now in Blackrock where I live, the Central Café specialises in 'Fish and Chips' and will accompany take away chips (equals French fries) with deep-fried fish or chicken or grilled burgers or sausages. In addition to the Central Café, I can buy a serving of chips from any one of five pubs, five Asian take-aways and one McDonalds. The latter does have its emblems burned at G8 conferences and is top of the list when virtually anybody wants to express an opinion on fast food and obesity. The other ten outlets in Blackrock don't get a mention. What are we 'against': chips or McDonalds? Make up your mind because it's a fundamental difference. McDonalds may be the convenient whipping boy of the Blackrock chip industry but the whipping experience is based on a value-laden analysis and not on the available evidence from the realm of public health nutrition. From the national dietary surveys in Ireland, the following is the hard evidence. In a typical survey week 85% of children will have consumed chips and only 18% will have consumed chips from McDonalds. Among those who eat chips, the average intake of chips from all sources was 40g while for chips from McDonalds it was 17g. Children or teenagers who consume McDonald's chips are a significant minority relative to the total sample of chip eaters. And among the latter, the average daily intake from McDonald's chips is a fraction, about one third, of the total chip-eating population. Quite clearly, if chip-intake is an issue, then McDonalds is a player but not the major player by a long shot. However, if corporate-bashing is the issue, then clearly the Central Café in Blackrock is not much help.

The key point being made here, and one that needs further elaboration given its central role in this debate, is that the global corporate component of the average diet, at least in many parts of Europe, is far less than is popularly believed. The following data from a national dietary survey of adults in Ireland show that the food categories, which are 'mainly corporate', together account for rather a limited 17% of the energy intake in Ireland. Some two thirds of calories come from foods that are local, most of which are commodities sold unwrapped and unbranded (bread, meat, poultry, fish, fruit, vegetables, cheese, eggs, potatoes etc).

Looking at TV advertising or listening to the food supply critics would not give that impression, but the reality is that a small number of very large global food corporations play the dominant role in the sales and marketing of a limited number of food categories. Thus, in the chocolate market, a handful of very high profile food companies (Nestlé, Cadbury, Kraft, Mars) dominate a market with a massive advertising budget for a food category that accounts for 2.5% of energy intake in Ireland, while the zero profile potato farmers of Ireland dominate a market (with zippo advertising) that accounts for 12% of energy intake.

Now whereas most Irish potato farmers do not trot the globe regularly promoting the wonders of potatoes, they are 'organised' into a farmers' union that is strongly linked to a national agency which has the promotion of potatoes as a major objective and, of course, the various national agencies are organised internationally into the 'global potato industry'. The same will be true of the 'global sugar industry' or the 'global dairy industry' etc. And in many instances, the global alliance of small farmers and local national processors can find one of the global food giants as an obvious ally. For example, sugar is central to the economy of Coca Cola and so that company necessarily has in interest in the affairs of the 'global sugar industry'. Equally, McDonalds, for whom beef is a major economic interest, necessarily aligns itself with the 'global beef industry'. A major difference, however, between the global organisation of a largely local set of producers and a global food giant is that the latter is autonomous and is rich and spends that budget on innovation, advertising and ruthless competition. The former are usually the opposite: broke, poorly organised and very non-competitive. Between them, the farmers and food industry constitute a major part of the supply side of the food chain. Another and influential part of that chain is the retail sector that portrays itself as being on the consumer side of the fence and not the supply side. Because they sit at the market interface between the consumer and producer, they can wield great power on the latter. Indeed the question has been asked: 'What is the difference between a terrorist and a supermarket chain buyer?' the answer to which is: 'One can negotiate with a terrorist'. The retail sector can ban additives, demand GM free produce, design its own labelling system and impose it on suppliers, set analytical standards higher than legally binding and basically set the scene so long as it suits the customer. Thus in summary of this overview, the industrial section of the food business is almost always portrayed as the dominant player in the human food chain, but that is not really the case. They may dominate advertising and be globally recognised for their brands. But in real terms their contribution is less than frequently believed. As we saw in chapter eight, it is easy to attribute obesity to junk food, but the truth is that all foods are implicated and most of these are not global brands (bread, milk, meat, cheese, eggs, fish, fruit, vegetables, potatoes, rice, pasta etc.). Now let's leave that side of the cast and move to a totally different set of players, the scientists in the food and health piece.

The Honest Broker: Making Sense of Science in Policy and Politics is the title of an excellent book by Roger Pielke on which I will draw heavily to illustrate how science interacts with the policy and politics of food and health.[1] What Roger Pielke has done in his book is to classify scientists into one of four main categories. The first is the 'Pure Scientist' who is wired to the laboratory with no interest whatsoever in connecting his or her work to social issues or to policy makers. The world couldn't function if all scientists were to behave like this. It is a privileged and also a selfish position to adopt, but many do. The second category, the 'Science Arbiter', is willing to move out of the laboratory to provide technical assistance to policy makers. He or she doesn't seek out the limelight and frankly would prefer to remain in the laboratory, but recognises the need for scientists to answer very specific questions, the answers to which will inform policy. The third category is the 'Honest Broker of Policy Alternatives', and here we have a group of scientists who, with gusto, roll up their sleeves and get stuck into the issue of interpreting scientific data to help policy makers make better decisions. This often means sitting on scientific advisory committees, which are often multi-disciplinary in nature. The key attribute of this group is that they have no scientific agenda and are willing to cover every angle, likely and unlikely, to make sure that no stone is left unturned in searching for the illusive 'truth'. The final category is entitled the 'Issue Advocate'. Here we have a category of scientists who do have an agenda and who will seek to steer debate away from anything that would distract from their agenda. That agenda can range from the Kyoto Protocol to genetic engineering, from malnutrition to biofuels . . . anything you like. In my own field of nutrition I can identify scientists who have very strong views on sugar or trans fats or the fortification of food with micronutrients and who will always manage to wind their way to the policy debate, carrying the outward gravitas of the independent scientist, often darlings of the media, but inwardly intent on limiting the debate to deliver a given outcome which they have favoured *a priori*. How is it possible, you might ask, that a scientist, supposedly cold, dispassionate and indifferent and in love with mere 'facts' should adopt such an apparently unscientific approach to a problem that society needs to address and which has a scientific dimension? Well, scientists are no different from the rest of society and some will develop bees in their bonnet on some topic or other and some will believe that they can save the human race from some disaster and take no hostages on the road they see needs to be travelled to do so. This is not for one second to imply that the Issue Advocate is dishonest; far from it. Such a scientist has developed a position on an issue and believes passionately that he or she is duty-bound to pursue it, openly and ruthlessly or, if needs be, as Roger Pielke points out, by stealth.

Although science is supposedly built on a 'conjecture and refutation cycle', the reality is that conventional wisdom becomes somewhat sacrosanct. One of the difficulties in the area of food and health is that if you challenge conventional wisdom, some part of the corporate food sector will visit you to tell you that you are doing a great job because their sector is 'threatened' by this conventional wisdom. The moment that happens, the Issue Advocates who want to uphold conventional wisdom will deem you to be 'a mouthpiece of industry', 'tainted' and no longer an 'independent' scientist. The only way to win in this debate is to continue to publish original research in high impact journals, funded from competitive public funds. That gives you an untouchable currency, which the Issue Advocates have to live with begrudgingly. One of the important contributions to the science–policy–politics debate from Roger Pielke's book is that scientists are rarely 'independent'. It does not mean that most scientists are recipients of the largesse of the food industry. It means that scientists like everybody else have values and views. Some hold the view that the food industry is driven by unfettered greed and must be policed into oblivion. Others believe that the food industry is by and large responsible and that consumers have the right to eat wrongly so long as they harm no one else. Ask these two extremes to sit on a committee to advise on food labelling and the outcome will be determined by who shouts louder and longer. Scientists cannot be independent of their mindset. What we must seek is not scientific 'independence' but scientific integrity. Those who make jet engines and those who regulate jet engines will visit only the world's experts on jet engines. Third-rate scientists with little research income and little research output may be as pure as the driven snow in terms of 'independence' from industry, but they will not be consulted on important cutting edge science. A perfect example of the failure of scientists to always be objective was seen in a study of the association between intake of sugar-sweetened beverages and obesity.[2] The authors picked two studies that had examined a relationship between consumption of sugar-enriched beverages and obesity and which had not found any *statistically* significant positive association between the intake of sugary beverages and obesity. Taken together, the findings of these studies were cited in a total of 239 subsequent research papers on this topic. The majority of these 239 papers described the original results of the two test papers 'in a misleadingly positive manner to varying degrees'. In other words, they ignored the main conclusion of a complete absence of a statistically significant effect of sugar-rich beverages and obesity. Instead they chose to cherry-pick aspects of the results which suited their own research publications. In the case of one of the original papers, its findings were cited correctly in only 13% of the subsequent studies. For the other it was 33%.

In the latter part of the last century we saw an enormous increase in the number of NGOs and their evolution from national to trans-national forces, largely empowered by the mass print and TV media. We have in fact evolved from a representative democracy to a participatory democracy where the power of NGOs is very significant. That NGOs have flourished as they have is itself proof of their need in civilised society where someone has to champion the unpopular, the unlikely and the unknown. Consider the Soil Association, a UK NGO which champions organic farming. It began during the Second World War, when in 1943 Lady Eve Balfour wrote a book entitled *The Living Soil.*[3] Three years later she was first president of the Soil Association. Today, some 60 years later, the enormous growth of organic farming can be directly traced back to the founders of this NGO for when, as it is said, it was neither profitable nor popular, this NGO was championing the forerunners of today's standards for organic agriculture. Everything that is legal and decent and supports the cause of organic farming will be embraced and espoused by this NGO and its sister NGOs across the globe. Everything that threatens organic agriculture will be opposed. And in this judgement, it will be the considered opinion of the Soil Association and the Soil Association alone that matters. Thus the chemical fertiliser industry is not an ally and the biotechnology industry is an open enemy. Dick Taverne, in his book *The March of Unreason: Science, Democracy and the New Fundamentalism*, describes many of the best-known NGOs (Friends of the Earth, Greenpeace, Green Watch, The Soil Association etc.) as eco-fundamentalists.[4] Their views are based on a political or ethical stance and science will simply not be allowed to get in the way. He points out that they constantly cite one another with no attempt to seek a balanced view. Thus, as he points out, they reject the reports from independent experts of the Brazilian, Chinese, Indian and Mexican Academies of Science, the Third World Academy of Science, the US National Academy of Science, four reports of the Royal Society and two reports of the Nuffield Foundation. In the UK upper house of Parliament (House of Lords), a select committee on EU regulations on GM foods asked the UK Executive Director of Greenpeace, Lord Melchett, the following question:

> Your opposition to the release of GMOs, that is an absolute and definitive opposition? It is not one that is dependent on further scientific research or improved procedures being developed or any satisfaction you might get with regard to safety or otherwise in the future?

He replied:

It is a permanent and complete opposition based on a view that there will always be major uncertainties.[5]

I once asked Lord Melchett what would happen if, hypothetically, the scientific case against GM foods were shown not to be true beyond any reasonable doubt. He replied: 'We'd always fall back on the moral and ethical aspect.' Lord Melchett is honest. NGOs are political organisations and adopt whatever scientific position they need to sustain their political stance. But there is a difference between an NGO with a political agenda and politics itself. Politics is the art of the possible and that requires flexibility in the way the world is viewed. Yesterday's terrorist is today's statesman. Many environmental NGOs are fundamentalist, dogmatic and entrenched. The problem they have is that they have 'branded' themselves so and thus there is no going backwards. The media see NGOs as dedicated and devoted to saving the planet and therefore the media dare not query them in any way. The villain is the food industry, always.

The final actors of the piece are the national governmental agencies and the global agencies of the UN, and it is the latter which merit most focus since many of the governmental policies are influenced by local issues, by electoral pressures and domestic commercial interests. The main UN players in food and health are the World Health Organisation (WHO), the Food and Agricultural Organisation (FAO) and the World Food Programme (WFP). We should include here the United Nations International Children's Emergency Fund (UNICEF) although strictly speaking it is not totally UN.

The UN agencies enjoy enormous trust among consumers but they, like scientists, industry and NGOs, tend to appear differently when put under the microscope. The prestigious medical journal, *The Lancet*, pointed out in an important editorial how UN agencies can play around with scientific outputs. It cites two examples where UN agencies, not especially happy with the outcome of a research programme, pre-empted the publication of the research in a peer-reviewed journal by releasing its own version of events, painting a somewhat different interpretation from that in the scientific paper. In one case the WHO issued a press release on the findings of a group of researchers from Kenya on the use of insecticide-treated bed nets to combat malaria. The WHO, who had full access to the impending publication, painted a picture of outstanding success whereas the scientific paper was more qualified. In a second such case, UNICEF pre-empted the publication of a scientific paper reporting disappointing progress in efforts to reduce childhood mortality by releasing material to selected journalists regarding a 'major public health success', claiming that the annual under-five-year child mortality had fallen below 10 million. The 'disappointment' of the scientific paper (which UNICEF had access to) was nowhere to be seen. *The Lancet* editorial concluded:

> Both of these examples show how UN agencies are willing to play fast and loose with scientific findings in order to further their own institutional interests. . .. But the danger is that by appearing to manipulate science, breach trust, resist competition and reject accountability, WHO and UNICEF are acting contrary to responsible scientific norms that one would have expected UN technical agencies to uphold'.[6]

These two instances can be put alongside a detailed analysis of how the WHO makes its decisions which was the subject of a major paper published in the *Lancet* in the same year (2007) as the pre-empting press releases were made. The paper reported on a piece of research carried out jointly by the Norwegian Knowledge Centre for the Health Services and the Centre for Health Economics at McMaster University in Canada and funded by the EU. It involved interviewing 29 directors or equivalents in the WHO on decision-making processes. The recorded interviews were transcribed and given back to the interviewees to check. The results were very disturbing. Systematic reviews were rarely used and the favoured way of developing a report was to use an expert committee or individual experts. A systematic review is, as the name implies, a comprehensive review of all that is known on the topic with strict a priori criteria for quality control for accepting or rejecting any given paper. The paper notes that: 'For example, systematic reviews and concise summary of findings are rarely used which means that the evidence is generally not retrieved, appraised, synthesised and interpreted using systematic and transparent methods.'[7] Little attention was seen to be given to the end-users of policy, those who have to adapt global policy to local needs. The use of the expert committee was highlighted in one interview: 'There is a tendency to get people around a table and get consensus – everything they do has a scientific part and a political part. This usually means you go to the lowest common denominator or the views of a 'strong' person at the table.' Of course, if a 'strong' expert has a hand in shaping the composition of the committee then you can effectively write the report before they ever meet. I had personal experience of the wrath of UN agencies. In the summer of 1992 the two leading agencies involved in the area, the FAO and WHO, undertook a Preparatory Committee (PrepCom in UN-speak) to prepare the way for the International Conference on Nutrition which is discussed in chapter twelve. The PrepCom is anything but your normal concept of a committee. It is in fact a full-blown UN event, with all UN members in attendance and with a remarkable retinue of NGOs (both Public Interest and Business Interest) in tow. In August 1992, I interrupted a family holiday in the US to travel to Geneva to act as co-rapporteur for this global event. I felt very honoured to have been singled out for such a role. However, honour was not being served for breakfast on the morning I arrived at the WHO headquarters in Geneva. I had been sacked – no longer the honourable co-rapporteur. My sin? I had been critical of the way in which international agencies were issuing dietary guidelines and had written many scientific papers outlining my reservations, not at the issuing of dietary guidelines, but at the way the WHO was executing the process. A colleague of mine at Trinity College Dublin, the late Peter Skrabanek, an iconoclast of international repute, asked me to prepare a lay-targeted article on the limitation of quantitative global goals based on my several peer-reviewed publications in the area. The article was for the UK Social Affairs Unit, which specialises in asking unpopular questions. The publication of my article and several related articles was released just before the PrepCom as a booklet entitled *Who needs WHO?* For that, I was fired. Apparently, the WHO doesn't take kindly to criticism in much the same way as the Kremlin or the Vatican. There is a policy stance and you dare not challenge it. Four years later, honour was restored when I chaired the joint FAO–WHO consultation on food-based dietary guidelines although I hadn't repented!

These are the players in the drama of food politics. It is no different from the dramas that influence the global development of many social phenomena from the Olympic Games, to the telecoms sector, the aviation industry or the international aid programme. These are all dramas played out with comparable players who are fundamentally good and committed to a particular cause or agenda. The problem is that whereas they may articulate the existence of a 'common overarching goal', the reality is that they all have their cards marked in racing parlance: they all know how to vote on whatever matter because they all know the underlying ethos of their cause. That cause may be the pursuit of independent scientific critiques, the promotion of organic beekeeping, the abolition of the use of animal experimentation, the collapse of economic capital globalisation, the pursuit of farmers' markets, the promotion of exclusive breastfeeding or whatever. In effect, put them in the same drama and they will immediately swirl into alliances and each alliance will know its allies but, most importantly, know its enemies.

By and large, this adversarial system involving civil society, governments and the food industry works. There are sufficient checks and balances to make sure that daft legislation is very much the exception and not the rule. But this only happens because all players in the piece have a role to play in ensuring a safe and nutritious food chain.

CHAPTER ELEVEN

My Food, Your Poison: Who Sees What in Food?

When our tree-loping hominid ancestors abandoned their forest dwellings and moved to the new vista of river basins as food supplies dwindled, they were taking a risk. Because some young males had slept the night out under the stars by the river basin, having gorged themselves on the abundant supply of fish, birds and eggs, the venture was a calculated risk, not a reckless one. That is one key lesson that we will come to dwell on in this chapter, that the descent of the human race required risk-taking and that always had a benefit to whoever was taking the risk. We should also note from this hominid scenario that the migration involved a group. Thus the second key lesson that we will also dwell on later is that risk is a social construct. But before we go down that road we need to get the process in order. In the risk analysis process there is a clear pathway that starts with risk assessment which is purely technical, moves to risk management which is mostly political, and ends with risk communication which is mostly ignored and almost always botched. We need to build slowly to understand the latter because it is central to the purpose of this book – helping the consumer to understand.

There are three parts to risk assessment, all of them highly interconnected. The first starts with hazard characterisation. Here the question starts because it simply sets out to ascertain exactly what the hazard is and to gain some insight into what it might be capable of doing to human health. In some cases the hazard is very well characterised, such as when a new chemical is being submitted to the regulatory authority for approval. In other instances, finding the hazard means very careful research. For example, when a few British cows started to act strangely in groups on particular farms, the hazard had to be found. Was it in the air, the drinking water, in medicines or the food? And if it looked as if it was in the food, what part of the food was it in? You have to identify the hazard with precision otherwise you may be chasing lost causes. Once you have identified the hazard, you now want to characterise it. You want to drown yourself in the metrics of the biological effects of the hazard because you will be eventually asked to make decisions, which might affect human health. Here there is a wide range of options not all of which are applied at all times. Thus one might start with a database if the hazard was a chemical. If its chemical structure was very close to a chemical of known toxicity, the search might end right there. We might then grow some bacteria in its presence to see if it has any interaction with DNA. We then move to cell studies to see what happens to the expression of genes or the metabolic signature, but eventually we would have to do some work with experimental animals. One day we may be able to model a whole animal, but right now that is not an option and either we abandon the search for new drugs or food ingredients which require animal testing or we engage in it in a highly regulated way. At the end of this process we will have quantitative data on how this hazard at different doses causes effects in a wide variety of organs and tissues. Now it is important to dwell on one word in the last sentence, 'effect'. This does not have to mean lethal, near lethal, pathological or sickening. It can do of course. This term, however, includes any observation of a metabolite or biological function, which has moved outside the normal range, irrespective of wellness or sickness. The toxicologist is not looking for the 'toxic' effect as most people understand that word. He or she is looking for any effect, because they are relying on the law of Paracelsus, a pompous Swiss physician who famously stated: 'Sola dosis venum facet' or 'the dose alone maketh the poison'. Everything is toxic at the right dose and in the right circumstances. So the toxicologist records all deviations from the norm, irrespective of whether it appears trivial or suggests a nasty effect. Armed with this avalanche of data, a particular effect that the toxicologists are interested in is selected. We then begin the dose-response studies. Usually the effect in question is not observed when the animals are fed with low doses. We then move upward in doses and still the effect does not appear. Then, BINGO! At some given dose we begin now to see the effect and as the dose gets higher so too does the effect we are studying until it levels off. The point just before we first observe the effect of the chemical under study is known as the No Observed Effect Level (NOEL). Everything in toxicology depends on this. In the test animal this is the point where nothing happens, and at this point the animals are indistinguishable from all the animals at lower levels of exposure. But men are not mice and so to take account of that the NOEL is divided by ten. And then, just to be safe, it is again divided by ten. So one hundredth of the NOEL is a point known as the Acceptable Daily Intake (ADI) and that is the safe dose humans can be exposed to over a lifetime.

This is the process, which has evolved and is now universally accepted. To put it in perspective, estimates of exposure to those pesticides detected in foods using very conservative exposure methods, which we will shortly discuss, are put at about three per cent of the ADI. That means that people have an habitual intake, which is 1 in 30,000ths of the effect that was seen in the test animals to be perfectly normal. This system has served consumer safety well, and when a chemical is assigned an ADI it will always be subject to re-examination if any new data come along to justify it. In some cases, the dose response remains so flat that no effect is ever seen. Many of the vitamins which are food additives (E numbers) have no ADI. The ADI tells us about the biological potency of a compound. Of course, if the compound never enters the food supply, it cannot constitute a threat no matter what its biological potency. If everybody eats it then that might colour our views. Thus human exposure studies provide the ultimate set of data: under worst-case conditions, what is the intake of the chemical among very high consumers of the relevant foods, and is the exposure level below the ADI? In all my years of researching human exposure to food chemicals, rarely have I seen extreme intakes exceed the ADI, and when this has been observed, moving just slightly away from worst-case conditions towards reality, the intakes plummet below the ADI. The bottom line is that in the highly regulated area of food chemicals, there is, effectively speaking, a zero risk to consumers from permitted food chemicals. The brouhaha that would say there is a risk is simply scare-mongering and distracting consumers from real public health issues.

This is the point where we move from the scientific dimension to the 'political' dimension. It is the political dimension which makes the ultimate decision to 'ban', 'withdraw', 'label' or otherwise seek to influence consumer choice in relation to some hazard. In an ideal world, the decision is easy because the scientific data are complete, compelling and robust. But often the scientific data fall short of the ideal and the risk manager has a decision to make which is not exactly 100% clear-cut. For decades, this situation was accepted and lived with and it served consumer protection well.

However, risk management entered an entirely new phase in the late 1990s after the BSE scare. Trust in science and the regulatory process vanished. We were told that beef was safe and now we see people suffering an awesome and terrible disease and a dreadfully slow death. Enter the 'Precautionary Principle'. Traditionally, risk assessment was 100% based on science and nothing else. The Precautionary Principle changed that on foot of BSE and, probably, the public backlash against GM foods. This concept began in Germany in the 1970s and gained legs at a number of global environmental forums such as the Rio Declaration of 1992 and the Wingspread statement of 1998. It was quickly taken up by EU risk management and caused a serious level of controversy. There are many definitions of the precautionary principle, but the best approach is to cite directly from the European Commission who championed this concept:

> Recourse to the precautionary principle presupposes that potentially dangerous effects deriving from a phenomenon, product or process have been identified, and that scientific evaluation does not allow the risk to be determined with sufficient certainty. The implementation of an approach based on the precautionary principle should start with a scientific evaluation, as complete as possible, and where possible, identifying at each stage the degree of scientific uncertainty. Decision-makers need to be aware of the degree of uncertainty attached to the results of the evaluation of the available scientific information. Judging what is an 'acceptable' level of risk for society is an eminently political responsibility. Decision-makers faced with an unacceptable risk, scientific uncertainty and public concerns have a duty to find answers. Therefore, all these factors have to be taken into consideration. In some cases, the right answer may be not to act or at least not to introduce a binding legal measure. A wide range of initiatives is available in the case of action, going from a legally binding measure to a research project or a recommendation. The decision-making procedure should be transparent and should involve as early as possible and to the extent reasonably possible all interested parties.[1]

The scientific community who ran the risk assessment process was deeply suspicious of attempts to dumb down their scientific deliberations. Industry, heavy users of the risk assessment process, feared an unequal playing field since there could be different interpretations of such concepts as 'potentially dangerous effects' or 'degree of uncertainty'. Most NGOs of course loved it and the risk managers who invoked the concept were also happy. The players in the politics of food fulfilled their stereotypes. The key words in the Precautionary Principle are 'uncertainty' and 'danger'. Risk assessment is effectively a statement of: 'If A, then B' or 'If A_1 and/or A_2, then B'. Uncertainty can apply either to A or to B. The EU's own experts have used figures of Greek mythology to illustrate the principles of uncertainty. Damocles was invited to dine with his king with a sword hanging by a thread over his head. If we were confident that the thread would hold, Damocles faced no risk, but in the event that it might break then we were certain about the outcome – curtains for Damocles. The risk assessment focused on the input to the risk, the thread. Pandora had a slightly different analytical scenario. She was given a locked box containing all manner of evil potential. So long as the box remained closed we were safe but if the box was opened, we knew we would have disastrous consequences; until we saw them they would remain unknown. The uncertainty was more about the outcome of the risk, the contents of the box.

As regards the danger side of the precautionary side, there are three major dimensions to danger. Could the danger give rise to an event that we would generally regard as catastrophic? Would such a danger be reversible? How widespread would the damage be? If we take two examples from the food scare library we can see the extremes. Acrylamide is a compound which at high exposure levels causes cancers in rats. As we have seen, Swedish scientists noted that high levels were produced when starch-rich foods (crisps, chips) were heated.[2] The danger is not catastrophic, although it was headline news for months given that you generate as much acrylamide in your kitchen as anywhere else (toast, pancakes etc.). The danger can be reversed by introducing new processing techniques and by advising consumers on cooking methods. Finally, on all sides of the danger, there was a high level of uncertainty. The effect was quite global. In contrast, the risk of developing CJD from eating beef, which might be infected with BSE prions, was laden with uncertainty in the probability that the meat would be infected and in the probability that a person who ate the meat would develop CJD. The danger (CJD), were it to be realised, was catastrophic and non-reversible and it had the potential to be global. Having chaired the EU working group on BSE in the height of the crisis of 1997–2000, I had sympathy with the risk managers in the introduction of the Precautionary Principle. The problem with the Precautionary Principle was that it had the potential to be abused and, indeed, it was abused by the very people who introduced it, the EU. European consumers didn't want their beef to be derived from animals treated with hormones to promote growth and so, in 1989, the EU banned the import of such beef which had a huge impact on the US meat industry and sparked a major trade row since both the US and the FAO/WHO risk assessment procedures found no reason to suggest any risk to human health from such beef. The EU had concerns on one hormone based on its scientific advice, but had no scientific basis for its expressed concerns on five others and for these the EU invoked the Precautionary Principle to support the ban. The US took the EU to the Appellate Body of the World Trade Organisation in 1996 and in 1998 the WTO ruled in favour of the US.[3] In effect, the EU had no reasonable scientific grounds to ban the import of beef from cattle treated with the five specified hormones. Its stance was based solely on a political position and to support it the EU called in the Precautionary Principle. This is the dangerous end of an apparently sensible risk management option. Issue-driven NGOs who shun the scientific consensus can mobilise the views of the public. There are votes in being greener than green, especially when it brings no disadvantage to the electorate.

Leaving the realm of risk management we now come to the third element of risk analysis – risk communication – which is by far the most misunderstood. The first part of risk communication is the message, and the manner in which a message is transmitted is one important aspect of how risk is perceived. In a study reported in the *New England Journal of Medicine,* three groups comprising patients, graduate students and physicians were asked to imagine they had lung cancer.[4] They were shown data in two ways for two different approaches to the treatment of lung cancer, surgery or radiation. One way the data was shown was 'positive' as survival rates and the second way was to present the same data in a 'negative' way as mortality rates. They were asked to choose one treatment form. The number of patients choosing radiation therapy over surgery fell from 44% to 18% when the data were framed in terms of mortality. The same pattern was also found for both the graduate students and the physicians. The data above are identical, each the mirror image of the other. Mortality was a word that seemed more threatening than survival and in the short term it had lower numbers. The above is a trick to illustrate how framing risk can influence perception of risk. However, the same data can be used differently to suit different agendas. Thus the coal-mining industry can state that deaths among miners per ton of coal mined have fallen. Using the same data, the unions can show that deaths per 1,000 miners have not fallen. Fewer miners are needed to mine the same amount of coal and hence the two ways of looking at the same data. Neither side is lying nor is either side cheating on the statistics. They are choosing to look at the same problem through different mindsets, which takes us now from the presentation of the risk data to the consumer's perceptions.

Most scientists, me included until I read the work of Paul Slovic of the University of Oregon, have a simple view of communicating with the ill-informed and unnecessarily concerned consumer.[5] Give them the data. Tell them the story. Then the penny will drop, they'll see the light and, hey presto, the problem is solved. Go forth and preach. As the song 'Galway Bay' says: 'They might as well go catching moon beams or light a penny candle from a star!' The following story has served me well in explaining why preaching is mostly doomed. A small group of highly intelligent rocket scientists are attending a meeting in some convention-type hotel. The speaker becomes momentarily speechless before screaming in a panic that there is a snake in the room. The rocket scientists propel themselves on mass into the large foyer. All hell has broken loose. At that point, an adjacent seminar on the life cycle of the cobra ends and the herpetologists (snake scientists) emerge smiling and pleased with the excellence of the research just presented. They catch the unease of the rocket scientists, and having been told of the snake in the adjoining room they proceed to investigate. They emerge grinning and tittering. 'You see', says the main man, 'although this is a potentially venomous snake and people have died from bites of this species, because of its age, gender (if snakes have them), because of the longitude and latitude, the time of year, the height above sea level, the price of oil . . . there is really a very, very insignificant risk of that snake biting any of you nice rocket scientists today. So, fear not. Continue with your seminar and have a nice day.'

I am not a rocket scientist but if I were and I was there I would tell the main man where to stuff his snake and insist on either another room with a snake-check in advance or bye-bye to the seminar. I would not care what reassurances I got, I simply do not want a snake loose in that seminar room. I am certain that most of my colleagues would agree. The snake is the danger and it is real. It can be measured, dissected, quantified, studied, modelled, displayed, demonstrated and so on. Against this real danger, two groups construct entirely different perceptions of risk: an unacceptably high level of risk among the rocket scientists and a quite acceptable level of risk among the herpetologists. As Paul Slovic has pointed out, whereas danger is real, risk is socially constructed. Risk is therefore very value laden – 'one man's food is another's poison'. When scientists think of the common person's inexplicable and irrational fear of a new technology, they see only one thing: the gap in knowledge between the informed (snake scientists) and the ignorant (rocket scientists). That being so, the mere provision of knowledge will not solve the problem. Humans have survived by taking successive calculated risks, gambling on achieving some expected benefit. In the case of the rocket scientists, there was simply no benefit, against some perceived risk. Their response of the rocket scientists to the risk from the snake was emotional, less rational than expected.

The risk managers see dangers in terms of uncertainty, catastrophic possibilities, reversibility and scale of impact. Paul Slovic tells us that the consumer has a different way of thinking about risk and that there are three main features which shape the consumer's perception of risk. I will use the relative risks to health from obesity and BSE to explain their role. The first of these is familiarity. Everybody knows several people who are obese and, although they may suffer social stigmatisation and not enjoy the vibrant life of the Hollywood norm, they all seem pretty happy. They read books on obesity and on slimming, see TV documentaries on it and actually diet. In contrast, I would hazard that almost nobody reading this book is familiar with BSE or has seen someone suffer the disease, or has seen its dreadful impact on friends and family. Remember HIV? Remember when the first headline cases emerged? Remember the movies on the topic? HIV is no longer headline news, partly because of medical advances in treating the disease but partly because it's just too familiar. The unfamiliar is rightly feared. The second feature is dread. Most thin people would not like to get fat and many battle long and hard either to lose weight or avoid weight gain. But, if you lose the battle, so what? You're only fat and, since many friends are also fat, what of it? But consider a disease, which literally eats away your brain to give it its pathologically 'spongy' form – that's truly dreadful. Does it hurt? Is it slow? What do you finally die from? The dreadful is dreaded. Finally, we have control. 'I'm the correct weight for my height and I can control that by weighing myself daily and constantly dieting and exercising.' 'I'm quite a bit overweight but fear not, whenever I choose to lose weight I will do it, just, not right now.' Ultimately, each individual controls his or her own weight. But when you buy a T-bone steak, you cannot tell whether the associated nerve tissue (dorsal root ganglia) is free of BSE prions. Even vegetarians have fallen victim to new variant CJD, possibly through contamination of bovine fat with spinal cord material. If there is a risk of BSE being around, you will find it difficult to shun the risk, however small. Exposure is a lottery. You have no control.

We can examine the consumer's perception of risk in another way, which draws on some elements of this dread – familiarity and control dimension. Consumers are given a wide range of risks to consider and to rank them in terms of the threat they make to society as a whole. They will rank risks high if the risks are dreaded, unfamiliar and outside their control. The ranking will have no correlation with the real scale of threat to society. Thus pesticides will be ranked as a bigger threat than obesity. But if the same questionnaire is repeated, this time asking them to rank risks to them *personally* as opposed to society as a whole, several areas of risk shift and all of these are the big killers, the big public health issues: obesity, poor nutrition, alcohol and smoking. The risks for society are always higher than for them personally. One can conclude that even if they are smokers, overweight with a poor diet and a fondness for alcohol, they do not rank these as high for themselves personally because they can control them themselves. They have the power to change whenever they decide to do so. However, the risks from dangers they cannot easily control (pesticides etc) don't change between themselves personally and society as a whole. For those of us interested in public health this is a huge challenge. To recap thus far in the consumer's perception of risk we have seen that there are certain attributes of danger that drive the consumer's view and, importantly, how consumers rank risk. What is driving this? When this question emerged in the midst of the technological revolution of the last century, the 'theory of the white male' surfaced. When risk perception is studied in different groups, white males always had the least fear of any given risk. The deduction was that white males were more likely to have studied science or engineering or to have worked in the science and technology sector and thus have a greater understanding of this danger and a lower perception of risk. Paul Slovic's work ended that theory.[5] He examined attitudes to risk among people who know a great deal about risks, toxicologists. Male toxicologist still had a different view of the same risk when compared to female toxicologists, both in the US and in Europe. Since they were all trained to the same level, the difference was gender not knowledge. That women see the world differently from men is well known. What was surprising at one level but not at another was that European toxicologists saw risk differently from US toxicologists. What therefore shapes views of risk? Paul Slovic brings us to the term 'worldview' that might be defined as 'A collection of beliefs about life and the universe held by an individual or a group'.[5] Psychologists have identified a number of categories of worldview and these are closely linked to how people see risk. 'Fatalists' have the view that, when your number is up, that's it and there's not much one can do about it. They therefore feel they have very little control over risks and thus frankly don't care. The second category involves 'hierarchy' which happily leaves the issue with experts. The third is 'individualism' and such individuals like to come to their own conclusions and are not happy to be directed hither or thither in their analysis of risk. Next we have the 'egalitarians' who are likely to want the perception of risk informed by an inclusive debate and discussion. Finally we have the 'technological enthusiasts' who clearly have great trust in the scientific process. People don't completely fall into any one of these boxes, but these are the main drivers of the way we see the world and thus how we see the risk. Worldviews are important but so too is 'affect' which in psychology means in a sense our first reaction to things. Whether we know it or not, we apply affect to everything. When we see a car we see an 'old car' or an 'expensive car' or a 'foreign car' or a 'black car'. We don't just see a 'car'. Studies show that affect is associated with risk perception.

Paul Slovic's research asked subjects for their first reaction to the term 'nuclear power'. Some had negative affective responses such as death, destruction, catastrophe, while others had positive affects: electricity, zero carbon footprint. The subjects were then asked to agree or disagree with the statement: 'If their community was faced with a potential shortage of electricity, a new nuclear plant should be built to supply that electricity.' Those with a positive affect of nuclear power were far more likely to agree with the statement. First impressions tend to last. All in all, consumers draw on their worldviews and, with regard to their first reaction to reach conclusions on risk, Paul Slovic points out that danger is real but risk is socially constructed. Thus whoever controls the definition of risk controls the rational solution to the problem at hand. Defining risk is therefore an exercise in power.[5]

And that brings us right back to the politics of food. Risk assessment is an adversarial exercise. The food industry innovates to compete to win the mouths of the consumer. The scientists are on the one hand part of this innovation but also part of the regulatory process. The regulators are caught between the precision of science and the politics of getting air time. The consumers are affluent, informed and mobilised through a network of NGOs. And none of them trusts one another. The informed, affluent and organised consumer mainly of the Northern hemisphere can demand the safest food that science can deliver and can shun new technological innovations in food, arguing that there is enough food and what we now need is a return to the romantic form of agriculture to save the Planet. That selfish attitude will ensure the continued North/South divide and will guarantee that global welfare will decline, faster of course in the south. It is to that issue of feeding a growing global population in a sustainable manner that we now turn.

CHAPTER TWELVE

How the Other Half Dies

Within one decade no child will go to bed hungry, no family will fear for its next day's bread, and no human being's future and capacities will be stunted by malnutrition. Every man, woman and child has the inalienable right to be free from malnutrition and hunger

World Food Conference, Rome, 1974[1]

As a basis for the Plan of Action for Nutrition . . . we pledge to make all efforts to eliminate before the end of this decade: famine and famine-related deaths; starvation and nutritional deficiency diseases in communities affected by natural and man-made disasters; iodine and vitamin A deficiencies.

World Declaration and Plan of Action for Nutrition, Rome, December 1992[2]

The Rome Declaration calls upon us to reduce by half the number of chronically undernourished people on the Earth by the year 2015 . . . If each of us gives his or her best I believe that we can meet and even exceed the target we have set for ourselves.

World Food Summit 1996[3]

Goal 1: Eradicate extreme poverty and hunger; Target 1. Halve, between 1990 and 2015, the proportion of people whose income is less than $1 a day; Target 2. Halve, between 1990 and 2015, the proportion of people who suffer from hunger.

UN Millennium Development Goals 2002[4]

In the 40+ seconds or so that it has taken you to read the above, seven children have died of hunger somewhere in the world. According to the WHO, 'nearly 9 million children under the age of five die every year according to 2007 figures. Over one third of them are linked to malnutrition.'[5] This translates into one child every six seconds. In this chapter we explore the global blight of widespread hunger, a situation that is worsening by the day as food prices soar.

Hunger leads eventually to malnutrition, which can manifest itself in several ways. The gaunt corpse-like children one sees on TV are suffering from an acute and immediate lack of calories. They have lost all their subcutaneous fat and they are thus 'skin and bones'. Acute malnutrition, which leads to this wasting condition known as 'marasmus', is often caused by some calamity such as conflict, drought or other causes of a sudden shortage of food. Whereas wasting gets TV time, the far more common form of malnutrition, stunting, doesn't hit the network news. It would appear that TV requires a high number of casualties per hectare per day to merit airtime. Stunting is an incorrect height for age (someone a lot smaller than they should be for their age), whereas wasting is an inadequate weight for height (someone who is notably thin and not the right weight for their height). Stunting occurs during development, beginning in the womb as we discussed in chapter six. Where there is a shortage of energy at a period of growth, a compromise has to be reached. In effect, the body has to ask whether all organs should suffer equally or whether some should be more protected than others. In the case of stunting, the decision has been made to retain as far as possible the really vital functions: fully functioning brain, immune system, lungs etc. By shrinking height by a few inches, the overall energy requirement falls and, effectively, the child has adapted to the harsh food environment. In the short term, that adaptation can be reversed when the rains fall and the crops eventually get harvested and the child can encounter a period of very high growth rate to catch up with their peers and thus be the right height for age. But there is a critical point of continued food deprivation beyond which this loss of height becomes permanent. This we saw in chapter six. A country with a high prevalence of stunting is definitely a country with a chronic food shortage and we will see examples of that shortly. There is another type of child one sees on TV – one whose face, arms and tummy look fat or bloated. Such a child is far from fat and is suffering from a form of malnutrition known as 'kwashiorkor'. In such cases, there is possibly enough energy to meet caloric needs but not enough protein to meet the needs of growth, which is characterised by the deposition of protein rich lean tissue. Chronic inadequate protein intake distorts overall body protein metabolism and leads to the movement of water into areas where normally the level of fluid would be regulated at a lower level. Thus the bloating one sees in such children is caused by the inappropriate accumulation of fluid underneath the skin and, if one presses the skin, the depression would remain for a few moments until the fluid rebalanced itself. We have all seen this personally with swellings we have received from sprains and knocks. The child on the TV with either marasmus or kwashiorkor, or indeed a mixture of both, is in the throes of an immediate food crisis, but we should always bear in mind that such children will almost always have experienced chronic under-nutrition and will have been denied their full genetic potential for height.

There is one more form of malnutrition, which goes by the name of 'hidden hunger'. In this scenario, children or adults but more often children have adequate calories, adequate protein and adequate nearly everything else bar one micronutrient. Thus they may look fine and healthy, but it would take a biochemist to analyse their blood to tell you they were on their way to serious trouble and hence the 'hidden' dimension to their hunger. The three dominant micronutrients are vitamin A, iodine and iron. Vitamin A and its dietary precursor carotene are involved in vision.

Vitamin A is central to the development of vision and, as the intake of vitamin A or its precursor beta-carotene decreases, vision will become impaired. At first, the ability to adapt to darkness is reduced and night vision becomes impaired, which is why children are told that if they don't eat their vegetables they won't be able to see in the dark. As the vitamin A status declines, things get worse and a disease of the eye known as xerophthalmia develops, leading eventually to irreparable loss of sight. Vitamin A is also involved in the integrity of the lining of the lung, so that respiratory infections go hand in hand with vitamin A deficiency. The statistics are shocking: up to half a million children go blind every year due to vitamin A deficiency (xerophthalmia). Half of these die within 12 months of going blind, leaving a global total of 14 million children blind because of malnutrition. About 150 million are at increased risk of mortality from infectious diseases annually directly from vitamin A deficiency (diarrhoeal and respiratory conditions).

The second micronutrient of hidden hunger is iron. It is the key element in the blood protein haemoglobin, which transports oxygen from the lungs to the various tissues in the body. As iron status falls, haemoglobin levels fall and thus the transport of oxygen falls. This is like rationing fuel and it simply means tiredness and an inability to cope with normal levels of physical activity, which in rural Africa are very high. Iron status can fall because of low iron intakes, but it can be confounded by worm infestation and thus correcting the latter is essential before the food police march in. Some 2 billion people, over 30% of the world's population, are iron deficient. An inadequate iron intake in the first few years of life, especially in a child born to a fairly anaemic mother, has long-term deleterious consequences on brain development. Iron is an important element for brain function and the brain's full allotment of iron isn't complete until age two or so. If that gap is missed, the damage of impaired cognitive function will be retained throughout life. The third major micronutrient contributing to hidden hunger is iodine. This is a micronutrient required by the thyroid gland and the hormone produced by that gland, the thyroid hormone. Many people will be familiar with the consequences of a malfunctioning thyroid gland in the form of fatigue, and that is one of the main symptoms of iodine deficiency. Iodine is also involved in the functioning of the nervous system and thus a deficiency of iodine in early life and up to three years of age can lead to permanent neurological damage with a loss of IQ of between 10 and 15 points. Some 740 million persons have iodine deficiency disease and about 13% of the world's population have goitre. These three micronutrient deficiencies are the main contributors to hidden hunger because they are the most visible. Others like zinc deficiency that lead, for example, to a reduced immune system or a reduction in growth become buried in the global issue of hunger, and because they don't lead to an identifiable disease (blindness, goitre, anaemia) tend to be forgotten. However, one can be certain that in any food insecure region, multiple micronutrient deficiencies will be present. The tiredness and the reduction in cognitive function that come with iodine and iron deficiency simply add to the lowering of human capital in poor countries. Blind children of course have little or no hope and tend to fall to the bottom with a very low life expectancy. Shortly we will see how malnutrition and infection go hand in hand.

Hunger, we cannot measure. We can, however, measure its consequences. Two leading aid agencies, Concern Worldwide and Deutsche Welthungerhilfe, and the International Food Policy Research Institute based in Washington, have developed the Global Health Index.[6] The index measures three things to obtain a global single figure for each country: the percentage of the population with insufficient dietary energy intake, the percentage of children under five who are underweight for age and the under-five mortality rate. Ethiopia, Sierra Leone, Eritrea, the Democratic Republic of the Congo and Burundi are the bottom five of the 118 countries considered. Thus for the worst countries in the Global Health Index league in 2007, some 60% of the population didn't have enough food to eat, 34% of those under five that survived to then were growth retarded, and of those born alive, 21% died before the age of five years. In comparison with the early 1990s, the situation had either become worse or stayed the same. This is the scale of the problem. The problem is awesome and it's likely to get worse as the earth's population expands to about 9.2 billion from its present level of 6.7, an issue we will consider in the next chapter. Paul Collier from Oxford University and formerly at the World Bank has written an excellent book on poverty entitled *The Bottom Billion*.[7] Some 70% of the bottom billion live in Africa. The rest are mainly found in Haiti, Bolivia, Laos, Cambodia, Yemen, Burma and North Korea. In the period between the end of the Cold War and 9/11, these countries showed a real decline in incomes of 5%. He identifies five causes of the poverty trap, out of which the bottom billion will never emerge without help. The first trap is conflict, particularly civil wars which last on average five years and which are then followed by about a decade of widespread violent crime including homicide. The second, oddly enough, is being endowed with significant natural resources such as oil or diamonds. As Collier puts it, oil is good for Norway but not so good for unstable countries. A valuable natural resource will drive up the value of the local currency and thus render all other exports uncompetitive, and the revenues for these valuable commodities are very volatile in a boom and bust cycle. The third factor is being landlocked with bad neighbours who make the movement of goods very uncertain, and the fourth factor is bad governance. So, a country with a history of civil war, with a valuable natural resource, which is poorly governed and which is landlocked, is going to be absolutely typical of dire poverty. Let us cast our minds back to the four worst countries – not in any economic measure – but in the measure of the Global Health Index, which measures caloric supply, infant growth and infant mortality. All fit more or less into Collier's poverty model. All have had seriously unstable governments. All have experienced dire conflicts. Ethiopia waged a war with Eritrea in the late 1990s. Sierra Leone had a civil war for ten years from 1991 to 2001. In the Democratic Republic of the Congo, over 5 million persons were killed in a five-year civil war starting in 1998. In Burundi, the Tutsi–Hutu civil war saw some 150,000 Hutus killed. Two of the bottom four are endowed with natural resources: Sierra Leone with diamonds and the Congo with copper and diamonds. All have troublesome neighbours and only one, Sierra Leone, has significant coast. They all fit Collier's model for the bottom billion.

Why is there such a shortage of food? In some cases there is insufficient investment in agriculture so that output cannot meet the national need for food. However, in some cases, there is adequate food but there are social and economic injustices and inequalities. Let us first look at the latter cause of hunger and malnutrition. India is the fourth largest economy in the world. Some 60 million of its children are stunted, having achieved an inappropriate height for age. Micronutrient deficiency has a health care cost of $US 2.5 billion annually with 75% of children iron deficient and 57% with vitamin A deficiency. Half of all childhood deaths are attributable to childhood malnutrition. According to an analysis of the World Bank, there are two problems with the approach of the Indian authorities to childhood malnutrition.[8] First, the wrong age group is being targeted. The focus is on four to six year olds whereas it should be on those under three since four years of age is too late a point to start intervention given that malnutrition will have done its damage by then. The second criticism is that there is a need to improve access to nutrition intervention programmes, particularly in the poorer states in rural regions and among girls and those from the lower castes. Thus India has ample food but has a social problem to ensure that all of its 967 million citizens get their rightful share. In contrast to India, Malawi had a simple problem. In 2005, Malawi suffered a severe drought and the World Food Programme estimated that half the population was seriously short of food. The maths is simple. Malawi needs just over 2m tons of maize to feed its population and in that year only 1.2m tons were available. A newly elected president Bingu wa Mutharika decided to make major subsidies to agriculture against the wishes of major donors, including the World Bank. As we will see shortly, investment in agriculture was not on the agenda of the Washington suits. Subsidies were introduced which reduced the price of fertiliser to one sixth and high-yielding seed prices to one twentieth of the normal price. A drive around rural Malawi doesn't require a skilled agronomist to spot where the fertiliser was applied. It is so visible. Malawi now had a national maize yield of almost 4 million tons and was able to provide food aid to other African states. We will return shortly to this issue of improving agricultural productivity in Africa.

But even with adequate food, malnutrition can so readily be precipitated by infection. The two go together in what is called the infection–malnutrition cycle. The main killers are HIV/AIDS and malaria. The former is a viral disease, the latter a parasite. Both lead to the vicous cycle of infection (and infestation) and malnutrition. If you have a pet, you will know that it is in poor health when it is off its food. Reduced energy intake is a hallmark of infection. There are three other visible signs that may be seen. One is vomiting and the second is diarrhoea. Now think about the nutritional balance books. The intake is down because of a loss of appetite and that is exacerbated by vomiting and diarrhoea, through which vital nutrients including water are lost. The third visible sign is fever, for when we are infected our basal metabolic rate rises and rises in proportion to the severity of the infection. So now we have a further loss of energy from the system. Finally and invisibly at first, we have a dramatic loss of muscle in a desperate bid to move vital components of protein, the amino acids, away from a not-so-necessary strong muscle to the vital organs such as the immune and digestive systems. This final route of loss will eventually become obvious when the unfortunate victim begins to visibly fade away through loss of energy from fat and the loss of muscle. If the balance book is that of a child, then there is an additional need to divert some protein and energy for growth or, alternatively, to adapt to the situation and stop growing. It takes medicine and nursing to get someone through an illness and back to health when all physiological factors return to normal – except when normal means inadequate nutrition. Where this occurs, the immune system becomes less effective and thus more susceptible to yet further infections.

The statistics on HIV/AIDS are both encouraging and shocking.[9] They are encouraging in that there is a downward trend in HIV deaths. In 2009, 2.6 million people died of AIDS across the globe, which is down from 3.1 million in 1999. In the period 2001 to 2009, HIV infections fell by more than 25% in 33 countries where HIV infection was widespread. The statistics are still shocking. Over 16 million children were orphaned due to AIDS in 2009 alone, the highest figure since statistics began to be collected. The sight of their dying parents and the family strife, which arises from land and property inheritance issues, traumatises these children. They are more likely to get sick, to become malnourished, not to attend school and basically have the most miserable of most miserable life trajectories. Of those that die from AIDS, it is often TB that gets to play the Grim Reaper. AIDS slashes the immune system and TB infection follows. Of course, because AIDS creates a reservoir for the TB virus, all forms of impaired immune function, such as that derived from malnutrition, now has the threat of TB.

Malaria is caused by a parasite of the species *Plasmodium* and is spread by mosquito bites. Each year globally about half a billion people become severely ill through malaria. A staggering 90% of these occur in Africa, mostly in under fives where it is the leading cause of mortality. A joint initiative of several UN agencies and the World Bank operates a programme, Roll Back Malaria, which aspires to get control of malaria by 2010.[10] They point out that in Africa 10% of the overall disease burden in Africa is malaria-based, accounting for 40% of public health expenditure and up to 50% of hospital admissions. In Africa, the predominant variety of the malaria parasite is *Plasmodium falciparum*, which is the most severe and deadly of all the Plasmodium family. In his book *The End of Poverty*, Jeffrey Sachs of the Earth Institute of Columbia University adds to this fact by explaining a little about the ecology of the parasite.[11] The hot climate of Africa guarantees that the parasite once engulfed by a mosquito will complete the full two-week life cycle to be ready to infect another victim. He points out that in India the predominant mosquito is as likely to bite cattle as a human. Thus for a human to be infected we need two bites from the mosquito, one to get the parasite and the second to transmit it. If one of those two bites is into a cow, then there is no threat to humans. In Africa, the predominant mosquito doesn't dine on cattle. Without doubt, poverty is one reason why Africa is the hub of the global malarial problem, but Africa drew a short straw when it came to which mosquito it would have as a pest. Malaria is believed to cost 1.3% of annual GDP. Over years, this adds up to dire economic performance. Thus food security is determined by the adequacy of inputs into agriculture, income and credit and by well-being. We've seen how food insecurity emerges when each of these goes wrong. Let's now look at how we might correct these problems.

First we must deal with those whose hunger threatens their health and well-being and afterwards we can address the needs of the population as a whole. In the case of micronutrients, there are two approaches. The first is the use of 'sprinkles' which is a multi-vitamin and multi-mineral mix which comes in sachets and which can be sprinkled on meals. The Helen Keller Institute used this approach in helping victims of the tsunami in Indonesia. A second emergency approach known as Community Therapeutic Care (CTC) targets children who are suffering from acute malnutrition and uses volunteers in the community to identify children at risk.[12] Pioneered by two aid agencies, Concern Worldwide and Valid International, children are brought to a centre, assessed and sent home with a highly nutritious food made locally with mostly local foods. The foods have a high oil and low water content and thus do not require refrigeration. In the past, such children required four to six weeks' residential treatment in a hospital and the success rate was low, only one in four of the needy getting treatment. The residential nature meant that mothers had also to be resident and, since African agriculture is entirely female based, success was never going to be high. In contrast, the CTC programmes are seeing three out of four needy children complete the programme. Moreover, since it is a bottom-up approach, the CTC model can embrace issues such as nutrition and health education. Both of these programmes are designed to meet the needs of those who are either at very high risk of acute malnutrition or have developed it. The next level is to engage in preventative programmes and, of these, fortification is the most promising. The fortification programmes generally target the three critically important micronutrients – vitamin A, iron and iodine. Some suitable staple food, which is widely consumed, is chosen as the vehicle for fortification, such as salt for iodine or vegetable oils for vitamin A. The fire-brigade approach that tackles the emergence of malnutrition is an essential means to save lives. But in the long term we need to see the poorer countries develop their agricultural output within a developing economic and social structure. That will need economic aid from the developed countries.

One would imagine that, in general, nutrition would be a high priority for the global aid agencies. It may be for some but for other significant players nutrition has only just been discovered. In 2005, the World Bank issued a paper entitled *Repositioning Nutrition as Central to Development: A Strategy for Large-Scale Action*.[13] The idea of repositioning nutrition from the Washington suits is intriguing. It implies correctly that nutrition has not been a priority in developing countries that are accused of failing to devote adequate attention to this issue. Governments are accused of having failed to recognise that pivotal role that malnutrition has on economic performance affecting the attainment of a number of Millennium Development Goals. And one of the reasons given is that because there are multi-organisational stakeholders in nutrition and food security, it often falls between the cracks of government – the partial responsibility of many government departments but the main responsibility of none. Now hold on here. Governments in developing countries prioritise what they have to prioritise to suit the suits so to speak. So this admonishment is a bit cheeky. And was it some Pauline Road-to-Damascus discovery of compassion that caused the bank to 're-position' itself in respect of nutrition? No, it was filthy money. The Copenhagen Consensus Conference (organised by the sceptical environmentalist Bjorn Lomborg) investigated a number of global crises and undertook very detailed analysis of the cost benefits of different interventions.[14] One of these global challenges was malnutrition. First they calculated that shifting one infant from being low birthweight to normal birthweight saved US$579.82. How precise is that? Half of that saving is due to the gain in economic productivity and the other half is due to reduced health care costs. They then looked at the cost of different interventions and computed a cost benefit ratio. The top level of benefit to risk ratio was US$520 for iodine fortification. In other words, $1 spent on iodine fortification returned $520 in better productivity and reduced health care costs. For vitamin A fortification the ratio was 43 at the most optimum of the models and for iron it was 14. Thus if 50% of the gain in moving a child from a low to a normal birthweight is associated with increased productivity and, if the cost benefit ratios are so high, it's a no-brainer for the Washington suits. Nutrition has been rediscovered. Remarkably, agriculture was also rediscovered.

Robert Paarlberg, in his book *Starved for Science*, makes the point that the declining confidence in scientific agriculture which began to develop in industrialised countries in the late 1980s, leading to a negative investment in agricultural R&D for the next decade, is the root cause of the failure of African countries to make the required investment in the public spend on agricultural research.[15] Freed of the influence of this form of thinking, Asian and Indian governments poured money into developing agriculture. Thus whereas Asia enjoyed a 2.3% growth in per capita food production between 1980 and 2000, in Sub Saharan Africa it was negative or zero at -0.01%. In the 20-year period from 1980 to 2000, China and India increased investment in agriculture by 80%. In sub-Sahara Africa, the comparable figure was 25%. In the US, a farmer in 2000 harvested some 9.3 tons of corn per hectare. In the same year it was 1.6 tons in Kenya and a mere 0.8 tons in Malawi. It is primarily due to low investment in agricultural inputs: lack of modern seeds (not GMOs), lack of fertiliser, herbicides and pesticides, mechanisation and storage. But subsidising agricultural inputs was decidedly disfavoured in the Thatcher–Reagan era of the 1980s and 1990s. Suits from the International Monetary Fund (IMF) would descend on cash-strapped poor nations with the 'formula': get the markets working, clear the debts and all will be right. This was all based on the so-called Washington consensus (Washington is home for the World Bank and the IMF), which set out strict fiscal rectitude measures. Subsidising agricultural production was simply passé. Thankfully, that has now changed.

On 5 July 2004 in the Ethiopian capital, addressing a group of African heads of state, the then Secretary General Kofi Annan launched a highly ambitious drive to energise agricultural production in Africa – The Alliance for a Green Revolution for Africa (AGRA):

Nearly a third of all men, women and children in sub-Saharan Africa are severely undernourished. Africa is the only continent where child malnutrition is getting worse rather than better. Hunger is a complex crisis. To solve it we must address the interconnected challenges of agriculture; health; nutrition; adverse and unfair market conditions; weak infrastructure; and environmental degradation. Knowledge is not lacking. What is lacking, as ever, is the will to turn this knowledge into practice. Success will require African governments to commit themselves wholeheartedly to the Millennium Development Goals, by developing national strategies consistent with the timeline and targets for 2015. We will also need more convincing action from the developed countries to support those strategies: by phasing out harmful trade practices, by providing technical assistance, and by increasing both the volume of aid to levels consistent with the Millennium Development Goals.[16]

The concept of a Green Revolution for Africa draws on what has been named the Green Revolution, which brought Asia from the brink of catastrophic hunger to an agricultural revolution. It began towards the end of the Second World War when the Mexican government asked for help in developing new varieties of wheat to meet the needs of a rapidly expanding population. With the assistance of the Ford and Rockefeller Foundations, the US agronomist Norman Borlaug established a number of new high yielding varieties that with the right irrigation and fertiliser usage showed dramatic increases in yields. In 1961, the Indian government, faced with the prospects of a dire famine, invited Borlaug to help India, initially by importing Mexican grain but then developing local varieties as he had done in Mexico. The Punjab was chosen as the first test area, but soon the whole of Asia was to benefit from new high yielding varieties of wheat and rice which also involved the International Rice Research Institute in the Philippines. The results were astonishing. Yields of wheat and rice grew tenfold in a matter of years. The term Green Revolution is attributed to a former head of USAID, William Gaud, who declared that:

> These and other developments in the field of agriculture contain the makings of a new revolution. It is not a violent Red Revolution like that of the Soviets, nor is it a White Revolution like that of the Shah of Iran. I call it the Green Revolution.[17]

The Green Revolution which saved the lives of maybe billions of persons over the last 50 years has its critics who argue that it has also brought poverty, social upheaval, loss of biodiversity, loss of soil organic fertility, increased soil salt level and so on. This to me is saying that we should not have invented and applied antibiotics because of problems on the farm, problems of allergy, problems of resistance, of super-bugs and so on. But the proponents of the Green Revolution in Africa are going to meet some stern opposition from two quarters: the organic food movement and the anti-GM lobby and they generally go hand-in-hand.

Robert Paarlberg describes the approach of the organic food movement to the problems of Africa. The chief scientist at Greenpeace, Doug Parr, believes we 'should help African farmers develop self-confidence in their traditional knowledge so that they do not immediately switch to chemicals once they can afford them'. The present very low to zero use of fertilisers, herbicides and pesticides in Africa apparently offers the organic movement an opportunity to make a large part of the globe self-sufficient on organic agriculture. Paarlberg cites a German organic movement in Kenya advising on the preparation of compost based on stinging nettle, chamomile and cow horn. You get a lot of those in Africa! The problem that organic agriculture faces is that every hectare devoted to food production requires another hectare of land to provide the grazing for livestock to produce manure or the use of cover crops to be subsequently ploughed into the earth. This reduces the efficiency of organic agriculture. Even if organic agriculture could deliver nitrogen at the rate of synthetic fertilisers (which it might on very knowledge-intense farms) this need for adjunct land will always make the system less efficient. The New Partnership for African Development (NEPAD) has set targets for African agriculture of a 6% growth per annum to 2015.[18] That will require the present use of artificial fertiliser to be increased fivefold. Whatever the agricultural romanticists believe, that won't happen with organic farming but that doesn't stop them offering false hope. An FAO sponsored report that says so is often cited as proof that the UN backs organic agriculture.[19] Some 2,350 NGOs have official status with the UN agencies. They wield huge influence and among them are many powerful organic farming NGOs. The FAO publication was organised by 15 of these NGOs. If you put 15 organic farming NGOs into a conference on farming and development, you should expect the inevitable answer you get.

If the introduction of modern agriculture into Africa is a challenge, introducing GM technology is an even tougher battle. However, there are little signs that the big guns are not about to lie down and let the anti-GMO lobby destroy true opportunities in Africa. In its 2008 Development Report on Agriculture, the World Bank is clearly stating that the denial of African farmers the right to access GM crops is something it will not tolerate:

> The international development community should stand ready to respond to countries calling for access to modern technologies, as in the recent declaration of the African Union. It should be prepared to meet requests to fund the development of transgenics with pro-poor traits and to underwrite the high initial costs for their testing and release.[20]

The World Bank's report highlights the benefits of GM technology: increased yields, increased profits and reduced pest and weed management sprays among the GM farming communities of Argentina, China, India, Mexico and South Africa. Equally, AGRA is not ducking the issue:

The Alliance for a Green Revolution in Africa (AGRA) supports the use of science and technology – in everything from field-based soil ecology to cyberspace-based market information systems – to aid Africa's smallholder farmers in their urgent efforts to end widespread poverty and hunger'. . . AGRA itself will be funding initiatives that strengthen Africa's scientific capacity at a number of levels. We do not preclude future funding for genetic engineering as an approach to crop variety improvement when it is the most appropriate tool to address an important need of small-scale farmers and when it is consistent with government policy.[21]

However, the opposition, derived from eco-fundamentalists, is relentless. We have already discussed this in chapter three, so I will not repeat it. The impact on Africa is quite impressive. Angola, Malawi, Mozambique, Nigeria, Zimbabwe and Sudan have all rejected food aid shipments on the grounds that they might contain GM grains. Several African states such as Ghana and Zambia have a formal policy on banning GM crops. As the Zambian president said: 'Simply because my people are hungry, that is no justification to give them poison, to give them food that is intrinsically dangerous to their health.'[22] This is in stark contrast to Asia, India, Latin America and South Africa, all of whom have embraced GM with considerable benefit as we have seen. How is it that most African states stand alone in the developed world in shunning a technology that would boost their agriculture? According to Robert Paarlberg, the answer is from an undue influence of the EU. The EU has more or less squashed any possibility of developing GM foods within its own agricultural structures based on a precautionary approach wrongly fed by what he sees as an anti-science eco-fundamentalist movement. As I write, two German universities have abandoned field trials of GM crops from eco-fundamentalist pressure.[23] So why if the EU shuns GM technologies should Africa not? Bear in mind the influence the EU has on Africa, its former colonies which speak mostly European languages. The EU buys €7 billion worth of goods from Africa (six times that of the US) and provides 50% of all aid to Africa (three times that of the US). Moreover, EU aid agencies actually fund either anti-GM programmes or programmes designed to implement the EU anti-GM legislation in Africa. The Women for Change NGO in Zambia, which is utterly opposed to GM technology is funded by Sweden, Denmark and Norway. The German aid agency GTZ funds Biowatch, which is active in the anti GMO lobby in Africa. GTZ also donated €2m to the African Union to develop GM regulations based on the EU model. Norway gave Zambia $400,000 to help them develop a GM-free policy. We should not be surprised at the African stance. But as a citizen of Europe, I feel utterly ashamed. Consider what is being shunned.

Scientists at Leeds University with funds from the public purse have developed a GM potato, which is resistant to an attack by parasitic worms (cyst nematodes).[24] They inserted the gene for a protein, cystatin, into the potato, which kills the parasitic worm. Cystatin is found naturally in many seeds such as rice, maize and sunflower, which is why these pests do not attack them. Cystatin is not foreign to humans since it is a natural component of our saliva. Potatoes with the cystatin gene will show huge increases in yield simply by reducing losses to these parasites. Sounds like common sense? Yes says the Bolivian government whose country is heavily reliant on potatoes. Not to the anti-GM lobby. Activists in Bolivia apparently warned farmers that transgenic potatoes might cause unwanted pregnancies or worse. Africa has unreliable rainfall, which is translated into an index of the risk of drought. But when you compare the drought risk in Africa to other parts of the world, things just don't add up (percentage of land at high risk of experiencing a serious drought: Africa 20; India 24; China 27; Latin America 31; US 44; Eastern Europe 56). Why with such a lower risk of a drought occurring in Africa are the consequences of a drought so much worse? The answer is simple. African agriculture is almost entirely rain fed and those rains are increasingly unreliable and very poorly managed. Investment in irrigation in South Asia and East Asia is high so that 40% of land is protected from the vagaries of drought conditions. In Africa, the investment is abysmal and the percentage of land irrigated is one tenth that of Asia at 4%. Faced with this challenge, the science of plant breeding has discovered genes that help in combating drought-related plant stress and now many transgenic drought-resistant crops exist.[25]

That anti-GM lobbies will oppose this technology is cast iron even though it is in development. Consider how they treated new GM rice produced by a duo of Swiss and Austrian university scientists that contained high levels of the precursor of vitamin A, beta-carotene. Vitamin A deficiency remains one of the great challenges to public health nutrition with some 500,000 persons going blind annually because of lack of vitamin A. We can obtain vitamin A in either of two ways. The first is to consume foods which contain vitamin A itself (animal fats, milk, meat, offal) or we can consume plant foods rich in beta-carotene which we then convert, albeit inefficiently, into vitamin A. Unmilled rice contains some beta-carotene, but unmilled or brown rice isn't suitable for long-term storage since the fat fraction in the bran can become rancid. White or polished rice contains little or no beta-carotene. Enter two scientists with the Swiss Federal Institute of Technology in Zurich and the University of Freiburg, Ingo

Potrykus and Peter Beyer.[26] They inserted two genes into rice, which led to the synthesis of beta-carotene. This has led to a global initiative to use this technology to eliminate or drastically reduce the incidence of diet-related blindness in developing countries. Their website, www.goldenrice.org, sets out their ambitions: 'Our goal is to be capable of providing the recommended daily allowance of vitamin A – in the form of beta-carotene – in 100 to 200 grams of rice, which corresponds to the daily rice consumption of children in rice-based societies such as India, Vietnam or Bangladesh.' The anti-GM groups don't like it and continue the argument that traditional methods if properly implemented would suffice without what they wrongly see are the risks associated with GM crops. So to discredit golden rice, a young activist is seen on the internet sitting in front of a plate of rice so large that it beggars belief. Thus the message is that that if golden rice is successful, this is the amount of rice one would have to eat to tackle the problem of vitamin A inadequacy.

Why is the anti-GM lobby so manipulative of the facts? The reference intakes for nutrients are not set at the average but at the top 2.5% of needs. That is not the figure used to assess diet and maybe the anti-GM groups didn't know that or maybe it suited their perverse argument to pretend not to know. The average requirement is what would be used. In the case of vitamin A, the basis of establishing that average requirement is the maintenance of the normal levels of vitamin A in the liver where it is stored. However, when a child loses his or her eyesight due to vitamin A deficiency, there is no vitamin A in the liver. A rather smaller amount than the average requirement to keep liver levels normal would be required simply to first prevent deficiency. Again, the anti-GM lobby chose to ignore this. They make matters worse by assuming that a child going blind from inadequate vitamin A intake (or its precursor beta-carotene) has no prevailing vitamin A or beta-carotene intake so that all has to be provided by golden rice. A deficiency does not mean a total absence and the inadequate diet is just that. The nutrient is there but not at the level needed. Again the GM opponents chose not to consider this. Thus because of the pressure from such groups, the regulatory framework makes the golden rice project proceed at a snail's pace. There are, however, clear signs of a change of mind by African governments, and if they do change their mind it will be serious trouble for the anti-GM NGOs. The Economic Community of West African States (ECOWAS) has set out a timetable to end in 2008, which will facilitate the development of modern biotechnology and has already completed a common biosafety protocol. Uganda has started its own GM trials of bananas, which have been bred using this new technology to resist a common pest of this food, which is a staple in this country. The BBC did a news feature on it and included an interview with Lord Melchett, a leading opponent of GM technology. His views were: 'If you're a subsistence farmer in Africa with any sense, and many of them are; you know you're being lied to. You know it's propaganda and hype. All of these benefits have been claimed for decades, and not one has been delivered.'[27] Which brings to mind the saying: 'The man who has bread has many troubles. He who has none has but one.'

And so, that is how the other half dies – too young and too easily. Besides the emergency food aid and the investment in agricultural inputs we have seen in this chapter, the other half also needs investment in schools, in hospitals, in roads, in medicines and in their future. In the next chapter we will see how a changing environment will threaten agriculture and the food chain. As with everything else in life, the poorer countries will most certainly fare the worst.

CHAPTER THIRTEEN

Mankind and Mother Earth

I was born in 1948. Then, there were just fewer than 3 billion inhabitants of planet earth. Today, we are just under 7 billion. In 2050, we will be just over 9 billion. These numbers alone do not portray the scale of the problem. In the period of my time on earth so far, the population of developed countries has gone from just below 1 billion to just above 1 billion. In contrast, in developing countries, the figure has jumped from 2 to 5 billion. Thus almost all of the growth in the earth's population has been in the economically less developed countries. Bearing in mind that we haven't a great track record in looking after the present bottom billion, there is a serious chance that when we reach 2050 it will be several bottom billions who will go hungry. There are further nuances to the data. Not only will we have more poor mouths to feed but we'll also have increasingly wealthier mouths to feed. Right now, the spiralling costs of food globally, attributed to the rising wealth in the Asia or the rising use of crops for biofuel, has hit the agenda of the G8 summit. Higher demands for livestock-based food (meat and dairy) will pose considerable challenges to the global food supply. And, finally, this expansion in the demand for food will have to be met from more or less the same area of land as is presently available. In this chapter, we will look at the issue of the human race and the sustainability of the planet from the perspective of those interested in food and health. We will look at the impact of the food chain on our environment and also the converse, the impact of climate change and other environmental phenomena on the food chain.

Predicting the future has always been a necessity of society and we have moved a long way from the soothsayer and the examination of the entrails of chickens. In religion, the confidence of the adherents in the predictions of the future is as rock solid as their belief in the explanations of present and past events. Outside of religion, we need to have some level of evidence to believe predictions of the future. Climate change is an area where predictions are seen by some as the end of the planet, by others as somewhat incredible and thus to be ignored and by others as a challenge to solve. That everyone doesn't buy into the predictions of the Inter-Governmental Panel on Climate Change should not surprise us. Consider the following predictions of doom and gloom.

Club of Rome: In 1972, a group of self appointed specialists produced a report entitled *The Limits to Growth*.[1] The report sold 30 million copies which is not surprising given the direness of the predictions. These included a prediction that oil would run out by 1992 and that all the earth's mineral and energy resources would be depleted by 2070. Obviously they got it wrong but, in getting it wrong, they began to sow doubts about those who would tell us that there were wolves at the door. They got it wrong for two reasons. Their models were flawed and they did not factor in that what is technologically not feasible now will become feasible when the present comfort zone is threatened. Rising oil prices sent technology scurrying in all directions to find alternative fuels and to make prevailing fuels more efficient.

Y2K: As the last millennium drew to a close, around the world governments prepared for the momentous day. They did so with signature projects from great monuments, great buildings and every manner of celebration. But they also prepared for a very grave event that would send the world spiralling into chaos. This was the millennium bug or the year 2000 project (Y2K). Computers were designed to go form 1997, 1998 to 1999 and then to 0000 with catastrophic effects on how computers would function. It was a brave person who chose to fly on the moment of the dawn of the new millennium. Lest anyone was in doubt, the gravity was clearly articulated by such people as John Hamre, US Deputy Secretary of Defense: 'The Y2K problem is the electronic equivalent of the El Niño and there will be nasty surprises around the globe.' The Y2K problem cost a small fortune, genuinely worried many and was a damp squib of enormous proportions. Quite simply nothing of even the most minor consequence happened.

In both instances the dire predictions either didn't happen or were averted by interventions based on a sound understanding of the science. The purpose of introducing these two case studies is to remind ourselves that these events have in some way or other shaped the worldviews of the present-day consumers when it comes to predicting the future. When arguing any aspect of the most serious of all problems facing the human race – the sustainability of the planet – there are two approaches. One is to argue the case laying out the pros and cons of this and that side of the argument. This is the role played by the 'Honest Broker of Alternatives' style scientist as outlined in chapter ten of which I am one. The other is to scare the wits out of people and have a 'trust me I'm a distinguished environmental scientist' approach which is the role played by the

'Issue advocate' type scientist of chapter ten. The following is a direct quotation from Professor Stephen Schneider of Stanford University and a major contributor to the Inter-Governmental Panel on Climate Change which received the 2008 Nobel Peace Prize:

> On the one hand, as scientists we are ethically bound to the scientific method, in effect promising to tell the truth, the whole truth, and nothing but – which means that we must include all the doubts, the caveats, the ifs, ands, and buts. On the other hand, we are not just scientists but human beings as well. And like most people we'd like to see the world a better place, which in this context translates into our working to reduce the risk of potentially disastrous climatic change. To do that we need to get some broad based support, to capture the public's imagination. That, of course, entails getting loads of media coverage. So we have to offer up scary scenarios, make simplified, dramatic statements, and make little mention of any doubts we might have. This 'double ethical bind' we frequently find ourselves in cannot be solved by any formula. Each of us has to decide what the right balance is between being effective and being honest. I hope that means being both.[2]

'Sexing up' the data may get headlines and rattle the cages of politicians. But trust is hard won and very easily lost. In the ensuing sections, I will try to avoid any bias to upgrade or downgrade the evidence. Climate change is about higher greenhouse gases and higher global temperatures. This is where we will focus first and later we will turn to the effect of climate change on rainfall and drought.

In 1958, Charles Keeling of the Mauna Loa Observatory in Hawaii started to record the levels of CO_2 in the atmosphere and his data, known as the Keeling Curve, shows a gradual rise in atmospheric CO_2 over ensuing years.[3] In 1958, the levels of atmospheric CO_2 were of the order of 315 parts per million (ppm). By 2000, the values had reached 368 ppm and, if the present trajectory continues, by 2015 we will have hit 400 ppm. If we continue as we are, the 'business as usual' model in Jeffrey Sachs's book *Common Wealth: Economics for a Crowded Planet*, we will hit 560 ppm by 2100 based on present data.[4] But if Asia continues to grow at its accelerated rate with its very high CO_2 output, then Sachs suggests that we might reach the figure of 560 by as early as 2050. Rising CO_2 output is the first fact in the chain of climate change. The second is the consequences of elevated levels of greenhouse gas emissions. From the sun's rays comes short-wave radiation that passes through the greenhouse gases of which CO_2 is the most important. Upon warming, the earth's surface causes the emission of long-wave radiation which does not easily or fully pass through the greenhouse gas cover but which hangs around to warm the earth. The greater the density of the greenhouse gas effect the greater the level of global warming. This is the second piece of hard evidence – the globe is getting warmer. The next step is by far the most difficult. It is the attempt to quantify the consequences of global warming. First let's consider the predicted range of increase in global temperature. Nicholas Stern of the London School of Economics, in his book *A Blueprint for a Safer Planet*,[5] predicts that the 'business as usual' model, which is where we hide our head in the sand about climate change and do nothing, will lead to a temperature rise of a 5°–6° increase above the 1850 figure by 2100. Even with a concerted global effort to abate CO_2 emissions, the expected rise in temperature will be of the order of 2°–3° above the 1850 value. All of this is based on the enormous amount of complex modelling of the Inter-Governmental Panel on Climate Change (IPCC) and of the Stern review which was a UK initiative led by Nicholas Stern.[6] So what has all this got to do with you and me? Rising temperatures will warm the earth's oceans and that means expansion of the volume of water with consequent rising sea levels. The IPCC predicts a rise of up to 0.6 metres. Asian coastal cities which are densely populated, such as Mumbai or Dhaka, are the most likely to witness catastrophic effects. In Miami and in New York, the economic costs are predicted to be very high although the risk to human life will be less. Because the oceans play such a pivotal role in regulating climate, we will witness a greater frequency of storms and hurricanes and cycles of severe heat waves and periods of extreme drought. This will also involve melting ice-caps and glaciers. We now turn to examine the human food chain in all of this. To what extent does the human food chain contribute to this imminent disaster? To what extent will climate change influence the viability of the human food chain and what steps might we take to abate the problem? We will begin with the first of these two questions.

Land-use change and forestry account for 18% of all greenhouse gas emissions. Agriculture itself represents 13% of these emissions.[7] Together they account for 31% of all greenhouse gas emissions. This is higher than the contribution of all forms of electricity and heating (27%) and 2.5 times that of all forms of transport (12%). Land-use change is effectively deforestation and peat burning, and the two go hand in hand. Burning forests not only burns trees but it also ignites the peat in the deep swamps on which forests grow. Peat fires can then spread over large areas in the post deforestation stage and Indonesia has in recent years witnessed widespread damage from this phenomenon. Rainforests in particular are enormous reservoirs of carbon dioxide. Indeed, the total output of CO_2 by humans across the globe from all sources still only represents about one tenth of that stored in the Amazon rainforest, its trees, vegetation and peat swamps.[8] The total output of greenhouse gases by deforestation is equal to the total annual output of such gases and the US is the second largest carbon polluter in the world. China tops that league and the two countries most responsible for deforestation, Indonesia and Brazil, are ranked second and third. Some 80% of Brazilian deforestation is related to beef farming, with Brazil the biggest beef exporter in the world. Brazil is the second-largest producer of soya beans in the world, a significant amount of which is used in beef production. In the case of Indonesia, the primary economic target of deforestation is timber with Indonesia being the biggest exporter of logs in the world.

There are, however, other areas of the human food chain which influence climate change besides deforestation. In terms of primary production, cattle and sheep exhale a considerable amount of the greenhouse gas methane and their manure too is a major source of both methane and nitrous oxide, another greenhouse gas. Rice production also yields considerable levels of atmospheric methane. Although carbon dioxide gets the headlines, these other greenhouse gases are of importance in the overall equation. Both methane and nitrous oxide have a greater 'Global Warming Potential' (GWP) than carbon dioxide because they are more efficient in trapping the reflected heat from the earth's surface. However, they are present in the atmosphere at much lower levels than carbon dioxide and so it is carbon dioxide which gets the limelight. Farming itself contributes to the carbon dioxide emissions. Inputs into agriculture such as animal feed, fertilisers and pesticides all originate from energy-dependent processes. Farm machines such as tractors and harvesters are energy demanding and agricultural practices such as ploughing release large amounts of CO_2. Pull a plough through an untilled field and you immediately lose between 20% and 50% of the soil carbon in the top metre.

There is one more area of the human food chain which might contribute to greenhouse gas emissions and that is the issue of 'food miles'. Although greenhouse gas emissions and water balance represent the greatest global challenge to the human food supply chain, there are pressure groups to have food miles labelled on food products to reduce the environmental impact of food. This 'buy local' philosophy is effectively anti-capitalism and anti-globalisation by another name and is the darling of the agricultural romanticists who oppose modern technology. The UK Department of the Environment, Food and Rural Affairs carried out an analysis of the issue of food miles. The car, which brings us to the supermarket (or farmers' market) accounts for 48% of all food miles. In terms of the impact of different routes to miles, heavy goods vehicles account for most of the CO_2 emissions associated with food miles. The report shows that food transport in total accounts for just 1.8% of the UK's total CO_2 emissions in any one year. That represents just 8.7% of the total CO_2 emissions of the UK road sector. They point out the difficulties of these calculations. For example, it is more efficient to grow tomatoes in Spain and fly them to the UK than to grow them under glasshouse conditions in the UK.[9] In another analysis of food miles from the US, a different approach was taken. Researchers at the Carnegie Mellon University calculated the true cost of putting your food in your mouth.[10] The UK study only calculated the cost from the supermarket to the table. The Carnegie Mellon researchers went back in the food chain to consider food mile CO_2 burdens as a proportion of the total CO_2 cost of growing, processing, distributing the food and the cost of the bringing it home. The total CO_2 burden of the food chain was dominated by the production phase at 83%. Transport as a whole contributed only 11% while what we see as food miles, from producer to retailer, accounted for just 4%. Indeed when one moves from food transport overall to specific food items, the situation becomes extremely complex. One study compared the energy costs of an apple under four scenarios: imported into the EU from New Zealand; importation into the EU from any Southern hemisphere country; EU-produced apples consumed outside the state of origin; EU-produced apples consumed within the state where they were grown.[11] The relative effect on energy inputs was found to depend greatly on the time of year. When New Zealand apples are harvested and shipped to the EU they do not bear the energy costs of full seasonal storage, only the costs of transport. However, at that time point the EU apples have consumed considerable energy in storage. In contrast, when EU apples are harvested, the opposite is seen. Food miles are far more complex than the simple models often used by activists in the field.

Having looked at the main problems to the environment from the food chain, we need now to turn to the opposite question – what will climate changes mean for global food production? We should first factor in the positive effect that increased atmospheric levels of CO_2 will have on crop yield by directly improving the process of photosynthesis, whereby the plant captures solar energy. This is referred to as carbon fertilisation. The C3 crops (rice, wheat, soybean, fine grain legumes, and most trees) show a positive response in terms of yield to increased atmospheric CO_2. C4 crops (maize, millet, sorghum and sugar cane) show no improvement in yield. The exact effect of elevated atmospheric CO_2 levels on crop yields is controversial. Under laboratory conditions it tends to be high. Under field conditions known as FACE (Free Air Carbon Enrichment), the effect of carbon dioxide is still to lead to increased yields but at lower levels than under laboratory conditions.

Whereas CO_2 will increase yields, rising temperatures will have negative effects. It is anticipated that climate change will lead to cyclic shifts to extreme temperatures. The impact on yields will depend on the period of the growth phase of the plant that this hot spell develops. Plant growth responds positively to rising temperatures up to a point and thereafter it fares worse. The maximum temperature tolerated by wheat will be 24°C for leaf growth and 35°C for grain filling.[12] All in all, most experts predict a fall in agricultural output. In developing countries, the fall will be about 21% and if carbon fertilisation from atmospheric CO_2 kicks in, output will fall by about 9%. In developed countries, on average, the fall could be as low as 6% and, if carbon fertilisation kicks in, it will result in higher yields, up to 7% higher. In the developed countries, parts of Southern US will see a fall in yields and Australia will be badly hit with a fall of 16% with the most optimistic models. The burden of lowered agricultural output will fall mainly on the bottom billions that the world will be home to in the latter part of this century. Thus there will be more mouths to feed, mouths which will be thirstier, with less food and with more climatic tragedies from flooding and drought. That this will happen in my granddaughter's life is alarming.

Let us now turn to the third question: What steps might we take to abate the problem? Well, if deforestation is at the heart of the problem it has to be central to the solution. According to Nicholas Stern, CO_2 output from deforestation and peat fires can be halved through the investment of $5 billion per year. However, as both Stern and Sachs point out, it does require concerted global action. If the deforestation problem is dealt with on an ad hoc basis, what is closed down in one area will open up in another, a phenomenon known as 'leakage'. This investment also makes economic sense. Halving emissions from deforestation would cost $5 per tonne, which compares with the $30 per tonne on the European Emissions Trading Scheme. There is a second route to reduce carbon losses from soils and that involves changes in tillage practices in those areas of the globe where modern tillage is practised. Soils as we have seen are fantastic carbon sinks. Plants capture CO_2 in photosynthesis and if left there will contribute much of that carbon to organic matter within the soil. The term conservation tillage refers to a form of agriculture where more than 30% of the crop residue remains on the surface after planting. There are many forms of conservation tilling from no-till to strip-till. In the former, the ground is broken by the machine at the exact spot to automatically insert the seed and fertiliser and the small hole is then closed up. In strip-till a machine breaks the surface of the soil but, unlike a plough, only does so to a width of about eight inches. The exact choice of conservation tillage chosen depends on many factors, including soil type and topography. This form of tillage does need new approaches to weed management and, although herbicide use may increase, this is not necessarily the case and the leading websites (www.notill.org or www. notill.com) advocate conservative approaches to weed management. In the US, the growth in no-till farming is staggering, rising from 2.2 million hectares in 1973, to 4.8 million in 1983 and jumping dramatically to 21.1 million hectares in 2001. The advent of herbicide resistant crops has greatly boosted the use of no-till farming. Methane production from ruminant fermentation can be reduced through diet and from manures by a variety of management techniques. More careful use of nitrogen inputs in feeds and fertilisers can help reduce nitrous oxide emissions from agriculture. Many other areas of agriculture may benefit from new technologies. Just as the motorist will reduce CO_2 outputs, switching to hybrid electric cars, so too will farmers switch to hybrid tractors. Fertiliser and pesticide production will become cleaner and smarter management of manures and other agricultural wastes will reduce the scale of the problem. And finally we return to the issue of food miles and the belief that buying local will be environmentally friendly. We saw previously how complex this issue is. The authors of the US study which considered food miles from field to plate and not supermarket to plate concluded:

> The results show that for the average American household, 'buying local' could achieve at maximum, around a 4 to 5% reduction in greenhouse gas emissions due to large sources of both CO_2 and non-CO_2 emissions in the production of food. Shifting less than 1 day per week's calories [i.e. one-seventh of total calories] consumption from red meat and/or dairy to other protein sources or a vegetable diet could have the same climate impact as buying all household food from local providers.[10]

The idea of buying local seems attractive and certainly all the leading restaurant chefs would insist on using local food. But it is simply not feasible for all of our food to be local unless we want to go back a long time when we did rely mostly on local food but which led to a poor diet. The breadth of variety we have today requires food miles and, from the available data, this is not a major factor in the overall CO_2 economy. Moreover, buying local could have a negative effect not just because production might be less energy efficient for climate reasons, but also because, from a nutritional point of view, foods which are important in this regard may not be capable of being locally produced – we don't grow citrus fruits in Ireland. Finally there is the issue of trade. Egypt imports its wheat. Saudi Arabia, having paid huge sums to irrigate very arid land, not only became self-sufficient in wheat but became a net exporter. So which is worse, the wheat miles en route to Egypt or the wheat miles out of Saudi?

Now let us turn to the issue of global water availability, which brings in present water use and the predicted impact on our water balance through effects of climate change. The water available to us is only a fraction of the total water on the earth. About 98% of all water is tied up in the oceans, the sea, in snow and in glaciers. The groundwater available to us for all our water needs accounts for a mere 0.75% of the earth's total water. The human food chain extracts 70% of the surfacewater and groundwater available to humans. It is by far the biggest consumer of water. If the world's population is to reach 9 or 10 billion by 2050 and if we continue our present business as usual approach to the management of water, then water will limit food production. In fact, water will be so precious that the Secretary General of the UN, Ban Ki-moon, warned the World Economic Forum in early 2008 that conflicts will arise as the population grows and as climate change factors kick in. He notes that there are 46 countries, home to 2.7 billion people (40% of the world's population), where water shortage 'constitutes a high risk of conflict'.[13] A further 56 countries with 1.2 billion (18% of the total global population) are at moderate risk. He points out that this will affect rich and poor countries. Lebanon, Syria, Jordan, Palestine and Israel share the River Jordan. The six rivers of the Indus that flow from Kashmir are divided at three each to India and Pakistan in a deal brokered by the World Bank. Within Pakistan, the state of Punjab, the breadbasket of Pakistan, has negated all water treaties with surrounding states. So precious is water that the Indian government will not release data on the flow of the Himalayan Rivers (The Indus, The Ganga-Brahmaputra and the Yangtze), because the water is shared by Pakistan, China, Bangladesh, Nepal and Bhutan. Bangladesh depends on India for 91% of its water flow.[14] China has a problem in that the highly populated north has access only to 25% of China's water, so China is now investing up to $60 billion in one of the largest infrastructure investments in the world to divert water from the Yangtze to the north, equivalent to the flow of another Chinese river, the Yellow River.[15] About one fifth of the earth's population lives in regions where the use of water exceeds the rate of re-charge. Mexico's coastal aquifer, Hermosillo, has a water withdrawal rate three to four times greater than that of recharge and as a result saltwater intrusion is progressing at the rate of 1 km per annum. The High Plains aquifer, also known as the Ogallala aquifer, in the US stretches across eight states from just south of the Canadian border to the Gulf of Mexico. It pours out 12 billion cubic metres a year, which is 18 times the annual flow of the Colorado River and most of it goes on irrigation. At today's usage, there are estimates that within 25 years the aquifer will be redundant. In China, the flow of the 3H Rivers (Hai-Luan, Huai, Huang) to the ocean has fallen 60% in the last 30 years and water tables are up to 90 metres lower than they were 40 years ago. Researchers at the National Center for Atmospheric Research in Colorado report in 2009 from a major study of over 700 of the world's rivers:

> Overall, the study found that, from 1948 to 2004, annual freshwater discharge into the Pacific Ocean fell by about 6 per cent, or 526 cubic kilometres – approximately the same volume of water that flows out of the Mississippi River each year. The annual flow into the Indian Ocean dropped by about 3 per cent, or 140 cubic kilometres. In contrast, annual river discharge into the Arctic Ocean rose about 10 percent, or 460 cubic kilometres. In the United States, the Columbia River's flow declined by about 14 per cent during the 1948–2004 study period, largely because of reduced precipitation and higher water usage in the West. The Mississippi River, however, has increased by 22 per cent over the same period because of greater precipitation across the Midwest since 1948[16]

Thus, unlike the environmental threat of global warming to which many countries are indifferent, water scarcity is a visible threat. The human food chain extracts the majority of all water used, mainly for livestock but also for irrigation. In the developing world there will be an increase of 12% in irrigation water use by 2025 while in the developed world there will be a fall of 1.5%. In the developing world the need for water for livestock will double in this period. Because the projected population growth is also centred in the developing world, that is where the water crisis will hit hardest. Water is, relatively speaking, not readily tradable like oil or food and so local needs have to be met from a local supply. However, virtual water is tradable. If a country imports wheat, it has avoided the need to have to hand the water needed to produce that wheat. Thus if Egypt were to replace its wheat imports with local production, it would require the use of water to the level of one sixth of Lake Nasser which feeds the Aswan dam.

This is the picture as we stand presently, but the effects of global warming will now exacerbate this truly perilous state of affairs. Melting mountain glaciers will increase flooding and landslides. Stern points out that the Himalayan glaciers supply 8 million cubic metres to several major Asian rivers: the Yangtze and Yellow rivers in China, the Ganges, Brahmaputra and Yamuna in India and Bangladesh and the Indus in Pakistan. The loss of such glaciers will lead to significant falls in the flow rates of these rivers. He cites evidence that, in the July to September period, the Ganges river flow would fall by two thirds with devastating consequences on the population and on agriculture. Notwithstanding changes in water balance due to melting glaciers and ice-caps, dramatically altered cycles of rainfall and drought are envisaged. Heavy rainfall will occur more frequently and more prolonged droughts will be seen. Predicting exactly which region will get more or less rain or drought and when that will occur is very difficult to predict. Bill Cline has attempted some pre-dictions.[17] Bangladesh and Central America have similar temperatures at present (28°c) and are predicted to have similar rises in temperature (15%). However, Bangladesh will have almost a 10% rise in annual rainfall whereas Central America will show a 5% fall in rain. Pakistan will see a 16% rise in rainfall while Syria will see a 16% fall in rainfall, both countries showing a 25% rise in temperature. Of course it should be added that this average annual rainfall doesn't exactly fall evenly. The projections are (*a*) that the timing of the rainfall will be more variable, making it difficult to match crop life cycle with rainfall patterns, (*b*) that the duration of a rainfall will be reduced and (*c*) that when it rains it will rain much more intensely.

However, there is now clear evidence of the link between global warming and droughts. The Sahel belt runs in a straight line across North Africa from Senegal in the west to Eritrea in the east. It runs for about 2,400 miles and is about 200–400 miles in depth. It is a semi-arid area which borders the Sahara desert to the north and the more fertile parts of Africa to the south. The Sahel belt receives about 200–600 mm of rainfall annually (0.55–1.65 mm/d) in the form of monsoon rains between May and September. However, this rainfall is subject to enormous annual variability. Up to the late 1960s, the monsoons arrived in varying quantities. Then around 1970 the tap was turned off and a drought ensued that would last until today, with the monsoons arriving in only three years since then. Between the early 1970s and the 1980s, one million people died and an estimated 50 million others were affected. This semi-arid swathe of land is home to semi-nomads and, when the dust blew in the winds and cattle and camel corpses were shown on TV, the grazing practices of the nomads were blamed. Centuries of overgrazing, taking out and putting nothing back had depleted the nutrients and organic matter of the soil. The disaster was to a great extent seen as self-inflicted. Then, in 2003, scientists at the National Center for Atmospheric Research in the US published a major paper which involved the creation of a climatic model stretching over 70 years and which involved NASA space technology.[18] The outcome was that the human impact on the soil structure of the Sahel was too insignificant to explain the drought. Instead, the researchers identified one single variable which was responsible for the decline in rain: rising temperatures in the Indian Ocean. This is the ocean with the highest rate of rise of temperature and a large part of the Sahelian drought could be correlated with rising temperatures in this ocean. Thus the predicted effects on temperature and rainfall globally are gradually gaining greater credibility.

Turning now to solutions, a report from the International Food Policy Research Institute and the International Water Management Institute entitled *Global Water Outlook to 2025: Averting an Impending Crisis* identifies a number of actions that will be needed to achieve a sustainable water balance.[19] Governments will have to increase investment in crop research to boost water productivity. The price of water to agriculture will gradually rise twofold in developed countries to threefold in developing countries. This will lead to on-farm investment in greater water efficiency. Groundwater extraction for agriculture will become strongly regulated and overuse will become uneconomical. Generally higher prices for water will help subsidise investment in piped water schemes, making the use of water in agriculture more efficient. There will be savings in areas outside agriculture as well as industries recycling their waste which will also apply to municipalities. In terms of agricultural production, the catch phrase for better water use is: 'More crop per drop'. In Africa, this will mean better capture of rainwater through simple technologies. It will also mean increased irrigation, but without the mistakes which have been made in Asia where 40% of soils are enriched in salt (salinated). This happens because all water including rainfall contains some salt. When plants take up water, the salt is left behind and the salt begins to accumulate. Even more irrigation is needed to wash the salt from the soils and make the soils more fertile. In Asia, it will mean much more efficient use of water for irrigation and one option is drip irrigation, where the delivery of water to the plant involves minimal waste.

In looking to the future, it might be useful to remind ourselves of one great environmental success. In 1986, scientists began to notice that the ozone layer in the stratosphere over the Antarctica was declining with the chilling prospects of a huge increase in our exposure to UV radiation. Soon evidence began to emerge that gases called CFCs (chlorofluorocarbons), which had been used since the 1930s in fridges and aerosols, were to blame and in 1987 the Montreal Protocol set out a timetable for their gradual elimination. At first industry resisted it but they could soon see that they either joined in or lost out to an ever increasing environmentally aware consumer. The effect of restricting the use of CFCs was remarkable, leading Kofi Annan to declare: 'Perhaps the single most successful international agreement to date has been the Montreal Protocol'. In 2007, scientists from the US Earth System Research Laboratory declared: 'In spite of variations caused by temperature, atmospheric dynamics, and other natural factors, we expect the ozone hole to gradually appear smaller and smaller over time and eventually not form at all.'[20] I would like to think that there might be a hope that the wider issue of climate change might follow similar paths. Sadly, I don't think it will.

CHAPTER FOURTEEN

Projections and Reflections

This is a chapter where I try to make some key points about food and health. In the course of this book we have covered some exciting and challenging science, covering all aspects of the food chain. We have also covered the controversies in food and health, some of which are of enormous public health significance and some of which are the main issues that obsess the 'worried well', that not insignificant part of society that cares about the things which really don't matter in terms of public health, be it food miles, food additives, organic food, farmers' markets or an intolerance of those hopeless cases who cannot manage their food intake and get fat. Disgraceful! Leaving aside the worried well and the media and politicians who follow them, there are two terrible failures of mankind with regard to the human food chain. One is an unacceptable level of overweight and obesity and the other is hunger.

Let me first deal with hunger. Several years ago I would not have used this term preferring the medical term 'malnutrition' or one of its sub-divisions. But to talk about malnutrition is to talk about a concept. To talk of hunger hits the heartstrings. One billion people each evening at sunset settle down to a night's sleep with an empty belly. And the chances are that the same will apply the next night and the next night. Hunger is something I have never experienced and I suspect that most of the readers of this book will also never have experienced involuntary, severe and protracted hunger. When one wakes up in the morning or more likely in the middle of the night, it's not of football, ballet, sex or God they think. It is about food and, specifically, its absence.

We face a world where the population will grow from 6 billion to 9 billion in the next 40 years. It is a world where climate change will wreak havoc on agricultural output, when water shortage will curb crop growth to such a level as to be a cause of military conflict, when food prices will soar and when the number that go to bed hungry every night at the moment will increase to terrible proportions. Do I personally think things will get better? My answer sadly is that they won't. When I look at the selfish way the great powers have behaved in relation to global warming, I am sceptical about their willingness to construct a global plan of action to eliminate hunger. The UN Millennium Goal number 1 has several components. Target 1C seeks to halve, between 1990 and 2015, the proportion of people who suffer from hunger. Far from improving, the situation has got worse and will deteriorate further without concerted international action. It may well be that the non-governmental sectors will make better inroads than governments, and at two levels. One is the philanthropic level led by the Bill and Melinda Gates Foundation. They are presently funding very large programmes in combating diseases that greatly reduce human capital, namely polio and malaria, and also a major initiative in maternal and childhood nutrition.[1] In addition they are funding plant-breeding programmes aiming to increase rice yields by 70% within 20 years by introducing varieties resistant to drought, to submergence, to high salt or iron in soils and to cold temperatures. Philanthropic foundations can work in ways that governments or international agencies cannot. They can agree to work in controversial areas, to set conditions on collaboration or to instantly abort projects, all of which might be needed and none of which are easy for governmental organisations. A second possible route to grow wealth and with it education and food security is commercial investment in, for example, sub-Saharan Africa. Companies recognise that this continent must be helped to develop economically, motivated by humanitarian reasons but also the commercial reality that, as Africa develops, the market for international brand will rise. Perhaps the recognition by the World Bank that agricultural development requires investment and also that good nutrition is essential for economic development will see an overall improvement in the development of adequate nutrition. Another glimmer of hope is the Scaling up Nutrition initiative of Ban Ki-moon.[2] This UN initiative is specifically aimed at the first 1,000 days of life from conception to two years of age. Having a defined focus on hunger of this nature may be more productive than the all-embracing strategy of the millennium goal of halving hunger by 2115. The scale of global hunger is daunting but it is a challenge that we must face at all costs.

The scale of global prevalence rates of overweight and obesity are equally daunting. However, there may be light at the end of the tunnel so to speak. When we talk about the epidemic of obesity, there is a possibility that some people might think that a significant fraction of the population would reach the weight of John Minnoch (credited in the *Guinness Book of Records* as being the heaviest male in history). At 6 feet 1 inch tall, he weighed 442kg, equivalent to a BMI of 128. That equates to the biomass of just 4.5 Irish adult males! That is not how it works. In an obesogenic environment, people will reach a weight which is genetically determined. Some will remain slim. Some will gain a little weight. Others will become overweight or obese. Each will reach their genetic potential and stay there. If that is the expectation, then at a certain point the rates of increase of obesity must level off. And that appears to be the case.

Researchers from the Institute of Preventative Medicine at Copenhagen gathered data on time trends in obesity over the period 1999 to 2010.[3] They set out a total of seven criteria, which had to be met if a published study was to be included in their analysis. For example, the sample size had to be greater than 5,000 and data on weight and height had to be measured directly and not self reported. Thus, out of 52 studies, only 44 met the seven inclusion criteria. They also graded the studies into very high, high, medium or low quality. Of the six studies graded very high quality data, five showed that obesity rates were stable during the period 1999 to 2010. These five were from France, Sweden, England, Greece and Australia and only in China did a very high-quality study show an increase in obesity. Among children and adolescents, there was a clear trend towards a stabilisation of obesity across continents and, while the pattern among adults was less clear-cut, stabilisation was nonetheless generally evident.

A related study comes from Australia, actually from a rather distinguished WHO Collaborating Centre for Obesity Prevention, and it looked at obesity trends in preschool children over the period 1999 to 2007.[4] They studied two cohorts, one aged 2 years old in 1999 (130,000) and the other 3.5 years old in 1999 (96,000), each of which was followed annually to the year 2007. Weight, height (and length for younger age groups) were measured annually. Whereas in 1999 some 2.5% of 2 year olds were obese, in 2007 this fell to 1.7%. For 3 year olds in 1999, the comparable figures were 4.5% and 2.9%. Similar trends were seen when obese children were combined with overweight children (from 13.5% to 12.4% in the 2-year-old cohort and from 18.5% to 15.4% in the 3.5 year old group over the period 1999–2007). Although the overall rate of obesity and overweight was higher in the lower socioeconomic groups, the rate of decline in fatness was highest in these groups.

The fact that obesity rates might be stabilised or even falling in children does not mean that we can relax our efforts to establish normal weight range for the entire population coupled with a significant increase in physical activity. As with global hunger, there is no quick fix to the problems of obesity and our sedentary western lifestyle. Sadly, politically attractive short-term solutions abound of which taxes are the most popular. For a food tax to be successful it must reduce the intake of a food known to have a causative role in obesity.

Identifying such a food is scientifically very difficult when we know that people under-report food intake, with the obese being the worst offenders. Even if we could identify such a food or suite of foods, we would have to be sure that the tax would in fact reduce the consumption of the target food without any adverse effects on other areas of food choice. If people opt to pay the tax, then they have less to spend on other foods and we have no data available to understand how it would work. The solution has to be long term and must somehow involve both the food chain and the built environment.

Food and health will always remain a hot topic, but it attracts an undue share of writers and opinion formers who have narrow agendas or a somewhat unscientific approach to the topic. Hopefully, this book will have shed some light on this topic for some if not most readers.

Notes

Chapter One: With Regard to Food

1 Fernandez-Armesto, F. (2002) *Food a History*. London: Pan Books.

2 Pollan, M. (2008) *In Defence of Food*. London: Penguin.

3 Orwell, G. (1959) *The Road to Wigan Pier*. London: Secker & Warburg, p. 192.

4 Barker, D. (2003) 'The midwife, the coincidence and the hypothesis'. *British Medical Journal*, 327 (7429): 1428–30.

5 Roberts, P. (2008) *The End of Food*. Boston: Houghton Mifflin.

6 Keys, A. Aravanis, C. Blackburn, H. W. (1966) 'Epidemiological studies related to coronary heart disease: characteristics of men aged 40–59 in seven countries'. *Acta Medica Scandanavia Supplement*, 460: 1–392.

7 Grande, F. Anderson, J. T. Keys, A. (1972) 'Diets of different fatty acid composition producing identical serum cholesterol levels in man'. *American Journal of Clinical Nutrition*, 25 (1): 53–60.

8 Caggiula, A.W. Christakis, G. Farrand, M. (1981) 'The multiple risk intervention trial (MRFIT). IV. Intervention on blood lipids'. *Preventive Medicine*, 10 (4): 443–75.

9 US Senate Select Committee on Nutrition and Human Needs. (1977) *Dietary Goals for the United States*. 2nd Ed. US Government Printing Office, Washington DC.

Chapter Two: Sugar and Spice and All Things Nasty

1 Ames, B.N. and Gold, L.S. (1997) 'Environmental pollution, pesticides and the prevention of cancer: misconceptions'. *Life Sciences Forum*, 11 (13): 1041–52.

2 McCann, D. Barrett, A. Cooper, A. (2007) 'Food additives and hyperactive behaviour in 3-year-old and 8/9 year-old children in the community: a randomised, double-blinded, placebo-controlled trial'. *Lancet*, 370 (9598): 1560–7.

3 Connolly, A. Hearty, A. Nugent, A. (2010) 'Pattern of intake of food additives associated with hyperactivity in Irish children and teenagers'. *Food Additives and Contaminants*, 27 (4): 447–56.

4 The Agricultural Marketing Resource Center is funded by the USDA and provides data on markets and industry trends for the US agri-business. The figure quoted for the growth of the organic food sector are available at their website: http://www.agmrc.org/markets__ industries/food/organic_food_trends.cfm (Accessed April 2011)

5   Winter, C. K. and Davis, S. F. (2006) 'Organic foods'. *Journal of Food Science*, 71 (9): 117–24.

6   Zhao, X. Chambers, E. Matta, Z. (2007) 'Consumer sensory analysis of organically and conventionally grown vegetables'. *Journal of Food Science*, 72 (2): 87–91.

7   Kristensen, M. Østergaard, L. F. Halekoh, U. (2008) 'Effect of plant cultivation methods on content of major and trace elements in foodstuffs and retention in rats'. *Journal of the Science of Food and Agriculture*, 88 (12): 2161–72.

8   Dangour, A. D. Lock, K. Hayter, A. (2010) 'Nutrition-related health effects of organic foods: a systematic review'. *American Journal of Clinical Nutrition*, 92 (1): 203–10.

9   Søltoft, M. Bysted, A. Madsen, K. H. (2011) 'Effects of organic and conventional growth systems on the content of carotenoids in carrot roots, and on intake and plasma status of carotenoids in humans'. *Journal of the Science of Food and Agriculture*, 91 (4): 767–75.

10 Foster, C. Green, K. Bleda, M. Dewick, P. Evans, B. Flynn, A. Mylan, J. (2006) *Environmental Impacts of Food Production and Consumption: A Report to the Department for Environment, Food and Rural Affairs*. London: DEFRA.

Chapter Three: Modified Foods

1   Gaskell, G. (2005). *Europeans and Biotechnology in 2005: Patterns and Trends Eurobarometer 64.3. A Report to the European Commission's Directorate General for Research*. Brussels: Eurobarometer.

2   Darwin, C. (1890) *The Variation of Animals and Plants under Domestication*. London: John Murray, p. 211.

3   Crow, J. F. (2001) 'Plant breeding giants: Burbank, the artist; Vavilov, the scientist'. *Genetics*, 158 (4): 1391–5.

4   Hugo de Vries's book, *Species and Varieties, Their Origin by Mutation* (Chicago: Open Court, 1905; London: Kegan Paul, Trench, Trubner, 1905), is no longer in print but is available as an e-book at the Project Gutenberg website: www.gutenberg.org (Accessed April 2011).

5   van Harten, A. M. (1998) *Mutation Breeding: Theory and Practical Applications*. Cambridge: Cambridge University Press.

6   The Nobel Prize Award Ceremony Presentation Speech given by Professor T. Caspersson of the Karolinska Institute at the award of the Nobel Prize to Professor Hermann J. Muller. Available at http://nobelprize.org/nobel_prizes/medicine/laureates/1946/press.html.

7   Ahloowalia, B.S. (2004) 'Global impact of mutation-derived varieties'. *Euphytica*, 135 (2): 187–204.

8   This records an interview between a *New York Times* journalist and leading scientists of the International Atomic Energy Agency discussing the agency's role in mutation breeding which is available at http://www.nytimes.com/2007/08/28/science/28crop.html (Accessed April 2011).

9   The story of the chance meeting of two scientists at midnight over a pastrami sandwich in a Waikiki deli at a conference which led to the birth of modern biotechnology is told in many places and I select the Nobel Prize website: http://www.nobel-prize-winners.com/cohen/cohen.html (Accessed April 2011).

10 Federoff, N. and Brown, N. M. (2004) *Mendel in the Kitchen: A Scientist's View of Genetically Modified Foods*. Washington: Joseph Henry.

11 These data come from the Lipgene project which was funded under the European 6th Framework Programme of which I was the co-ordinator. The home page of the project is available at www.ucd.ie/lipgene (Accessed April 2011)

12 Napier, J. A. and Graham, I.A. (2010) 'Tailoring plant lipid composition: designer oilseeds come of age'. *Current Opinion in Plant Biology*, 13 (3): 330–7.

13 Food Standards Agency (2004) *Advice on Fish Consumption: Benefits and Risks*. Norwich: Stationery Office.

14 National Academy of Sciences (2004) *Safety of Genetically Engineered Foods; Approaches to assessing Unintended Health Effects*. Washington: National Academy Press.

15 Mensinga, T. T, Sips, A. J. Rompelberg, C. J. (2005) 'Potato glycoalkaloids and adverse effects in humans: an ascending dose study'. *Regulatory Toxicology and Pharmacology*, 41 (1): 66–72.

16 McMillan, M. Thompson, J. C. (1979) 'An outbreak of suspected solanine poisoning in schoolboys: Examinations of criteria of solanine poisoning'. *Quarterly Journal of Medicine*, 48 (190): 227–43.

17 In March 1986, the National Institute of Occupational Safety and Health (NIOSH) received a request to evaluate cases of dermatitis among the employees of a food company. Twenty-one cases of photo-dermatitis were identified and contact with psoralen-containing produce items followed by UVA exposure were deemed to be responsible for the observed cases. This is documented in the NIOSH Health Hazard Evaluation Report, no. 86–246 and is available at the website: http://www.cdc.gov'niosh/hhe/reports/pdfs/1986–0246–1736.pdf (Accessed April 2011).

18 Nordlee, J. A. Taylor, S. L. Townsend, J. A. (1996) 'Identification of a brazil-nut allergen in transgenic soybeans'. *New England Journal of Medicine*, 334 (11): 688–92.

19 National Academy of Sciences (2002) *Environmental Effects of Transgenic Plants: The Scope and Adequacy of Regulation*. Washington, DC: National Academy Press.

Chapter Four: The Metrics of Food and Health

1 Prentice, R.L. Caan, B. Chlebowski, R.T. (2008) 'Low-fat dietary pattern and risk of invasive breast cancer'. *Journal of the American Medical Association*, 295 (6): 629–42.

2 Sacks, F. M. Obarzanek, E. Windhauser, M. M. (1995)'Rationale and design of the dietary approaches to stop hypertension trial (DASH): A multicenter controlled- feeding study of dietary patterns to lower blood pressure'. *Annals of Epidemiology*, 5 (2): 108–18

3 Neuhouser, M. L. Tinker, L, Shaw, P.A. (2008) 'Use of recovery biomarkers to calibrate nutrient consumption self-reports in the Women's Health Initiative'. *American Journal of Epidemiology*, 167 (101): 1247–59.

Chapter Five: Personalised Nutrition

1 Horigan, G. McNulty, H. Ward, M. (2010) 'Riobflavin lowers blood pressure in cardiovascular disease patients homozygous for the 677C T polymorphism in MTHFR'. *Journal of Hypertension*, 28 (3): 478–86.

2   This is based on an abstract presented to the joint conference on 'Cardiovascular Disease Epidemiology and Prevention' and 'Nutrition and Physical Activity and Metabolism', 2010, under the title 'Genetic phenotypes predict weight loss successes: The right diet does matter' with M. D. Nelson, P. Prabhakar, K. S. Kornman and C. Gardner as authors.

3   Hazra, A. Kraft, P. Selhub, J. (2008) 'Common variants of FUT2 are associated with plasma vitamin B$_{12}$ levels'. *Nature Genetics*, 40 (10): 1160–2.

4   The quotes from President Clinton and Prime Minister Blair and Lord Sainsbury are taken from the BBC website http://news.bbc.co.uk/2/hi/science/nature/807126.stm Mike Dexter's quote is taken from a news article in *Nature* 405 (29 June 2000), 983–4 (Accessed April 2011).

5   The website www.sciona.com was accessed in January 2008 from which this quotation was extracted. The website no longer exists given the bankruptcy of Sciona.

6   The Institute of the Future (2003) *From Nutrigenomic Science to Personalized Nutrition: The Market in 2010*. Palo Alto: Institute of the Future.

7   Available at http://www.directlife.philips.com

Chapter Six: Plastic Babies

1   Morgan, E. (1994) *The Descent of the Child: Human Evolution from a New Perspective*. London: Souvenir.

2   Cunnane, S.C. (2005) *Survival of the Fattest: The Key to Human Brain Evolution*. World Scientific: New Jersey.

3   Morgan, E (1982) *The Aquatic Ape*. London: Souvenir.

4   Barker, D. (2003) 'The midwife, the coincidence and the hypothesis'. *British Medical Journal*, 327 (7429): 1428–30.

5   Langley-Evans, S. C. Phillips, G. J. Jackson, A.A. (1994) 'In utero exposure to maternal low protein diets induces hypertension in weanling rats, independently of maternal blood pressure changes'. *Clinical Nutrition*, 13 (5): 319–24.

6   Hales, C. N. Barker, D. J. Clark, P. M. (1991) 'Fetal and infant growth and impaired glucose tolerance at age 64'. *British Medical Journal*, 303 (6809): 1019–22.

7   Barker, D. J. P. Bull, A.R. Osmond, C. (1990) 'Fetal and placental size and risk of hypertension in adult life'. *British Medical Journal*, 301 (6746): 259–62.

8   Barker, D. J. P., Eriksson, J. G., Forsén, T., Osmond, C. (2002) 'Fetal origins of adult disease: strength of effects and biological basis'. *International Journal of Epidemiology*, 31 (6): 1235–9.

9   Ravelli, G. P. Stein, Z. A. Susser, M. W. (1976) 'Obesity in young men after famine exposure in utero and early infancy'. *New England Journal of Medicine*, 295 (7): 349–53.

Chapter Seven: Your Inside is Out

1   Gershon, M.D. (1998) *The Second Brain*. New York: HarperCollins.

2   Best, R. R. and Orator, V (1932) 'The vagus nerve and its relation to peptic ulcer'. *Annals of Surgery*, 96: (2): 184–91.

3   Forchielli, M. L. Walker, W.A. (2005) 'The role of gut-associated lymphoid tissues and mucosal defence'. *British Journal of Nutrition*, 93 (Supplement 1): s41– s48.

4 Sansonetti, P. J. (2004) 'War and peace at mucosal surfaces', *Nature Reviews*. 4 (4): 953–64.

5 Bäckhed, F. Ley, R.E. Sonnenburg, J. L. (2005) 'Host-bacterial mutualism in the human intestine'. *Science*, 307 (5717): 1915–20.

6 Gilmore, M. S. Ferretti, J. J. (2003) 'The thin line between gut commensal and pathogen'. *Science*, 299 (5615): 1999–2002.

7 Coyne, M. J. Reinap, B. Lee, M. M. (2005), 'Human symbionts use a host-like pathway for surface fucosylation'. *Science*, 307 (5716): 1778–81.

8 Deplancke, B. and Gaskins, H. R. (2001) 'Microbial modulation of innate defense: goblet cells and the intestinal mucus layer', *American Journal of Clinical Nutrition*. 73 (Supplement 6): 1131–41.

9 Zoetendal, E. G. Akkermans, A. D. L. Akkermans-van Vliet, W. M. (2001) 'The host genotype affects the bacterial community in the human gastrointestinal tract'. *Microbial Ecology in Health and Disease*, 13 (3): 129–34.

10 Ley, R. E. Bäckhed, F. Turnbaugh, P. (2005) 'Obesity alters gut microbial ecology'. *Proceedings of the National Academy of Sciences*, 102 (31): 11071–5.

11 Bäckhed, F. Ding, H. Wang, T. (2004) The gut microbiota as an environmental factor that regulates fat storage'. *Proceedings of the National Academy of Sciences*, 101 (44): 15718–23.

12 Turnbaugh, P. J. Ley, R. E. Mahowald, M. A. (2006) 'An obesity-associated gut microbiome with increased capacity for energy harvest'. *Nature*, 444 (122): 1027–31

13 Ley, R. E. Turnbaugh, P. J. Klein, S. (2006) 'Microbial ecology: Human gut microbes associated with obesity'. *Nature*, 444 (7122): 1022–3.

14 This quotation is taken from the Nobel Prize Award Ceremony given by Professor Staffon Normark of the Karolinska Institute at the ceremony where Barry Marshall and Robin Warren received their Nobel Prize in Medicine in 2005. http://nobelprize.org/nobel_prizes/medicine/laureates/2005/presentation-speech.html (Accessed April 2011).

Chapter Eight: A Tsunami of Lard

1 These data are taken from a data briefing of the UK National Obesity Observatory entitled: 'Adult obesity and socioeconomic status', dated October 2010. It is available from the website http://www.noo.org.uk/uploads/doc/vid_7929_Adult_Socioeco_DataBriefing_October_2010.pdf (Accessed April 2011).

2 Stunkard, A.J. Harris, J.R. Pedersen, N.L. (1990) 'The body-mass index of twins who have been reared apart'. *New England Journal of Medicine*, 322 (21): 1483–7.

3 Bouchard, C. Savard, R. Després, J. P. (1985) Body composition in adopted and biological siblings'. *Human Biology*, 57 (1): 61–75.

4 Poehlman, E. T. Tremblay, A. Després, J. P. (1986) 'Genotype-controlled changes in body composition and fat morphology following overfeeding in twins'. *American Journal of Clinical Nutrition*, 43 (5): 7723–31.

5 Saris, W. H. M. (2004) 'Focus on the fire of life'. *Current Opinion in Clinical Nutrition and Metabolic Care*, 7 (4): 595–7.

6 Wardle, J. Carnell, S. Haworth, C. M. (2008) 'Evidence for a strong genetic influence on childhood adiposity despite the force of the obesogenic environment'. *American Journal of Clinical Nutrition*, 87 (2): 398–404.

7   Semmler, C. Ashcroft, J. van Jaarsveld, C. H. (2009) 'Development of overweight in children in relation to parental weight and socioeconomic status'. *Obesity*, 17 (4): 814–20.

8   This is taken from a working paper number 11177 of the National Bureau of Economic Research, authored by P. M Anderson and K. F. Butcher and issued in March 2005. It is available at http://www.nber.org/papers/w11177.pdf

9   Hansberger, F. X. (1959) 'Behavior of transplanted adipose tissue of hereditarily obese mice', *Anatomical Record*, 135 (2): 109–13.

10 Friedman, J. M. Halaas, J. L. (1998) 'Leptin and the regulation of body weight in mammals'. *Nature*, 395 (6704): 763–70.

11 Farooqi. I. S. (2008) 'Monogenic human obesity syndromes'. *Frontiers in Hormonal Research*, 36: 1–11.

12 Council of Scientific Affairs of the American Medical Association (1988) 'Treatment of obesity in adults'. *Journal of the American Medical Association*, 260 (17) 2547–51.

13 Prentice, A. M. Jebb, S. A. (1995) 'Obesity in Britain: gluttony or sloth'. *British Medical Journal*, 311 (7002): 437–9.

14 Hu, F. B. Li ,T. Y. Colditz, G. A. (2007) 'Television watching and other sedentary behaviours in relation to risk of obesity and type 2 diabetes mellitus in women'. *Journal of the American Medical Association*, 289 (14): 1785–91.

15 Church, T. S. LaMonte, M. J. Barlow, C. E. (2011) 'Cardiorespiratory fitness and body mass index as predictors of cardiovascular disease mortality among men with diabetes'. *Archives of Internal Medicine*, 165 (18): 2114–20.

16 Hill, J. O. (2004) *The Step Diet: Count Steps, Not Calories to Lose Weight and Keep it off Forever*. New York: Workman.

17 Latner, J. D. Stunkard, A. J. (2003) 'Getting worse: The stigmatization of obese children'. *Obesity Research*, 11 (3): 452–6.

18 Wooley, S. C. (1987) 'Psychological and social aspects of obesity'. In: A. E. Bender, and L. J. Brookes eds, *Body Weight Control: The Physiology, Clinical Treatment, and Prevention of Obesity*. Edinburgh: Churchill Livingstone, pp. 81–9.

19 Sachs, J. (2008) *Common Wealth: Economics for a Crowded Planet*. London: Penguin, p. 28.

20 Keith, S. W. Redden, D. T. Katzmarzyk, P. T. (2006) 'Putative contributors to the secular increase in obesity: exploring the roads less travelled'. *International Journal of Obesity*, 30 (2006): 1585–94.

21 Costa, D. and Steckel, R. H. (1997) 'Long-term trends in health, welfare, and economic growth in the United States'. In R. H. Steckel and R. Floud eds, *Health and Welfare During Industrialization*. Chicago: University of Chicago Press.

22 Olsen, L.W. Baker, J. L. Holst, C. (2006) 'Birth cohort effect on the obesity epidemic in Denmark'. *Epidemiology*, 17 (3): 292–5.

Chapter Nine: Greying Matters

1   European Parliament, *White Paper on Nutrition, Overweight and Obesity Related Health Issues*. European Parliament resolution of 25 September 2008 (2007/2285 [INI]).

2   House of Commons (2004) *Commons Select Committee on Health. Third Report*.

3   Powell, J. L. *Ageing in the Americas*. Published in the Sincronia Archives and available at http://sincronia.cucsh.udg.mx/powellspring2011a.htm (Accessed April 2011).

4   Villareal, D.T. Banks, M. Siener, C. (2004) 'Physical frailty and body composition in obese elderly men and women'. *Obesity Research*, 12 (6): 915–20.

5   Roubenoff, R. (2004) 'Sarcopenic obesity: the confluence of two epidemics'. *Obesity Research*, 12 (6): 887–8.

6   Roberts, S. B. Fuss, P. Heyman, M. B. (1994) 'Control of food intake in older men'. *Journal of the American Medical Association*, 272 (20): 1601–6.

7   Murphy, C. Schubert, C.R. Cruickshanks, K. J. (2002) 'Prevalence of olfactory impairment in older adults'. *Journal of the American Medical Association*, 288 (18): 2307–12.

8   Towheed, T. Maxwell, L. Anastassaides, T. (2009) 'Glucosamine therapy for dieting osteoarthritis', *Cochrane Database of Systematic Reviews*. Available at http://onlinelibrary. wiley.com/doi/10.1002/14651858.CD002946.pub2/abstract (accessed April 2011).

9   Reichenbach, S. Sterchi, R. Scherer, M. (2007) 'Meta-analysis: chondroitin for osteoarthritis of the hip or knee'. *Annals of Internal Medicine*, 146 (8): 580–90.

10   Youl, P.H. Janda, M. Kimlin, M. (2009) 'Vitamin D and sun-protection, the impact of mixed public health messages in Australia'. *International Journal of Cancer*, 124 (8): 1963–70.

11   Chong, E.W. Wong, T.Y. Kreis, A. J. (2007) 'Dietary antioxidants and primary prevention of age-related macular degeneration: systematic review and meta-analysis'. *British Medical Journal*, 335 (7263): 1–8.

12   Hin, H. Clarke, R. Sherliker, P. (2006) 'Clinical relevance of low serum vitamin B_{12} concentrations in older people: the Banbury B_{12} study'. *Age and Ageing*, 35 (4): 416–22.

13   van Gelder, B. M. Tijhuis, M. Kalmijn, S. 'Fish consumption, n-3 fatty acids and subsequent 5-year cognitive decline in elderly men: The Zutphen elderly study'. *American Journal of Clinical Nutrition*, 85 (4): 1142–7.

14   Whitmer, R. A. Gunderson, E. P. Quesenberry, C. P. (2007),'Body mass index in midlife and risk of Alzheimer disease and vascular dementia'. *Current Alzheimer's Research*, 4 (2): 103–9.

Chapter Ten: Food and Health

1   Pielke, R. A. (2007) *The Honest Broker: Making Sense of Science in Policy and Politics.* Cambridge: Cambridge University Press.

2   Cope, M. B. Allison, D. B. (2010) 'White hat bias: examples of its presence in obesity research and a call for renewed commitment to faithfulness in research reporting'. *International Journal of Obesity*, 34 (1): 84–8.

3   Balfour, Lady Eve (1948) *The Living Soil*. London: Faber and Faber http://www. soilandhealth org/01aglibrary/01aglibwelcome.html (Accessed April 2011).

4   Taverne, D. (2006) *The March of Unreason: Science Democracy and the New Fundamentalism*. Oxford: Oxford University Press.

5   Quoted in Trewavas, A. Leaver, C. (2001) 'Is opposition to GM crops science or politics'. *European Molecular Biology Organisation*, 2 (6): 455–9.

6   Lancet editorial. (2007) Science at WHO and UNICEF: the corrosion of trust'. *Lancet*, 370 (9592): 1007

7   Oxman, A. D. Lavis, J. N. Fretheim, A. (2007) 'Use of evidence in WHO recommendations'. *Lancet*, 369 (9576): 1883–9.

Chapter Eleven: My Food, Your Poison

1   Commission of the European Communities (2000) *Communication from the Commission on the Precautionary Principle* (COM, 2000).

2   Stadler, R.D. (2005) 'Acrylamide formation in different foods and potential strategies for reduction'. *Advances in Experimental Medicine and Biology*, 561: 157–69.

3   The opinion of the Appellate Body of the WTO is available at http://www.wtoorg/english/tratop_e/sps_agreement_cbt_e/c5s3p1_e.htm (accessed April 201).

4   McNeil, B. J. Pauker, S. G. Sox, H. C. (1982) 'On the elicitation of preferences for alternative therapies'. *New England Journal of Medicine*, 306 (21): 1259–92.

5   Slovic, P. (2000) *The Perception of Risk*. London: Earthscan.

Chapter Twelve: How the Other Half Dies

1   Kapsiotis, G. D. (1975) 'An international programme for famine relief: Food Policy and Nutrition Division, United Nations Food and Agriculture Organization Rome Italy'. *Proceedings of the Nutrition Society*, 34: 195–9.

2   World Declaration on Nutrition (1992). This quotation is from the World Declaration on Nutrition issued by the Ministers of 159 states at the International Conference of Nutrition in Rome. http://www.fao.org/docrep/U9920t/u9920t0a.htm (Accessed April 2011).

3   *Monitoring Progress since the World Food Summit* (1996). This is a quotation from Romano Prodi, President of Italy and Chairman of the World Food Summit held in Rome in November 1996. It is available at http://www.fao.org/wfs/main_en.htm (Accessed April 2011).

4   To mark the millennium in 2000, the UN issued a series of eight goals known as the Millennium Development Goals (MDG) to be achieved by 2015. Goal number one is to eradicate extreme hunger and poverty. The MDGs are available at http://www.undp.org/mdg/goal1.shtml (Accessed April 2011).

5   Getting accurate data on mortality from malnutrition and hunger is not easy with many sites offering different estimates based on different definitions and criteria. I have opted to base my data on the WHO Fact Sheet number 178 issued in November 2009 and available at http://www.who.int/mediacentre/facesheets/fs178/en/ (Accessed April 2011).

6   The Global Hunger Index is a widely used annual measure of the level of hunger across 135 countries. Details are available at http://www.ifpri.org/publication/2010–global-hunger-index (Accessed April 2011).

7   Collier, P. (2007) *The Bottom Billion: Why the Poorest Countries are Failing and What Can Be Done about It*. Oxford: Oxford University Press.

8   The World Bank issued a report entitled '*India: Undernourished Children: A Call for Reform and Action*', which is available at http://www.go.worldbank.org/TUTLNHSPKO (Accessed April 2011).

9   Each year, UNAIDS issues it Report on the Global AIDS Epidemic, the most recent being that of 2010 from which these statistics were taken. It can be accessed at
http://www.unadis.org/globalreport/global_report.htm (Accessed April 2011).

10 Roll-Back-Malaria is a global partnership of 500 governmental and non-governmental organisations committed to actions to achieve the MDG. http://www.rollbackmalaria.org/ (Accessed April 2011).

11 Sachs, J. D. (2005) *The End of Poverty: Economic Possibilities for Our Time*. London: Allen Lane, 2005.

12 Collins, S. Dent, N. Binns, P. (2006) 'Management of severe acute malnutrition in children'. *The Lancet*, 368 (9551): 1992–2000

13 World Bank (2005) *Repositioning Nutrition as Central to Development: A Strategy for Large-Scale Action* Washington: World Bank.

14 Behrman, J. R. Alderman, H. and Hoddinott, J. (2004) 'Malnutrition and hunger'. In Lomborg, B. ed., *Global Crises, Global Solutions*. Cambridge, Cambridge University Press, pp. 443–98

15 Paarlberg, R. (2009) *Starved for Science: How Biotechnology is Being Kept Out of Africa*. Cambridge MA, Harvard University Press.

16 Speaking at a special meeting of African heads of state and leading policy makers organised by the Ethiopian Government and the Hunger Task Force of the UN Millennium Project, Secretary General Kofi Annan jointly with former US President Jimmy Carter in calling for a green revolution in Africa. His speech is available at http://www.earth.columbia.edu/ news/2004/story07–06–04.html. (Accessed April 2011).

17 The Honourable William S. Gaud of USAID delivered a speech to the Society for International Development (8 March 1968) in which he coined the term 'Green Revolution', His speech is available at http://www.agbioworld.org/biotech-info/topics/borlaug/borlaug-green.html (Accessed April 2011).

18 These projections were made by the leaders of the Comprehensive Africa Agriculture Development Programme at a joint meeting of the African Union Commission and the New Partnership for Africa Development in Cape Verde, November 2010. The material is available at http://www.org/system/files/CapeVerde (Accessed April 2011).

19 An International Conference on Organic Agriculture and Food Security was held at the FAO headquarters in Rome in May 2007. The proceedings are available at http://www. fao.org/paia/organicag/ofs/OFS-2007–5.pdf (Accessed April 2011).

20 World Bank (2008) *World Development Report Agriculture for Development* Washington: World Bank.

21 This quotation is taken from the website of the Alliance for a Green Revolution in Africa http://www.agra-alliance.org/section/about/genetic_engineering (Accessed April 2011).

22 This quotation was taken from an online version of the BBC and is available at http://www.bbc.co.uk/1/hi/world/africa/2233839.stm (Accessed April 2011).

23 Schiermeier, Q. (2008) 'German universities bow to public pressure over GM crops'. *Nature*, 453 (7193): 263

24 Professors Atkinson and Urwin of the University of Leeds Centre for Plant Sciences give an excellent outline of this GM potato research at the following website http://www.plants.leeds.ac.uk/people/groups_atk.hp (Accessed April 2011).

25 Pennisi, E. (2008) 'The blue revolution, drop by drop, gene by gene'. *Science*, 320 (5873): 171–3

26 Beyer, P. Al-Babili, S. Ye, X. (2002) Golden Rice: introducing the beta-carotene biosynthesis pathway into rice endosperm by genetic engineering to defeat vitamin A deficiency. *Journal of Nutrition*, 132(3): 506s–510s.

27 From the BBC reports on GM foods available at the following website: http://news. bbc.co.uk/2/hi/africa/7428789.stm (Accessed April 2011)

Chapter Thirteen: Mankind and Mother Earth

1   Meadows, D. H. (1972) *A Report of the Club of Rome's Project on the Predicament of Mankind*. Washington: Potomac Associates.

2   This quotation from Professor Stephen Schneider has become quite controversial because the exact words used in his interview with *Discovery Magazine*'s Pulitzer Prizewinning writer Jonathan Schell have been distorted by several journalists. The quotation I use is exactly as   laid out by Schneider on his own media website 'Mediarology'. It can be accessed at: http:// stephenschneider.stanford.edu/Mediarology/MediarologyFrameset.html. (Accessed April 2011).

3   Keeling, C. D. (1978) 'The influence of Mauna Loa Observatory on the development of atmospheric CO_2 research' in John Miller, *Mauna Lao Observatory: A 20th Anniversary Report* (National Oceanic and Atmospheric Administration Special Report, September 1978) (Boulder, CO: NOAA Environmental Research Laboratories.

4   Sachs, J. D. (2009) *Common Wealth: Economics for a Crowded Planet*. London: Penguin.

5   Stern, N. (2009) *A Blueprint for a Safer Planet: How to Manage Climate Change and Create a New Era of Progress and Prosperity*. London: Bodley Head.

6   The website of the Inter-governmental panel on climate change contains a wealth of predictions on the consequences of climate change. http://www.pec.ch (Accessed April 2011).

7   FAO, *Livestock's Long Shadow: Environmental Issues and Options* (Rome: FAO, 2006).

8   Nepstad, D. C. Stickler, C.M. Soares-Filo, B (2008) 'Interactions among Amazon land use, forests and climate: prospects for a near-term tipping point'. *Philosophical Transactions of the Royal Society*, B 363 (2008): 1737–46.

9   Department of the Environment, Food and Rural Affairs (2005), *The Validity of Food Miles as an Indicator of Sustainable Development* (Report no. ed50254).

10   Weber, C. L. Matthews, H. S. 'Food miles and relative climate impacts of food choices in the United States'. *Environmental Science and Technology*, 42 (10): 3508– 13

11   Jones, D. (2002) 'An environmental assessment of food supply chains: a case study on dessert apples'. *Environmental Management*, 30 (4): 560–76.

12   Tubiello, F. N. Soussana, J. F. Howden, S. M. (2007) 'Crop and pasture response to climate change'. *Proceedings of the National Academy of Sciences*, 104 (50): 1986– 90

13   The speech of Ban Ki-Moon to the World Economic Forum is available at the UN News Centre at the following Internet address: http://www.un.org/apps/news/story.asp?NewsID= 25398&Cr=davos&Cr1 (Accessed April 2011).

14   The Indus Waters Treaty was concluded by India and Pakistan on 19 September 1960. The deal was brokered by the World Bank and the treaty is available at: http://go.worldbank.org/WHGZVDDCB0 (Accessed April 2011).

15   This story was reported on http://www.economist.com/node/744971 (Accessed April 2011).

16 This major study funded by the National Science Foundation was published by the National Centre for Atmospheric Research and extracts are available at: http://www2.ucar.edu/news/854/water-levels-dropping-some-major-rivers-global-climate-changes (Accessed April 2011).

17 Cline, W. (2007) *Global Warming and Agriculture: Impact Estimates by Country.* Washington: Centre for Global Development and the Peterson Institute for International Economics.

18 Giannini, A. Saravanan, R. Chang, P. (2003) 'Oceanic forcing of Sahel rainfall to inter-annual to interdeccal time scales'. *Science*, 302 (5647): 1027–30.

19 Rosegrant, M. W. Cai, X. Cline, S.A. (2002) *Global Water Outlook to 2025: Averting an Impending Crisis*. Washington: International Food Policy Research Institute.

20 His quote is taken from a report of the US Earth System Research Laboratory in 2007. It is accessible at http://www.esrl.noaa.gov/news/2007/ozone2007.html (Accessed April 2011).

Chapter Fourteen: Projections and Reflections

1 Available at: http://www.gatesfoundation.org/topics/Pages/nutrition.aspx.

2 Available at : http://www.scalingupnutrition.org.

3 Rokholm, B. Baker, J. L. Sørensen, T. I. (2010) 'The levelling off of the obesity epidemic since the year 1999 – a review of evidence and perspectives'. *Obesity Reviews,* 11: 835–46

4 Nichols, M. S. de Silva-Sanigorski, D. M. Cleary, J.E. (2011) 'Decreasing trends in overweight and obesity among an Australian population of preschool children'. *International Journal of Obesity*, 35, 916–24

Index

Recent Reviews

Something to Chew On
978-1-906359-67-6

'There were many points made in *Something to Chew On* that are really original and impressive and Professor Gibney has produced 170 pages of fantastic 'brain food'. His detailed arguments on food and health controversies are very clear and exciting and, refreshingly, he is not someone to sit on a fence ... this book is a masticatory joy and is highly recommended.'

NHDmag issue 80, December 2012/January 2013

'I strongly recommend the book for public health policymakers and the media, who are confronted by these controversial topics daily. For classes that include food and nutrition controversies, reading assignments from this book and from "blame" books would provide an excellent foundation for class discussion.'

The American Journal of Clinical Nutrition, 2013

'Professor Gibney brings his vast scholarship to the subject, pulling together reports and studies from around the globe filtered through his own argumentative and common-sense-approach to one of the most important subjects in the world today.'

Sunday Independent

'Aimed at the general public, this work should be required reading for all concerned citizens. Summing Up: Highly recommended.'

Choice, February 2013

'This book covers a comprehensive range of fascinating topics regarding food and health and highlights many common myths and misconceptions among the general public . . . [It] is suitable for anyone with an interest in nutrition, food and health, who would like a reliable source of evidence-based information on key food and health issues, as well as students studying in this area.'

Nutrition Bulletin, December 2012